The Last Grand Duchess

Her Imperial Highness Grand Duchess

Olga Alexandrovna

1 June 1882 – 24 November 1960

IAN VORRES

KEY PORTER BOOKS

Acknowledgments

I gladly take this opportunity of expressing my gratitude to all those who helped me complete this study of Grand Duchess Olga: to her son, Goury Koulikovsky, to H. R. H. the Duchess of Mecklenburg, to H. H. the Duke of Leuchtenberg, the late Nancy, Viscountess Astor, the late Sir Edward Peacock, Vice-Admiral T. N. James, C.B., M.V.O., L. W. Brockington, Q.C., Lieutenant Colonel Bartley Bull, Mr. James Armstrong, Mr. Edward Ewing, Mr. Arnold McNaughton, Sir Thomas H. Preston, Bt., Mr. A. H. Creighton, and Mrs. R. B. Messervy. I am also indebted to Mr. Colin McCullough for revisions and corrections in the text and to Margaret Foster for typing the manuscript.

Finally, I gratefully acknowledge my debt to my parents, Andrew and Stephanie Vorres, whose personal encouragement and financial assistance enabled me to carry on with the research required for this book and to finish writing it.

—Ian Vorres

Canadian Cataloguing in Publication Data

Vorres, Ian
  The Last Grand Duchess

ISBN 1-55263-302-0

1. Olga Aleksandrovna, Grand Duchess of Russia, 1882-1960. 2. Nicholas II, Emperor of Russia, 1868-1918 – Family. 3. Russia – Kings and rulers – Sisters – Biography. 4. Russia – History – Nicholas II, 1894-1917. I. Title.

DK254.O4V6 2000   947.08'3'092   C00-931647-7

The publisher gratefully acknowledges the assistance of the Canada Council and the Ontario Arts Council.

We acknowledge the financial support of the Government of Canada through the Book Publishing Industry Development Program (BPIDP) for our publishing activities.

Key Porter Books Limited
70 The Esplanade
Toronto, Ontario
Canada M5E 1R2
www.keyporter.com

Design: Patricia Cavazzini

01 02 03 04 6 5 4 3 2 1

to Olga

Contents

The Romanov
Family Tree

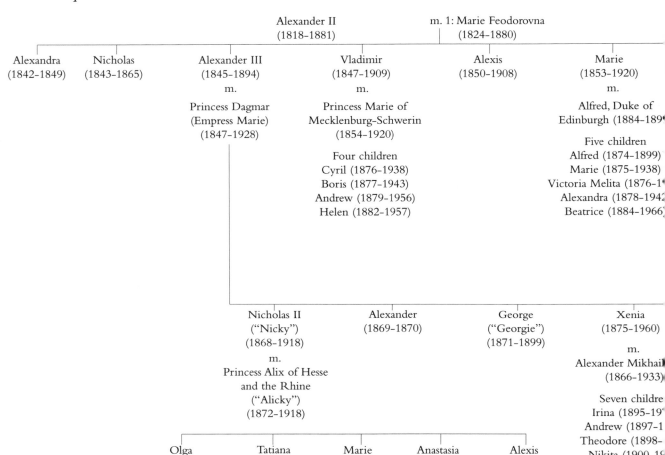

Alexander II
(1818–1881)

m. 1: Marie Feodorovna
(1824–1880)

Alexandra
(1842–1849)

Nicholas
(1843–1865)

Alexander III
(1845–1894)
m.
Princess Dagmar
(Empress Marie)
(1847–1928)

Vladimir
(1847–1909)
m.
Princess Marie of
Mecklenburg-Schwerin
(1854–1920)

Four children
Cyril (1876–1938)
Boris (1877–1943)
Andrew (1879–1956)
Helen (1882–1957)

Alexis
(1850–1908)

Marie
(1853–1920)
m.
Alfred, Duke of
Edinburgh (1884–189?)

Five children
Alfred (1874–1899)
Marie (1875–1938)
Victoria Melita (1876–1?)
Alexandra (1878–194?)
Beatrice (1884–1966)

Nicholas II
("Nicky")
(1868–1918)
m.
Princess Alix of Hesse
and the Rhine
("Alicky")
(1872–1918)

Alexander
(1869–1870)

George
("Georgie")
(1871–1899)

Xenia
(1875–1960)
m.
Alexander Mikhail
(1866–1933)

Seven childre
Irina (1895–19?
Andrew (1897–1
Theodore (1898–
Nikita (1900–19
Dimitri (1901–1?
Rostislav (1902–1
Vassily (1907–19

Olga
(1895–1918)

Tatiana
(1897–1918)

Marie
(1899–1918)

Anastasia
(1901–1918)

Alexis
(1904–1918)

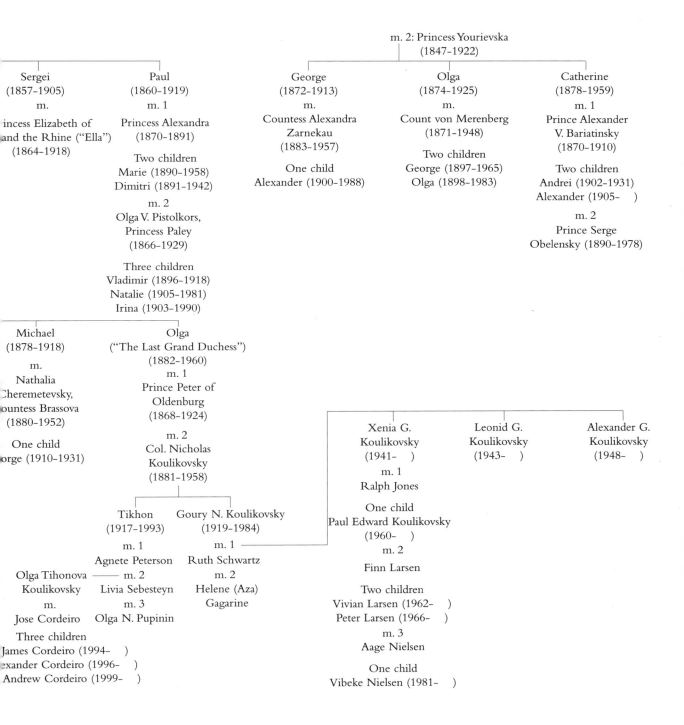

m. 2: Princess Yourievska
(1847-1922)

Sergei
(1857-1905)
m.
[Pr]incess Elizabeth of
[Hesse-]and the Rhine ("Ella")
(1864-1918)

Paul
(1860-1919)
m. 1
Princess Alexandra
(1870-1891)

Two children
Marie (1890-1958)
Dimitri (1891-1942)

m. 2
Olga V. Pistolkors,
Princess Paley
(1866-1929)

Three children
Vladimir (1896-1918)
Natalie (1905-1981)
Irina (1903-1990)

George
(1872-1913)
m.
Countess Alexandra
Zarnekau
(1883-1957)

One child
Alexander (1900-1988)

Olga
(1874-1925)
m.
Count von Merenberg
(1871-1948)

Two children
George (1897-1965)
Olga (1898-1983)

Catherine
(1878-1959)
m. 1
Prince Alexander
V. Bariatinsky
(1870-1910)

Two children
Andrei (1902-1931)
Alexander (1905-   )

m. 2
Prince Serge
Obelensky (1890-1978)

Michael
(1878-1918)
m.
Nathalia
[C]heremetevsky,
[C]ountess Brassova
(1880-1952)

One child
[Ge]orge (1910-1931)

Olga
("The Last Grand Duchess")
(1882-1960)
m. 1
Prince Peter of
Oldenburg
(1868-1924)

m. 2
Col. Nicholas
Koulikovsky
(1881-1958)

Xenia G.
Koulikovsky
(1941-   )
m. 1
Ralph Jones

One child
Paul Edward Koulikovsky
(1960-   )
m. 2
Finn Larsen

Two children
Vivian Larsen (1962-   )
Peter Larsen (1966-   )
m. 3
Aage Nielsen

One child
Vibeke Nielsen (1981-   )

Leonid G.
Koulikovsky
(1943-   )

Alexander G.
Koulikovsky
(1948-   )

Tikhon
(1917-1993)
m. 1
Agnete Peterson
m. 2
Livia Sebesteyn
m. 3
Olga N. Pupinin

Goury N. Koulikovsky
(1919-1984)
m. 1
Ruth Schwartz
m. 2
Helene (Aza)
Gagarine

Olga Tihonova
Koulikovsky
m.
Jose Cordeiro

Three children
James Cordeiro (1994-   )
[Al]exander Cordeiro (1996-   )
Andrew Cordeiro (1999-   )

Principal Connections Between the Royal Families of
Russia, Denmark, Great Britain, Germany and Greece

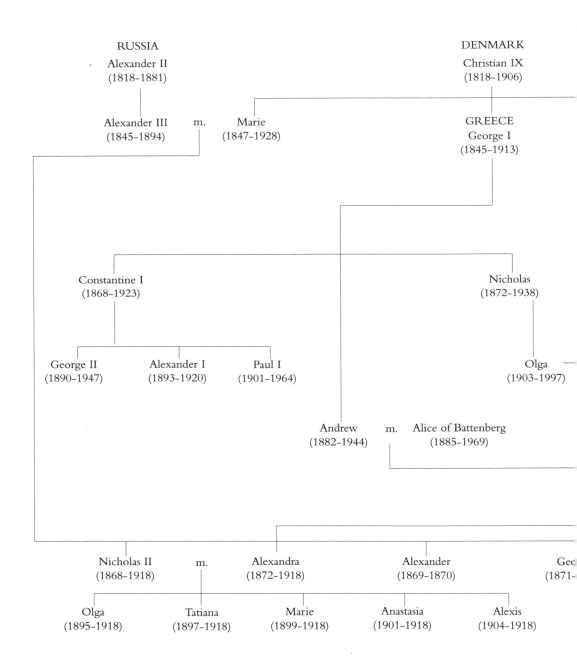

RUSSIA
Alexander II
(1818-1881)

DENMARK
Christian IX
(1818-1906)

Alexander III   m.   Marie
(1845-1894)   (1847-1928)

GREECE
George I
(1845-1913)

Constantine I
(1868-1923)

Nicholas
(1872-1938)

George II   Alexander I   Paul I
(1890-1947)   (1893-1920)   (1901-1964)

Olga
(1903-1997)

Andrew   m.   Alice of Battenberg
(1882-1944)   (1885-1969)

Nicholas II   m.   Alexandra
(1868-1918)   (1872-1918)

Alexander
(1869-1870)

Geo
(1871-

Olga   Tatiana   Marie   Anastasia   Alexis
(1895-1918)   (1897-1918)   (1899-1918)   (1901-1918)   (1904-1918)

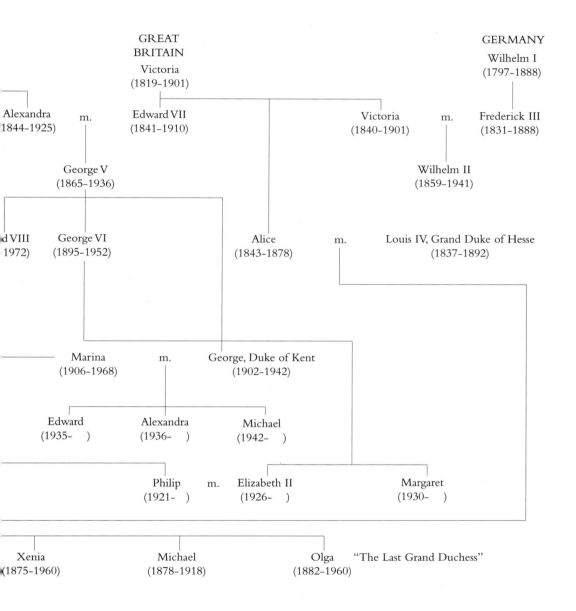

GREAT
BRITAIN
Victoria
(1819–1901)

GERMANY
Wilhelm I
(1797–1888)

Alexandra
(1844–1925)   m.   Edward VII
(1841–1910)

Victoria
(1840–1901)   m.   Frederick III
(1831–1888)

George V
(1865–1936)

Wilhelm II
(1859–1941)

d VIII
1972)   George VI
(1895–1952)

Alice
(1843–1878)   m.   Louis IV, Grand Duke of Hesse
(1837–1892)

Marina
(1906–1968)   m.   George, Duke of Kent
(1902–1942)

Edward
(1935–)   Alexandra
(1936–)   Michael
(1942–)

Philip
(1921–)   m.   Elizabeth II
(1926–)   Margaret
(1930–)

Xenia
(1875–1960)   Michael
(1878–1918)   Olga
(1882–1960)   "The Last Grand Duchess"

The Romanov Dynasty
1913-1917
Duration of Reigns

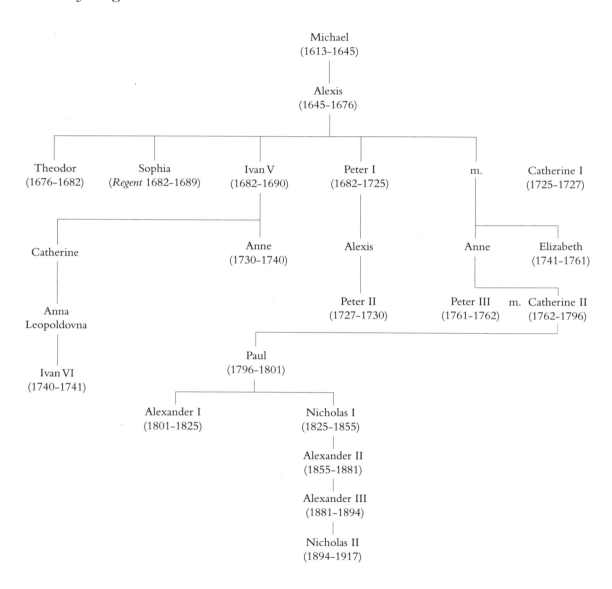

Michael
(1613–1645)

Alexis
(1645–1676)

Theodor
(1676–1682)

Sophia
(*Regent* 1682–1689)

Ivan V
(1682–1690)

Peter I
(1682–1725)

m.

Catherine I
(1725–1727)

Catherine

Anne
(1730–1740)

Alexis

Anne

Elizabeth
(1741–1761)

Anna
Leopoldovna

Peter II
(1727–1730)

Peter III
(1761–1762)

m. Catherine II
(1762–1796)

Ivan VI
(1740–1741)

Paul
(1796–1801)

Alexander I
(1801–1825)

Nicholas I
(1825–1855)

Alexander II
(1855–1881)

Alexander III
(1881–1894)

Nicholas II
(1894–1917)

Foreword

It is the author of this book, Mr. Ian Vorres, who, in the twilight of my life, succeeded in convincing me that it was my duty both to history and to my family to reveal the true events connected with the last Romanov reign. Fate, usually so cruel to members of my family, perhaps purposely spared me for so long to give me a chance to break my silence and vindicate my family against so many calumnies and distortions of facts leveled at them. I thank God for giving me such an opportunity on the eve of my death. My only grief is that I shall not see the publication of this book.

Because of many infirmities due to old age it is impossible for me to write my memoirs in person. For over a year I have continuously discussed all the aspects and happenings of my life with Mr. Ian Vorres, who enjoys my full confidence. I have made available to him all the letters and photographs in my possession and I have given him all the information needed for the writing of this book. May these pages cast a true light on two Romanov reigns—both so mercilessly misrepresented by rumor and irresponsible writing. May Mr. Vorres' book enable the reading public to reappraise at least some of the characters and events closely connected with one of the most splendid and tragic dynasties of Europe.

Her Imperial Highness
Grand Duchess
Olga Alexandrovna
Canada, 1960

Preface to the Fourth Edition

his book, the official biography of Grand Duchess Olga, youngest sister of the ill-fated Tsar Nicholas II, was first published in England in 1964 and in the United States in 1965. It enjoyed worldwide acclaim. It was written while the Grand Duchess was still alive with her full consent and cooperation. She died in exile in Toronto, Canada, on December 16, 1960.

Much has been written on the last imperial reign of Russia by members of the court, by tutors of the imperial children, by foreign diplomats serving in St. Petersburg at the time and by numerous relatives of the doomed family. The unique historic value of this book, however, lies in the fact that it is the first and only official biography ever released by a direct member of the ruling imperial family itself. Grand Duchess Olga was also the last surviving member of the family. This book has served, and is still serving, as an authoritative source for several biographies on the last Romanovs written in recent years. This is understandable because Grand Duchess Olga was particularly close to her brother, the Emperor, and her reclusive sister-in-law, Empress Alexandra, and was allowed to live with them in the Alexandra Palace in Tsarskoe Selo up to the bitter end. This book is based on the many intimate conversations I had with the Grand Duchess, over a a year-and-a-half, in her home near Toronto.

This book has also been used as conclusive proof against Mrs. Anna Anderson who attempted to pass herself off as Grand Duchess Anastasia, Grand Duchess Olga's beloved niece. Mrs. Anderson eventually took her case before the Supreme Court of Germany, though her claim to the title was ultimately rejected. I am indeed satisfied that this official biography helped render historical truth and justice.

A multitude of irresponsible and historically biased publications dealing with the last imperial family of Russia make it increasingly difficult today to sift fact from fiction. "It is legend that ultimately creates history," Jean Cocteau once said. Unfortunately, the Romanov legend continues to inspire new publications even today, including most recently a superfluous biography on Grand Duchess Olga based mostly on hearsay. The reissuing of a fourth edition will help, I hope, restore historical truth.

Judged today, the life of the Tsar's sister personifies an ancient Greek tragedy in which its heroes are led to their downfall by superior forces they cannot control, despite their determined actions of courage and compassion. Grand Duchess Olga's life, in fact, constituted a double tragedy. She was not only haunted by the real drama of her family, but also by the constant appearances, all during her lifetime, of numerous imposters claiming to be members of the doomed family, especially Grand Duchess Anastasia and the young Tsarevich.

When writing this book, I recall meeting two other women claiming to be the Grand Duchess Anastasia, besides Mrs. Anderson. I also met two men claiming to be the Tsarevich and numerous individuals personifying a variety of Russian Grand Dukes, Grand Duchesses and Countesses, all of whom purported to be relatives of the ill-fated family. All of them profited financially and socially from their assumed roles and added, needless to say, to the courage and discomfort of the Grand Duchess Olga.

"People simply want to believe all the tales written about my family, especially about my beloved Anastasia, and that repulsive Rasputin. I often feel it doesn't help what I have to say," I recall the Grand Duchess telling me once in despair. She has, however, patiently dwelt on both in length for this book.

"History has made our lives difficult," the late President John Kennedy once declared in an address to the American people. In Grand Duchess Olga's case, history succeeded in making her life more unbearable than most. "If I ever start crying, I will never stop," she once told me. It is to her everlasting credit that she kept smiling to the bitter end.

Ian Vorres
Canada, 2000

Preface to the First Edition

In 1958 I started to organize an exhibition of Byzantine art in Toronto. I had of course heard that Grand Duchess Olga was living in Cooksville, about ten miles away. I supposed she would have some Russian icons in her possession, but I must admit that I started on that brief journey without a shred of certainty in my mind. I had heard about the Grand Duchess being pestered by idly curious tourists and by journalists in search of copy. I had also heard of her love of solitude. I could not be sure of even being allowed to cross the threshold of her cottage. Dispossessed, exiled, she remained a Romanov. Her family could be charming. Equally, they could be aloof enough to freeze a stranger into silence.

Cooksville, once an isolated hamlet, now a growing suburb of Toronto, has but a few thousand people. It was easy to find that small brick cottage, surrounded by a garden and standing on a few acres of uncultivated land. I came nearer and saw a small, thin woman busily gardening. She wore a long old-fashioned dark skirt, a frayed sweater, a very plain blouse, and stout brown shoes. Her hair, combed straight back into a bun, had hardly any silver in it. Her face, though deeply wrinkled, did not look old, and her light brown eyes, for all the sadness in them, were not those of an old woman. As she moved toward me I was struck by the beauty of her carriage, and her manner soon put me at my ease; she was every inch "imperial," and in her case the word implied a nobility which, remaining itself, has nothing to say to condescension or vapid pride.

She invited me into the house and we discussed the matter of icons. We sat in a small living room crowded with furniture, books, papers, and all kinds of mementos. The floor was littered with flowers and plants in pots, stacks of drawing paper, brushes and tubes of paint, and I discovered soon enough that gardening and painting were the Grand Duchess's main occupations. A faded pink sofa, which she used as seat and desk, stood by the window. The walls were covered with paintings, a big portrait of her father, Alexander III, hanging over the fireplace. The little tables were crowded with family photographs, one of them being that of Anastasia, the Grand Duchess's favorite niece and god-daughter. It was rather a paradox of a room: at once wildly chaotic and orderly.

There we sat and talked about icons, and occasionally she would smile, and every moment I felt drawn closer to her. She was shabby enough and so was the room, but the spacious and splendid background of many palaces was reflected in her manner; its simplicity disarmed, its flawless dignity commanded respect.

I stayed on. We talked about art, the state of the world, gardening—I cannot now remember all the subjects she and I broached at the first interview. But I do remember that time flew so fast that it was a shock to realize that I had been there nearly three hours. She asked me to come again and I knew that she meant it, and I did come again—not as a casual caller but a friend. There was a difference of forty years between us, but the link grew and deepened. After each visit to Cooksville I returned to Toronto, conscious that the Grand Duchess's kindness, moral strength, and, above all, her unshaken faith in God and in people were an inspiration to remain with me all through my life.

I think that the heart of the link between us lay in my nationality and our shared faith. Greece had always been dear to Russia; our first Queen, wife of George I, was another Grand Duchess Olga, my hostess's greatly beloved cousin.[1] Queen Olga's daughter, Alexandra, was the Grand Duchess's aunt by marriage, and a son of Queen Olga's, Prince Nicholas, also married a Russian Grand Duchess, Helena, Olga's first cousin.

The Romanov family ties with Greece were strong enough, but a shared faith was an even stronger link. In 988, Vladimir, Grand Duke of Kiev, married Princess Anna, and received baptism at the hands of Greek bishops.

Later there came rivalries between patriarchs and many petty dissensions, but the core of the matter remained inviolate. The great schism of 1054 left all the Russian principalities firmly adhering to orthodoxy. The end of the Byzantine Empire, the attempt made by Rome to bring Muscovy into "a union"—none of it weakened the Russian adherence to orthodoxy. Grand Duchess Olga and I were not aliens to each other when we spoke of church art and beliefs. The icons she had were not kept as collector's pieces. To her they meant what they still mean to any orthodox believer— so many outward expressions of faith in Christ, His Mother, and the company of the Saints.

As months went on, I became more and more conscious that the Grand Duchess's memories were a rich storehouse. I knew that she had refused many tempting offers from editors and publishers. Yet I felt that if her silence was broken, it would do much toward removing at least some of the grotesque fantasies, not to say calumnies, woven around the Romanov tragedy by sensational writers. The Grand Duchess knew things about Rasputin which no one had ever mentioned in print. Her memories of her martyred brothers carried a refreshing immediacy and the stamp of the authentic. Her strictures on other members of the dynasty, severe as they were, carried no malice. But, above all, this most unusual Romanov lady, as I was to learn later, knew her country to an aching degree of intimacy. To listen to her was to walk in the gardens of history.

At last I dared greatly and suggested that she should write her memoirs. I pointed out that her memories had a great historical value. I urged as many reasons as I could muster. Except for her sister, Xenia, already an invalid, living in England, she, Olga, was the very last Grand Duchess, granddaughter, daughter and sister of Tsars, born into a splendor hard to imagine today, acquainted with griefs and privations which do not fall to every lady's lot, accepting her exiled obscurity with all her inborn grace and gentleness, and finally succeeding in keeping her faith intact in the teeth of bitter disasters. Surely, I argued, such a story would be of immense worth today when the majority of people cared little for spiritual values.

The Grand Duchess listened patiently enough. I finished. She shook her head.

"What sense would there be in my writing an autobiography? Far too much has been written about the Romanovs, far too many lies have been spoken, far too many myths have been created. Think of Rasputin alone! Nobody would ever believe me if I told them the truth. Surely you know that people believe nothing except what they want to believe."

I confess I felt disappointed, but I had too much respect for the stand she had taken to continue with my persuasion.

And then, one morning a little later, she greeted me with one of her rare smiles and asked:

"Well, when do we start?"

"When do we start what?" I asked.

"Why, work on my memoirs, of course."

"You mean you have decided to write them?"

"It is you who will write them," the Grand Duchess replied very gently. "I believe that fate brought you and me together so that you could write the story of my fife. I feel convinced that you can do it because you under-stand me far better than most people."

I cannot remember what reply I made. We were still standing by the lit-tle doorway. The Grand Duchess wore the same shapeless old skirt and the same shabby sweater. We were standing on Canadian soil thousands of miles away from her beloved country which she would never see again, the humble cottage behind her her very last home. I could say nothing. I bowed.

"Well." She smiled. "And when do we start?"

"This very moment," I replied.

We went into the cluttered living room and the Grand Duchess sat down on the faded pink sofa.

"To begin with," she said, "I started thinking of all you said the other day and I realized that I am indeed an historical phenomenon of sorts. Except for my sister, who is very ill in London,[2] I am the last Russian Grand Duchess, and more than that—I am the last member of the dynasty who was born in the purple."[3]

Such was the way that I started on the work which was to continue until the death of the Grand Duchess.

There was no room for sentimentality, but deep within me I felt that the shabby, cluttered room in no way warred against her proud beginnings. All the outward grandeur had gone, but the sense of race remained unassailable. Granddaughter, daughter, and sister of Emperors, she was true to her high origins. Day by day as she unfolded her story to me, I grew more and more amazed at something akin to genius in that little old woman. It was a genius indeed—her gift of coming to terms with life which had buffeted, wounded, and mocked at her, and yet left her unvanquished, and unembittered. The first Peter and the second Catherine would indeed have been proud of such a descendant.

The Grand Duchess's memory was extraordinarily vivid. Many incidents were etched so sharply that it was almost possible to imagine they had happened a day or two before. As our work progressed, I knew that she became more and more satisfied with the decision she had taken. She was particularly keen on accuracy and she often insisted on writing in her own hand some of the incidents, such as, for instance, her account of the train disaster at Borki.

The work meant consulting nearly every book written about the Romanovs during the last forty years. Her views on Rasputin, the Ekaterinburg massacre, and the claim of Anna Anderson to be Grand Duchess Anastasia will be given in their place. Here let it be said that the Grand Duchess was the last person living able to sift fact from fable. Her disgust and anger at the colorful calumnies about the Romanov family, which have been printed all over the world, knew no bounds.

She approached every problem as objectively as was possible. There was no vanity in her realization that her memoirs were important. She was vindicating both her family and her country. Yet, as we worked together, the sense of urgency grew and grew.

One afternoon she said to me:

"We must work harder because there is not much time left."

She must have had a premonition. Soon enough all the privations and sufferings, faced with such consummate courage, began taking their toll. She could no longer busy herself in the garden. Her world became the cluttered living room. But her memory did not fail her.

It is not for me to say whether I have acquitted myself well of the task the last Grand Duchess of Russia laid on me, but it is for me to assure my readers that I have written this book with a sense of deep dedication and gratitude that I should have been honored with the friendship and the confidence of one of the most courageous and noble-minded women of her day.

Ian Vorres

Born in the Purple

 n the spring of 1865 the entire Romanov family gathered together at Cannes. The twenty-two-year-old Nicholas, eldest son and heir of Tsar Alexander II, "the hope and comfort of our nation," to quote the poet Tiutchev, lay dying of pneumonia. His fiancée, Princess Dagmar, hurried south from Denmark, and she came in time. Contemporary records tell us that the dying Grand Duke asked that everybody, except his fiancée and his brother Alexander, should leave the room. What followed was known to none except those present, but a legend persisted that Nicholas's hand took Alexander's and Dagmar's and joined them on his breast. The young Tsarevich (Alexander was born in 1845) and the Danish girl were married the following year.[1]

Tsar Alexander III, Grand Duchess Olga's Father.

It might not appear an auspicious beginning, but it proved miraculous. Alexander, who succeeded his father in 1881 as Alexander III, was the first Romanov sovereign to prove himself a good husband and father, and the exigencies of court discipline never elbowed out the warmer aspects of family life. Alexander and Dagmar, now Grand Duchess Marie, had indeed a great grief at the beginning of their married life—their first born died in infancy—but another son, the future Nicholas II, came in 1868, and a third, George, in 1871, followed by the arrival of a daughter, Xenia, in 1875, and yet another boy, Michael, in 1878.

The '70s were eventful years for Russia. In 1875 the adroit policy of Alexander II averted yet another conflict between France and Germany. A couple of years later, he fought Turkey with the result that the Balkan Peninsula was freed of the Turkish yoke forever. For this and for the

Empress Marie Feodorovna, Grand Duchess Olga's mother, 1847–1928.

Empress Marie with three of her children. Nicholas II (the future Tsar of Russia), born in 1868, George, born in 1871, and Xenia, born in 1875, in the Empress's arms. Michael and Olga are not yet born.

Gatchina Palace (an early aeriel photograph).

abolition of serfdom in Russia in 1861 he was called "Tsar Liberator." But conditions were far from tranquil in the Empire. One by one, revolutionary groups were formed. With one or two exceptions, they were terrorist and they hoped to achieve their aims by murder. Several loyal servants of the Crown lost their lives. Several attempts were made on the Emperor's life, and one of them succeeded: on 13 March 1881 Alexander was killed by a bomb in St. Petersburg, and Olga's father, aged 36, became Tsar Alexander III. The murderers, including a girl born of a noble family, were caught, brought to trial, and hanged in public. Alexander III could not afford to show clemency. He had inherited an Empire deeply scarred by all the turmoils and violences of the '70s.

For all the drastic measures taken, unrest remained, and Alexander III left the Winter Palace in St. Petersburg for Gatchina, some fifty miles to the west of the capital. There he brought up his family, exchanging the great palace at Gatchina for the smaller one at Peterhof during the summer months, and there he worked, "the busiest man in the Empire," as one of his cousins, Grand Duke Alexander, called him.

Under Alexander III the Empire, for all the unrest within, enjoyed an unbroken spell of peace without. He had fought in the Balkans in 1877–78 and he called all war "an infamy." "It should be possible for all nations to settle their differences without a single gun being fired," he said.

So Russia remained at peace and had an opportunity to observe a phenomenon hitherto unfamiliar to her people—the young Tsar's home life.

It was a pattern never before seen in a Romanov household. To Alexander III marriage vows were

inviolable and children were the crown of a husband's happiness. He had reigned little more than a year when, on the first of June, 1882, the Empress Marie was delivered of a daughter at Peterhof. Within a few minutes all the belfries at Peterhof broke into a triumphant peal. Within an hour or so the thunder of the traditional 101-gun salute from the ramparts of the SS. Peter and Paul Fortress in St. Petersburg announced the news to the capital. Telegraph wires were kept busy and the salute was fired in every city and town of the Empire.

The baby, given the name of Olga, seemed very delicate. Her mother, following the advice of her sister, the then Princess of Wales, and the precedent established by her mother-in-law, decided to have an English nurse, and Elizabeth Franklin, her valise full of starched caps and aprons, came from England.

"Nana," said the Grand Duchess to me, "was my protector and adviser all through my childhood, and my loyal companion in later years. I have no idea what I should have done without her. All she had done for me enabled me to go through the chaos of those revolution years. She was

Tsar Alexander III and Empress Marie on the Royal Yacht in the Black Sea with Xenia, George, and Nicholas.

Grand Duchess Olga playing with her father, Alexander III, in the park at Gatchina Palace.

capable, courageous, tactful; she was there as my nurse, but her influence was felt by my brothers and sister."

The word "protector" here used by the Grand Duchess carries a particular significance. A sovereign's children were naturally guarded against all possibility of the least mishap befalling them, but Mrs. Franklin's concern was not with that particular kind of protection. She ruled supreme in the nurseries, but she had many underlings to help her, and Russian servants were notoriously loquacious. Gossip seeps into the best-regulated household. Imperial palaces were no exception. That some of the bloodcurdling stories of revolutionary violence did reach Olga was evident from her account of the disaster at Borki,[2] yet Mrs. Franklin's ignorance of Russian conditions must have proved a good antidote, and she could calm the child as no one else could.

Many fairy stories have been written about the luxury and opulence of the life led by the Romanovs. Certainly, the court was brilliant. But the splendor did not reach the imperial nurseries. At the Winter Palace in old Petrograd, at Tsarskoe Selo, Gatchina and Peterhof, it was possible, as late as 1922, to see the children's quarters. They slept on camp beds with one hard, flat pillow and a very thin mattress. A modest carpet covered the floor. There were no armchairs or sofas. Bentwood chairs with very straight backs and cane seats, most ordinary tables, and whatnots for books and toys summed up the furniture. The only rich detail could be noticed in the so-called "icon" corner where the face of the Virgin and Child would be surrounded by pearls and other gems. Their food was of the plainest and, since the days of Olga's grandmother, wife of Alexander II, English customs had been introduced: porridge for breakfast, cold baths, and plenty of fresh air.

Olga was the only baby in the nurseries, her brother Michael being four years older, but hers was by no means a lonely babyhood. The two eldest brothers, Nicholas and George, her sister Xenia, and, of course, Michael had the freedom of the nurseries, always so long as they recognized Mrs. Franklin's authority.

Gatchina was the Emperor's favorite palace. In her turn, Olga preferred it to all the others, and most of her childhood was spent there. The palace had nine hundred rooms; it consisted of two colossal quadrangles joined together by a narrow, curved colonnaded wing of several floors, its roof studded with two towers. It was there that the great art collections were kept in separate galleries. In the Chinese gallery were kept priceless pieces of porcelain and jade collected by earlier sovereigns. The Chesmé gallery commemorated the great naval victory over the Turks in the Bay of Chesmé in 1768, and its walls were hung with tapestries and paintings of the battle.

Unlike the Hermitage, the Gatchina galleries were not then open to the public, but nothing prevented the Tsar's children from visiting them—particularly on wet days.

"And what fun we had there," remembered the Grand Duchess. "The Chinese gallery was ideal for hide and seek! We would crouch behind some huge Chinese vase. There were so many of them, some twice our size. I suppose their value was immense, but I don't remember that any of us ever damaged them."

A formal photograph taken at Gatchina Palace of Grand Duke Michael, age eleven, and Grand Duchess Olga, age seven.

The great park lay outside with its river and several artificial lakes dating back to mid-eighteenth century. At some distance from one of the quadrangles were the stables and kennels, in themselves a little world, with their army of grooms, stable boys, kennel men, and such like; and facing the front door of the palace stood a great statue of Paul I.[3]

Paul I, Catherine the Great's only son and Grand Duchess Olga's great-great-grandfather, proved a most restless ghost: he haunted St. Michael's Castle and the Winter Palace in St. Petersburg, and he haunted Gatchina too. His bedroom in one of the towers, so the Grand Duchess told me, was kept just as it used to be in his lifetime, and all the servants insisted that they had seen Paul's ghost.

Tsema Gallery, one of the numerous vast galleries at Gatchina Palace, named after a famous sea battle between the Russians and the Turks. The enormous paintings lining the walls depict the engagement.

"I never did," said the Grand Duchess, "and it made me despair; contrary to all that has been said about him, Paul was a dear fellow and I would have liked to meet him."

This was a most original comment on the unfortunate Emperor, whose qualities were anything but endearing, and the Grand Duchess seems to have been the only member of her family to hold such a kindly opinion of a tyrannical and suspicious ancestor, considered insane by some of his contemporaries.

Every corner at Gatchina spoke of Russia's great past under the rule of

the Romanovs. The achievements of soldiers and sailors under Peter the Great, Anna, Elizabeth, Catherine the Great, and Alexander I were commemorated in tapestry, painting, and engraving. Later Olga would start proper history lessons, but from her earliest years she seems to have absorbed the sense of Russia.

Gatchina teemed with servants. Olga told me there were more than five thousand of them, including the men at the stables, on the farms, and in the gardens and the park, but it may well be that her memory failed her in this instance. Alexander III had to keep up eight establishments—Gatchina, Peterhof, two large palaces at Tsarskoe Selo, the Anitchkov and Winter Palaces in Moscow, and Livadia in the Crimea—Nicholas II, Olga's brother, kept seven,[4] and the total of men and women employed in the imperial

Tsar Alexander III feeding ducks with Grand Duke Michael in the great park at Gatchina Palace. Grand Dukes George and Nicholas and a member of the naval attachment who tended the palace grounds are standing behind them.

Grand Duchess Olga and Grand Duke Michael in the company of sailors who looked after the rivers and lakes at Gatchina Palace.

household rarely exceeded fifteen thousand. It is hardly likely that a whole third of that number would have been kept at Gatchina.

Nonetheless, there were crowds of them. All were chosen most carefully. A great many came from families which had served the Romanovs for generations.[5] Numbers of them were known to the children—and not by name only. Respect, faultless service, and affection on one side and concern and love on the other bound the children and the servants together. They were not all Russians. Abyssinians, Greeks, Negroes, Finns, Circassians, and others were among them. Olga's mother had Abyssinian servants, who wore gold-braided black jackets, baggy red trousers, yellow shoes and white turbans. The others wore raspberry-colored coats and white breeches.

These people were all loyal to the very marrow of their bones. Nonetheless, the gossip was never-ending.

"I don't think they eavesdropped," said the Grand Duchess, "but they knew far more about us than we did ourselves. Even when I was quite small, news seeped into the nurseries—and that in spite of Nana's vigilance—before breakfast time. I would hear about my brothers' latest pranks and what punishments were meted out to them, about my sister's cold, Papa leaving to attend a review or Mama giving an important party, and what visitors were expected at the palace."

So there was Gatchina with its nine hundred rooms, its army of servants, its immense park; but, court functions apart, there was no pomp under its roof. Olga's father, the Emperor of all the Russias, was up at seven every morning, washed in cold water, dressed himself in peasant's clothes, made his own coffee in a glass percolator, filled a plate with cracknels, and, his breakfast eaten, he went to his desk and settled to the day's work. He disturbed none of the servants. Some time later his wife joined him, and a small table was brought by two servants. Husband and wife shared a breakfast of boiled eggs and rye bread and butter.

Did they share it in peace? It was precisely at that time that their baby daughter made her appearance. The Empress, her breakfast finished, would leave, but the baby Grand Duchess stayed with her father.

Olga's nurseries at Gatchina were very near the Emperor's study. There were four rooms: her bedroom, Mrs. Franklin's, a sitting room and a dining room. That tiny kingdom was under Nana's exclusive care, and all the servants had to obey her orders—particularly about baby Olga's food.

"We all grew up on a very plain diet," the Grand Duchess told me. "For tea, we had jam with our bread and butter and English biscuits—cake was served very seldom. We liked the way our porridge was cooked—Nana must have taught them how to do it. Mutton cutlets with peas and baked potatoes seems to have been our staple dinner, or else roast beef, but even Nana could not make me like it—particularly when it was underdone! But all of us were brought up in the same way: we ate whatever we were given."

In those early childhood years the day's greatest excitement came after breakfast when Mrs. Franklin brought her little charge into the Emperor's study. Once there, little Olga crawled under his desk and kept very quiet, the Emperor's big sheep dog Kamchatka by her, until her parents had finished their breakfast.

"My father was everything to me. Immersed in work as he was, he always spared that daily half-hour. As I grew a bit older, my privileges increased. I remember the day when I was first allowed to put the imperial

An early, formal photograph of Grand Duchess Olga (left) at age three with her sister Grand Duchess Xenia, age ten, at Gatchina Palace.

seal on one of the big envelopes which lay in stacks on the desk. It was a very heavy seal of gold and crystal, but how proud and delighted I felt that morning. I was appalled at the amount of work Father had to do every day; I think a Tsar was the hardest-worked man on earth. Besides audiences and state functions, every day he was faced with stacks of edicts, ukases and reports which he had to read and sign. Many times Father would furiously scribble his indignant comments on the margins of the documents: 'Idiots!' 'Fools!' 'What a beast he is!'"

There were occasions when the Emperor unlocked a special drawer in his desk, and, excitement dancing in his eyes, would show his "treasures" to his favorite child. The "treasures" were a collection of miniature animals made of china and glass.

"And once my father showed me a very old album full of most exciting pen-and-ink sketches of an imaginary city called Mopsopolis, inhabited by Mopses.[6] He showed it to me in secret, and I was thrilled to have him share his own childhood secrets with me."

As I listened to those early memories, I was struck by one detail: the foreground of that stage was occupied by the Emperor, Nana, Olga's brothers and sister, and behind them stood a vast crowd of servants, soldiers, sailors, and all manner of common folk. But the Grand Duchess had very little to say about her mother; the intimate conversations in the study would not begin until the Empress had gone. Again the great palace was crowded with members of the household, but the earliest memories do not seem concerned with any of them. There must have been a long procession of foreign royalty, ladies-in-waiting, chamberlains, equerries. She would have met them all. She must have heard about them. But to her, ever since her childhood, warm realities had meant much more than the gorgeously patterned splendor of court. The memory of those mornings burned bright and clear to the very midnight of her life.

"My father had the strength of a Hercules, but he never showed off when other people were present. He told us that he could bend horseshoes and cutlery quite easily, but did not dare do it because my mother would have been furious. Yet once in the study he bent an iron poker and then straightened it out. I remember how he kept his eyes on the door in case someone were to come in!"

At the beginning of autumn 1888 Olga left her dear Gatchina for the first time. The whole imperial family went to visit the Caucasus. In October they were due to be back in the North.

On the twenty-ninth of October, the long imperial train was traveling fast towards Kharkov. The Grand Duchess remembered how grey the day was, wet snow shrouding the countryside. About one o'clock the train was approaching the small town of Borki. The Emperor, the Empress, and four of their children were having lunch in the dining car. The pudding was being brought in by an old butler called Leo when the train lurched violently, and then again, so that everybody fell on the floor. Within a second or two the dining car was torn open and the heavy iron roof caved in just a few inches above the passengers' heads. They were all, in fact, lying on the ground, the thick carpet between them and the permanent way. The explosion had sliced off the wheels and the floor of the car. The Emperor was the first to crawl out from under the roof. This done, he held it up so that his wife, children, and the others were able to get clear of the wreckage. It was truly a Herculean effort on Alexander's part and, though nobody knew it at the time, it was to cost him dear.

Mrs. Franklin and Olga were in the children's coach immediately behind the dining saloon. They were waiting for the pudding which never came.

"I remember clearly how two pink glass vases fell off the table and were smashed at the first shock. I was frightened and Nana took me on her knees and put her arms about me." There followed another crash and something heavy fell on them both. "And then I felt wet earth against my face...."

Olga seemed all alone. The violence of the second explosion had thrown her clear of the wreckage. She rolled down the steep embankment and panic clutched her. The world became an inferno. Some coaches further down the train were still moving, crashing against those in front, and pitching sideways. The deafening noise of iron clanging against iron and the screams of the injured made the six-year-old child more frightened than ever. She had forgotten to think either of her parents or Nana. All she wanted was to run away from the horror she saw. She ran stumblingly, blindly. A footman, one Kondratiev, ran after her and picked her up in his arms.

"And I was so frightened that I scratched his face. . . ."

From the footman's arms Olga went into her father's, and he took her to one of the few carriages left intact. There lay Mrs. Franklin, who had two ribs broken and a severe internal injury. All the children were left together while the Emperor and Empress, and all the uninjured members of the retinue, helped the household doctor to tend the wounded and the dying who lay on the ground near enormous bonfires lit to keep them warm.

"Later I heard," said the Grand Duchess, "that my mother had been heroic, helping the doctor with a real nurse's zeal. . . ."

Indeed it was so. Once she knew that her husband and children were safe, the Empress Marie forgot all about herself. She had been cut about her arms and legs by splintered glass and bruised all over, but she told everybody that nothing was the matter with her, ordered her personal luggage to be brought out, made bandages out of her underwear, and looked after as many wounded as she could. At last a relief train arrived from Kharkov. Neither the Emperor nor the Empress, for all their fatigue, would come aboard until all the wounded were settled in and all the bodies, decently covered, were taken on board. There were two hundred and eighty-one casualties, twenty-one of them fatal.

The Borki disaster was indeed a tragic landmark in at least one very young life. An inquiry never established the cause. Everybody was convinced that the Railway Regiment, in whose care lay the safety of imperial trains, had been negligent and that two bombs had been placed on the permanent way. A rumor went about that the leader of the guilty revolutionary group had met his own death in the explosion, but nothing came to be proved.

Grand Duchess Olga was inclined to think that the accident had been
due to the train splitting a defective piece of the permanent way. Yet her
own words rather contradicted her acceptance of that theory.

"I was only six but I became conscious of a danger lurking somewhere.
Much later someone told me that when I began running away from the
wreckage, I kept screaming, 'Now they'll come and kill us all!' This may
well be true. I was far too young to know anything about revolutionaries.
'They' was a composite symbol, something of an image of an enemy."

Many members of the household were either dead or crippled for life. Kamchatka, her father's favorite dog, was crushed by a piece of fallen carriage roof. Count Sheremetev, officer commanding the Cossack Guards and a personal friend of the Emperor, was among the dead. But above the sharpness of concrete losses stood the frightening intangible sense of peril. The happy, carefree childhood days were ended on that murky October afternoon, the wreckage of the imperial train streaking the snowy landscape with black and crimson. The little Grand Duchess could have found no words to express all she felt, but something deep inside her made her understand much more than should ever have been grasped by one so young and so sheltered as she was: the gravity so often seen on her father's face and the look of tension in her mother's dark eyes.

Olga's parents had witnessed the death of Alexander II. They had seen that horribly mutilated body, the bomb having been thrown just as he was returning from an errand of mercy and comfort.[7] Alexander III had few delusions, but he continued making his public appearances, though he well knew that the most thorough police precautions could not but leave a loophole for a millionth chance of a mishap.

Back at Gatchina the outward rhythm of life beat to its familiar measure, but little Olga knew nothing was the same for her. "It was then that I began being afraid of the dark," she told me.

The shadowy reaches of the galleries and corridors now made her uneasy, and for the first time she understood why mounted police kept watch 'round about the park walls. Late in the evening one could see the bobbing lights of the police lanterns which were strapped to the heads of the horses. She also understood why a guards regiment, the famed Blue Cuirassiers, was stationed within the Gatchina precincts, their barracks close to the imperial stables. In addition, a composite regiment acted as the Tsar's bodyguard. It comprised representatives of all the regiments of the guard and was stationed at Gatchina as well. Yet such was the Grand Duchess's nature that little by little she came to accept all those men as her friends. Their presence, as it were, came to heal some of the wounds received at Borki.

"I made friends with as many as I could," she said, "and it was fun when

Michael and I slipped away into the barracks and listened to the men's songs. My mother strictly forbade such pranks, and so did Nana, and every time we carried it off we felt we had achieved something. The men used to play games with us and toss us in the air. Peasants though they were, they never behaved roughly. I felt safe with them. It was after Borki also that I first became aware of the Cossacks of the household standing guard outside our private apartments at Gatchina. Hearing them tiptoe at night outside my door in their soft leather socks gave me a wonderful sense of security. They had been especially selected for this duty because of their physiques and they soared above me like creatures from Gulliver's Travels."

Soldiers and sailors were friends indeed.[8] But there were others whose presence often irked the Emperor's children: plainclothes men so ubiquitous that one could not escape them. That winter of 1888–89 Olga seems to have become conscious of them for the first time.

"I suppose they were necessary, but my father could not bear them, and they looked so very obvious we nicknamed them 'naturalists' because they kept darting in and out from behind trees and shrubs."

She was not yet seven. She had not yet made a single public appearance. The splendid functions given by her parents at Gatchina and St. Petersburg meant nothing to her. The small, well-ordered world of the nurseries, her father's private study, the palace galleries, and the park—such was her orbit. Yet the sunny simplicities of that daily life, under the wise rule of an English nanny, were already marked by a shadow which came and went—to return again and yet again.

The Schoolroom and the World

Olga's room at Gatchina remained the same, but the dining room became her classroom as soon as she passed her seventh birthday. There she and her eleven-year-old brother, Grand Duke Michael, were kept at their lessons from nine till three every day, and from then on brother and sister became inseparable.

"He and I had so much in common," the Grand Duchess said to me. "We had the same tastes, liked the same people, shared many interests, and we never quarreled."

When she did happen to be prevented from being with him, she was in despair. On such occasions she always managed to have a servant smuggle a note to him, a practice that grew into a regular habit. Sometimes she would bombard him with two or three letters a day, and she once showed me some of the notes, scribbled on imperial stationery, which she had sent to him at Gatchina.

My dear old Mikael: How is your throat? I am not allowed to see you; I will send you something! Now goodbye. I kiss you, Olga.

Dear Misha: Mama won't let me go tomorrow because I went [out] this morning. Please see her again. I am terribly sorry. Olga.

The young Olga had several pet names for Michael, but her favorite was "dear darling Floppy," an endearment that remained with him through the years. Later, when they both had become adults and attended official

Grand Duke Michael, "Floppy," in 1893.

Grand Duchess Olga with her brother Grand Duke George, "Georgie."

functions, Olga would often forget herself and dumbfound nearby dignitaries by addressing her brother as "darling Floppy."

As I listened to the description of those remote days in the schoolroom, I felt that however well Alexander III's children were brought up their education as such must have been rather elementary.[1] The Grand Duchess mentioned many masters, all carefully chosen by the parents—Mr. Heath and M. Thormeyer for English and French, and an unnamed gentleman who taught them geography and who annoyed them by taking himself too seriously. Although he had never ventured beyond St. Petersburg, he would talk about other countries with absolute authority, describing minutely their landscapes and flowers with the air of a world traveler. Grand Duke George, however, would always deflate the poor man's ego. Every time he spoke of another monument or flower in a distant land, George would politely ask: "Did you see it yourself? Did you smell that flower?" To which the poor man could only answer meekly, "No."

Georgie, according to his sister, was a terrible tease. His study was adjacent to that of Nicholas, the Tsarevich, who was kept in fits of laughter listening to George torture his tutors. If Nicholas had difficulty concentrating on his books it was because George always kept him distracted, she added. "In fact, Georgie's humor was such that whenever he cracked a particularly good joke, Nicky would write it down on a scrap of paper and file it in a 'mystery box' along with other souvenirs of his childhood. He kept this box in his study when he became Tsar and would often have a hearty laugh rereading his secret source of collected humor.

"To make matters worse, Georgie had a colorful accomplice in his green parrot, Popka, who for reasons unknown to me hated Mr. Heath. Every time the poor English master entered Georgie's room, the bird would fly into a rage and then imitate Mr. Heath with the most exaggerated British

Grand Duchess Olga with her brother Grand Duke George, "Georgie."

accent. Mr. Heath finally became so exasperated that he refused to enter Georgie's room until Popka had been removed."

They were taught dancing, Russian, and drawing. "Dancing was one of the important 'chores' Misha and I performed together. Our dancing master was Mr. Troitski, an artistic and very dignified gentleman who wore white whiskers and stood as straight as an old officer. He always wore white gloves and insisted that a huge pot of fresh flowers always be placed on the piano used by his accompanist.

"Misha and I had to bow and curtsy to each other before stepping into the *pas de patineur*, the waltz, or the polka, which I hated. We both felt such fools and were self-conscious, especially since we knew that despite our orders the Cossacks standing on guard outside the ballroom were peeking through the keyholes. They always greeted us with broad grins after the lesson, a fact which only increased our embarrassment."

History and drawing alone seemed to attract the little Grand Duchess. Neither Michael nor she played any pranks during their history lessons.

"Russian history," she said, "was something like a part of our real lives—all intimate family matters—and we could enter into it without the least effort."

The morning visits to the Emperor's study became shorter and shorter. Yet their content gained in color and interest. Olga was old enough to listen to stories of the past—the days of the Crimean War, the triumph of the Emancipation, the great reforms carried out by her grandfather in the teeth of so much opposition, and the Russo-Turkish War of 1877, which broke the Turkish yoke in the Balkans.

But there remained many lacunae. As will be seen later, Olga followed her family from one palace to another in the North of the Empire; she came to know the Crimea and also Denmark on her regular annual visits to her Danish grandparents, King Christian IX and Queen Louise. But the palaces at Peterhof, Tsarskoe Selo, and Gatchina were in that part of the country which had been wrested from Sweden by Peter the Great; the farms were all tenanted by *chukhny*, an old Russian term for the population on the eastern fringe of the Baltic lands. Neither Olga nor any of the others knew much about the way of life as it was lived in the heart of the country. Their horizon was narrowed by precaution even more than by etiquette. They traversed the whole of Russia on their way from St. Petersburg to the Crimea, but they traveled in closely guarded imperial trains, the entire length of the permanent way policed by the men of the Railway Regiment. In a word, they had no chance to learn their native land. It is a matter for wonder that the Grand Duchess so early began developing her love of the common people. She knew them because she never lost an opportunity of making friends.

"They called my father the Tsar—*moujik*," she said to me once, "because he did understand the peasant mind. Like Peter the Great he detested all pomp and luxury, had simple tastes, and told us he never felt so much at ease as when, all alone, he could wear ordinary peasant clothes. And I know that, contrary to everything that has been said, he was loved. You should have seen soldiers' upturned faces at maneuvers or after a review. It was not an expression assumed at an officer's command. Even as a child I was conscious of that devotion."

After 1889, Olga no longer dined and supped in the nurseries every day. There were many occasions when, at the Empress's order, Mrs. Franklin changed the little girl's frock at noon, brushed her hair with extra care, and the Emperor's youngest daughter had to make the long journey to one of the palace dining rooms, to lunch with her parents and the guests that happened to be invited that day. At Gatchina, except on formal occasions when meals were served in the great banqueting

Formal portrait of Grand Duchess Olga, age eight, at Gatchina Palace.

hall near the throne room, the imperial family dined in a big bathroom on the ground floor, its windows opening out into the rose garden. The room had indeed been used as a bathroom by the Empress Alexandra, wife of Nicholas I, and the enormous white marble bath, with four great mirrors at the back, stood against one of the walls. Grand Duchess Olga's mother had it filled with masses of varicolored azaleas.

"I was not shy," the Grand Duchess said, "but those meals with the family soon became an ordeal. My brother Michael and I were always hungry and Mrs. Franklin never allowed eating between meals."

"Hungry?" I could not help my amazement.

"Oh yes," she went on. "There was plenty of food and, though plain enough, it looked far more exciting than the dishes served in the nursery,

Formal portrait of Grand Duchess Olga, age eight, at Gatchina Palace.

but, you see, strict precedence was observed: my parents were served first, then the guests, and so on. Michael and I, being the youngest, had the last turn. In those days it was considered very bad form either to hurry or to finish the food on your plate. By the time our turn came, there was just time to have one or two bites. Even Nicky was once so hungry that he committed a sacrilege...." She explained that every child of the Romanov family had a gold cross given it at its baptism. The cross was hollow and filled with beeswax. An infinitesimal relic of the True Cross was embedded in the wax. "...He opened his cross and ate the contents—relic and all. Later he felt very ashamed of himself but admitted that it had tasted 'immorally good.'

"I was the only one who knew about it. Nicky would not even tell George and Xenia. Our parents would have been shocked beyond words. As you know, we were all brought up very strictly in religious matters. There were the regular weekly services, and many fasts, and every national occasion would be marked by a solemn Te Deum—all of it was as natural to us as the air we breathed. I can't remember that any of us ever discussed religion, and yet"—the Grand Duchess smiled—"my eldest brother's sacrilege did not shock us at all. I just laughed, and later whenever we had something nice to eat we would whisper to each other, 'It's immorally good,' and nobody knew our secret."

I said again that it seemed incredible for an Emperor's eldest son to be hungry at a palace where kitchens, larders, and storerooms were full of good things.

"Ah, but everything was strictly appointed," the Grand Duchess explained. "There was breakfast, lunch, tea, dinner, and evening tea—all severely in accordance with the palace stewards' instructions, and some of them had not been changed since the days of Catherine the Great. Why, there were some small saffron buns which appeared daily with the evening tea in 1889. They were of the same kind served at court in 1788. My brother Michael and I hardly ever ceased playing most mischievous pranks, but we just could not have sneaked into one of the pantries to ask for a sandwich or a bun. That would have been one of those things which were not done."

But, in spite of short commons at her parents' table, those occasions were good for the little Grand Duchess. She might not talk. But she could listen, and she listened greedily to every conversation. Members of the family, foreign royalty, her father's ministers, diplomats—her small world kept enlarging week by week. Some of the thumbnail portraits she sketched for me by no means reflected the colors used by future historians. Nonetheless, those portraits were based on her impressions and they were part of her own truth. For instance, there was General Cherevin, head of the dreaded Okhrana, a very frequent guest at the Emperor's table. His devotion to Alexander and Marie turned him into a personal friend of the family, but I could not help wondering whether Grand Duchess Olga knew anything about the work of the Okhrana when she said of him: "Friendly, generous, and humble. He was very popular in St. Petersburg."

What would she have said if she had known that thousands of mothers in the capital and its environs used to frighten their children with Cherevin's name!

The Grand Duchess met someone else in the dining room at Gatchina, the famous Pobedonostev, once her father's tutor, now the powerful Procurator of the Holy Synod. She admitted to me that he was feared throughout the Empire.

"Yet people were not altogether fair to him," she complained. "He had an ascetic air and his eyes could look steel-cold on occasions. I know that he stood for autocracy, anti-Semitism and Pan-Slavism. But there were warmer traits in his make-up. I would often see him being kindly to children. And he could be funny. There was at least one flaw in his armor: he was terrified of ghosts. He and his wife lived in a flat in Liteynaya Street in St. Petersburg. The building was haunted. Pobedonostev had priests to exorcise the ghost. Nonetheless, an unseen monster's claws took to tearing off the blankets on his bed. Pobedonostev was panic-stricken, but he stayed on, and not until his wife had left did he change his mind and follow her to another house. He told the story himself. I often think that if the public knew how frightened Pobedonostev could be, they would have changed their opinion of him."

"Was he not known as the power behind the throne?" I asked. She shook her head.

"I believe people were apt to exaggerate his influence. I do remember that my father listened to him more attentively than to other ministers, but my father usually arrived at his decisions independently of anyone's advice. You see, he worked so hard. Those brief morning sessions with him left a deep impression on my mind! His desk was literally stacked with papers. And later I learned that he would often work till the small hours. His days were crowded with giving business audiences to ministers, bishops, governors from the provinces, and others. When in the Crimea, he was supposed to be on holiday, but even there state papers appeared, and an endless procession of couriers and messengers kept him in touch with his government.

"I can't say," added the Grand Duchess, "that I ever understood his work in all its details, but I do know that it made superhuman demands on his time and energy. He so loved purely family occasions, but how he grudged even a few hours given up to formal entertainment! In that he resembled Peter the Great."

Those were red-letter days when, the palace clock striking three, the Grand Duchess and her brother Michael received a message that His Imperial Majesty would take them for a walk in the Gatchina woods.

"We would set out for the deer park—just the three of us—like the three bears in the fairy tale. My father always carried a big spade, Michael had a smaller one, and I had a tiny one of my own. Each of us also carried a hatchet, a lantern, and an apple. If it was winter, he taught us how to clear a tidy path through the snow, and how to fell a dead tree. He taught Michael and me how to build up a fire. Finally, we roasted the apples, damped down the fire, and the lanterns helped us find our way home. In the summer, he taught us how to distinguish one animal spoor from another. We often fetched up near a lake, and he taught us how to row.

He so wanted us to read the book of nature as easily as he read it himself. Those afternoon walks were the finest lessons we could have."

After the walk, at about five in the afternoon, the children would have tea with the Empress. Occasionally, a group of ladies from St. Petersburg would join the Empress and then tea time became a rather formal affair. The ladies would sit in a semi-circle around the Empress, who would pour tea from a beautiful silver service placed before her by her impeccable servant Stepano. On one occasion, though, the practical joker, George, upset the dignity of the tea-time ceremony in rather spectacular fashion. He stuck out his foot just as Stepano was walking into the room with his usual air of magnificence, and there was a look of pained disbelief on Stepano's face as he found himself flat on the floor with cups and plates, silverware and cakes and biscuits clattering and rolling around the room, to the horror of the imperial gathering.

"Georgie was the only one who could get away with such terrible tricks, for Mother had a great weakness for him," said the Grand Duchess. This was probably a mother's tender premonition, for when Grand Duke George was just twenty, he contracted tuberculosis and died seven years later at Abbas Touman, in the foothills of the Caucasus.

Sunday was a happy day for young Olga and Misha. It was the day they were allowed to invite other children, young members of the nobility, to visit Gatchina. They would arrive by train from St. Petersburg for tea and a couple of hours of play. A suite of thirteen rooms in a remote part of the palace—part of the apartments of Paul I—was set aside for the youngsters.

The Emperor rather than the Empress stood closer to his two younger children. The Grand Duchess admitted the existence of a gulf between her mother and herself. The Empress Marie fulfilled her functions admirably, but she was always an Empress even when she entered the nurseries. Olga and Michael were afraid of her. Her very manner suggested that their little world and its small problems did not greatly interest her. The Grand Duchess never dreamt of going to her mother for comfort and advice.

"As a matter of fact, going to her rooms was a duty laid on me by Nana. I never felt at my ease. I tried to be on my best behavior. I could never bring myself to speak naturally. She had a horror of anything beyond the frontiers of etiquette and propriety. Only much later did I realize how jealous she was of Nana, but my attachment to Nana was not the only barrier. When Michael and I were caught in a forbidden prank, we would get punished, but, the punishment over, my father would roar with laughter—as, for instance, that evening when Michael and I climbed to the roof of the palace because it was so much fun to see the great park by moonlight. But my mother could not even smile when she heard of such pranks. It was indeed fortunate that her days were so crowded that few of our escapades came to her notice."

And yet there were at least two interests shared by mother and daughter, and they might so easily have forged a link between them. The Empress Marie had a love for painting, though neither in Denmark nor in Russia did she have proper lessons. A picture of hers, a life-size portrait of a coachman, later came to be hung in a gallery. Her youngest daughter showed her talent at so early an age that the Emperor decided to have expert tuition given to her.

"Even during geography and arithmetic lessons I was allowed to sit with a pencil in my hand. I could listen far better whilst drawing a cornstalk and some wild flowers."[2]

The other common interest between the Empress and the Grand Duchess was animals, horses in particular. "Riding was the favorite sport of us children. We all adored horses: each of us had a high-ranking officer from the imperial guard as riding instructor. We all took to riding like fish to water. Mother also adored horses but Father hated them," said the Grand Duchess.

Imperial horses were very badly trained and had a tendency to bolt. She recalled the occasion at Gatchina when the Empress had brought her lovely small pony chaise around to the entrance to pick up the Emperor for a drive. As Alexander III stepped in, the two horses reared back and he instantly jumped out. "Come back in!" shouted the Empress, but the Emperor snapped: "If you want to kill yourself, you can do it alone!" The Grand Duchess added: "My mother personally looked after the affairs of the imperial stables and General Arthur Grunwald was in charge. He was a kind old gentleman, not entirely suitable for the job. Once Mother wanted a pair of larger horses for her pony chaise. Later, when she asked to see them, old General Grunwald said, '*Oui, je les ai achetés, mais je conseillerais Madame de ne pas les conduire.*'" (Yes, I bought them, but I would advise Madam not to drive them.)

The Empress rode and drove superbly, and all the children were mounted almost as soon as they could walk. But horses were by no means the only animals to engage the children's affection. Had they been allowed to keep all the animals sent to them by relations and friends, the palace might have grown into a zoo. Dogs, bear cubs, rabbits, wolf cubs, hares, even elks and lynxes were sent as presents. Except for the dogs, they went to the Zoological Gardens in St. Petersburg and Moscow.

One of the Grand Duchess's favorite pets was an albino crow given her by her father. There was also a wolf cub, kept in a paddock in the grounds and brought up on a diet of fruit and milk, and Kuku, a wild hare, grown so tame that it followed its mistress everywhere.

But shooting she detested.

"Michael was given his first rifle one Christmas when he was ten, I think. The next day he shot a crow in the park. We saw it fall, ran up, and found it wounded. We both sat down in the snow and cried bitterly. My poor Floppy was so unhappy that day, but his shooting certainly improved. He had an excellent teacher and ended by becoming a crack shot. But I never liked it. Neither my sister nor I were taught to shoot...."

The two greatest landmarks of the year were Christmas and Easter, and the Grand Duchess's memories of both festivals were warm and colorful. First and foremost, they were happy family occasions, but on those two days in the year the family was by no means limited to parents, children, and the great crowd of relations. The family meant thousands of servants and personal retainers, of soldiers and sailors, of members of the household and others in possession of the entrée. Presents had to be given to them all.

And presents meant a very peculiar problem. Etiquette forbade any member of the imperial family to enter a shop in any town. The shop-keepers had to send their wares to the palace. Alexanders,[3] Bolin, Cabussue, Scipion, Knopp and others sent case after case to Gatchina.

Xenia and Michael dressed for a costume ball.

"But," remembered the Grand Duchess, "they kept sending the same things, year in, year out. Once something was bought, they got the idea that we always wanted the same thing and somehow there was never enough time to send the things back to St. Petersburg. Moreover, cooped up in the palace, we had no idea about any novelties in the market. Really important shops did not advertise in those days. Even if they did, we children would not have seen the advertisements: newspapers were taboo in the nursery. The one present I always gave to my father was my own handiwork—a pair of soft red slippers, cross-stitched in white—and it was such a pleasure to see him wear them."

The Emperor's children had no pocket money. Whatever they chose for their personal presents was paid for out of the privy purse. They had no idea about values as such. Olga's elder sister, Grand Duchess Xenia, a great favorite with her mother, happened to be in the Empress's rooms when two ladies-in-waiting were unpacking cases of jewelry and bibelots sent by Cartier from Paris. Xenia, aged thirteen, had not yet decided what she would give her mother. But suddenly she saw a filigree scent bottle, its stopper studded with sapphires. She snatched at it and begged Countess Stroganov not to give her secret away. That scent bottle must have cost a small fortune, and Xenia duly presented it to her mother on Christmas Day. A little later the Empress made it known that boxes arriving from Cartier and other jewelers could be admired by the children and no more.

Alexander III hated all vulgar ostentation. He might well have showered jewels on all his children every Christmas, but the presents they got were toys, books, gardening implements, and suchlike.

Yet, for all the imperial thrift, Christmas cost a lot. The lists prepared in the Emperor's private chancery ran into many thousands, and all the cards attached to the gifts bore the imperial signature. So many presents could hardly have been chosen individually. They were mostly pieces of porcelain, glass and silver. Relations and intimate friends received jewelry.

For several months before Christmas the palace was in a turmoil—messengers arriving with mysterious parcels, gardeners bringing numbers of Christmas trees, cooks driven off their feet. Even the Emperor's private study was littered with packages, which Olga and Michael were forbidden to look at. In the small kitchen-pantry at the back of the nurseries, Mrs. Franklin was engaged in the sacrosanct business of making plum puddings. The imperial cooks might easily have made them, but Mrs. Franklin would not hear of delegating the duty to the kitchen servants.

By Christmas Eve everything was ready. Something of a hush fell over the palace in the afternoon. All the servants stood by the windows waiting for the star to appear. At six, the bells of the Gatchina church rang for vespers. The service was followed by a family dinner.

"We ate it in a room adjoining the banqueting hall. The doors of the latter were closed, Cossacks standing on guard. We felt we could eat nothing—such was our excitement—and, oh, how difficult it was to keep silent! I would stare at my knife and fork and carry on an imaginary conversation with them. We all, even Nicky, by then a young man in his early twenties, lived for the moment when, the unwanted dessert cleared away, the parents would get up and go into the banqueting hall."

But the children and all the others had to wait until the Emperor rang a handbell. Then, all etiquette, let alone formality, was thrown to the winds and there was a stampede toward the doors of the banqueting hall. Once those were flung open, they found themselves in a magic kingdom. Christmas trees, each glimmering with multi-colored candles and glittering with gilded and silver fruit and ornaments, seemed to fill the hall. No wonder! There were six trees for the family and many more for relations and the household. Near each tree stood a small table covered by a white cloth and laden with presents.

On that occasion even the Empress did not frown at the bustle and hustle. What with the fun in the banqueting hall and the evening tea that followed, and the singing of the traditional songs, it would be nearly midnight before Mrs. Franklin could lead the excited children back to the nurseries. Three days later came the dismantling of the trees, and the children did it themselves. All the servants together with their families came into the banqueting hall, and the Emperor's sons and daughters, all armed with scissors, climbed stepladders and denuded the trees down to the very last ornament. "All the exquisite tulip-shaped candlesticks and all the beautiful ornaments, so many of them made by Bolin and Peto, were given to the servants, and weren't they happy, and weren't we happy in their happiness!"

The second landmark of the year came at Easter, its festivities being enjoyed all the more because they followed seven weeks of rigorous abstinence—not only from meat, butter, cheese, and milk but from any form of entertainment. The Grand Duchess's dancing lessons were suspended during Lent. There were no balls, concerts, or weddings. The period was called *Veliky Post* (The Great Fast), and the name fitted.

Beginning with Palm Sunday, they went to church morning and evening. Easter Eve brought the first breath of freedom. Mrs. Franklin might retire at her usual hour, but Olga, no longer considered a baby, stayed up. For the great midnight service known as *Zautreniya*, which lasted more than three hours, she was dressed as for a great court occasion: an empearled *kokoshnik* on her small head, the embroidered veil falling down to her waist, the silver brocade sarafan and a kirtle of cream satin. Full court dress was worn by all attending the service. On an imaginative child such a service held at an unaccustomed hour must have produced an indelible impression of awe, expectation, and joy.

"I can't remember if we ever got tired, but I do remember how we all waited, breath suspended, for the first triumphant 'Christ Is Risen' chanted by the combined imperial choirs."

Snow might lie thick and firm outside, but the words ended the winter. Big and small annoyances, disappointments, and anxieties all vanished at that

first "Christ Is Risen." Everybody in the church stood, a lit candle in hand. All gave themselves up to that triumph. The rigors of Lent behind them, the Emperor's children ran into the banqueting hall for the traditional *razgovlyatsya* where delicacies forbidden since Carnival Sunday awaited them.

"And on the way we kept stopping every minute to exchange the traditional three kisses with butlers, footmen, soldiers, maids—anyone we met on the way."

Easter Day was hardly a day of rest for the imperial family. It started with a reception in one of the great halls of Gatchina. The Emperor and Empress stood at one end, and everybody connected with the palace came up in turn, to receive the traditional Easter greeting together with an egg made either of porcelain, or jasper, or malachite.

"I particularly enjoyed standing near my father when it came to the choir boys' turn. Some of them were quite small, and footmen would lift them up onto a stool. It would have been impossible for my father to stoop several times a minute to kiss the boys."

The entire day was taken up with these ceremonies. In the afternoon, the Emperor, accompanied by his youngest children, visited all the barracks in the palace precincts and beyond. As she grew older Olga was permitted to hold the tray with the china eggs.

"What a busy, happy day! And how it reflected the truth of an ancient saying of ours, 'As precious as an egg on Christ's own day.'"

When in 1817 Grand Duchess Olga's great-grandfather Nicholas, later Nicholas I, was married to Princess Charlotte of Prussia, the future of the Romanov dynasty seemed to depend solely on him. His father, Paul I, had ten children, but, of his four sons, Alexander I had two daughters, both dying in infancy, Constantine was childless, and Michael, the last of the four brothers to marry, would have one daughter. It was with Nicholas I that the Romanov family escaped the danger of extinction. Nicholas's four sons between them gave him seventeen grandsons.

By the time Olga was ten, she could scarcely count all the members of the family. To the Romanovs proper were added the Princes of Mecklenberg-Strelitz and of Oldenburg, and the Dukes of Leuchtenberg, all of whom, having married into the Romanov family, gave up their alien nationality and were accepted into what was known as the Imperial House (*Imperatorsky Dom*). There were also ties of blood with several German houses—Prussia, Coburg-Gotha, Hesse, Baden, and Würtemberg—with the Danish royal family, and, through the latter, with Greece. In 1874 Alexander III's only sister, Marie, married the Duke of Edinburgh. In brief, the only reigning houses unallied to the Romanovs were those of

Hapsburg, Bourbon, and Braganza, whose profession of the Roman Catholic faith created an insuperable barrier in the eyes of the Russians.

Alexander III was very much a patriarch; he looked upon that enormous Romanov clan as one family unit, and during his reign little was heard of any factions, quarrels, or rivalries. Even his younger brother, the hot-tempered Grand Duke Vladimir, and his imperious wife had to accept a policy which unified, if only on the surface. Alexander III, who hated all grandeur and ostentation, held fast by the family ties. Christenings, weddings, and funerals, to say nothing of other occasions, meant summonses to all the Romanovs to meet together, and the peasant Tsar proved himself a consummate host.

Such meetings were not always at Gatchina. The latter always remained closest to Olga's heart and there she had spent all her early years, but, with the nursery book closed, she began following the family on their appointed annual peregrinations.

To the northwest of St. Petersburg, on the shores of the Gulf of Finland, lay Peterhof, its world-famous fountains created by a Scotsman, Cameron, at the command of Catherine the Great. Peterhof was built on land wrested from Sweden by Peter the Great. Determined to bring Western ways to his country, he had ordered a sign to be placed in the palace that read: "*Ladies and Gentlemen of the court caught sleeping with their boots on will be instantly decapitated.*"

"I had heard of the existence of such a sign but I never saw it," Olga said. However, she did hear, from the servants as usual, that her father once caught her brother Nicky sleeping on his bed at Peterhof with his boots on after a particularly long ride. "It was indeed fortunate for Nicky that Father was not Peter the Great," she laughed.

To Peterhof the imperial family went for about six weeks in the summer. Complete informality reigned there despite the grandeur of the gardens and the Great Palace. According to the Grand Duchess, all the surrounding area teemed with the so-called *datchniki* (cottagers) from St. Petersburg. Most of them were elderly, semi-retired citizens of the middle class who spent most of their time lounging around in crumpled old pajamas.

"There was something contagious about the casualness of the *datchniki*,"

Grand Duchess Olga, about sixteen, at Peterhof with her aunt and godmother, Queen of Greece. (The author's aunt was the Queen of Greece's Lady in Waiting.)

said Grand Duchess Olga. From the moment the imperial family disembarked from the royal yacht they seemed infected by the carefree abandon of the area. As they rode in open carriages to the privacy of the imperial estate, they often would pass groups of fat women with their children, all of them naked, wading in the shallow streams around Peterhof.

"Our arrival would not upset them in the least. The screaming and laughing children would be silent only momentarily; their mothers would bow slightly and smile in acknowledgment to their Tsar and then they would continue enjoying their bath."

Even the troops billeted in and around Peterhof seemed to adopt the easy and casual ways of the *datchniki*. The Grand Duchess recalled that when the family was riding through the park, they would often see nude soldiers washing themselves and their clothes in the rivers. At the sudden approach of the imperial carriages, pandemonium would reign. Caught by surprise, the men would scramble out of the water, not to get their clothes, but to grab their caps which they would jam on their wet heads. Then, smartly standing at attention, they would salute and shout.

Only Nana, with her proper British ways, thought the sight "revolting" and looked the other way.

"We never stayed at the Great Palace," the Grand Duchess told me. "I know my father was glad of that annual escape from the vastness of Gatchina, and the Great Palace of Peterhof was even bigger. State receptions and banquets would be given there—but you could never turn it into a holiday home."

They stayed at a villa overlooking the sea. Built by Nicholas I for his wife, it was called Alexandria, and Olga came to love it even though some of the rooms were rather dark because of stained-glass windows. Its innumerable balconies were endearing. Its many stairs and unexpected landings and alcoves were good for games on inclement days. And there were no lessons for the younger children, no tiresome duties for the older ones. They were all together, and it was at Peterhof that the Tsarevich and Olga drew closer to each other, for all the fourteen years between them.

"I was about ten or eleven, but I grew to love him dearly. He was kind and generous to everyone he met. I never saw him trying to push

himself forward, or getting angry when he lost at some game or other. And there was always his faith in God. I still remember one hot summer day when he asked me to go with him to the chapel of the Great Palace. He never told me why he wanted to go, and I asked no questions. I think a service was going on because I remember some priests moving about. He and I stood very still and suddenly there came a violent thunderstorm, and something like a ball of fire glanced off one icon after another along the great iconostas, and then it moved towards us and seemed to stop right over Nicky's head. He grasped my hand tight, and something within me knew that he was going through a difficult spell and that I, however small, could be of some comfort to him. I felt both proud and humbled."

The date she mentioned helped to explain the incident to me. The period 1892–93 was when the Tsarevich, deeply in love with Princess Alice of Hesse, felt that he would never win her. She kept refusing him because she could not face having to change her Lutheran creed for orthodoxy. Nicholas was indeed "going through a difficult spell," and it seems that the little sister alone of all his family could best understand him.

Life at Alexandria was rooted in simplicity.

"My father would get up very early and go after mushrooms and bring a big basket for our lunch. Sometimes one of us went with him. We were all free from morning till night, but a Tsar's work allowed for no holiday in the real sense. Every morning ministers and other officials arrived from St. Petersburg, and my father was kept as busy as ever."

The glory of the place lay in its fountains. The great park was open to the public; sightseers and tourists went in the thousands, and plainclothes men must have got very weary towards the end of the imperial stay. The Emperor's children hardly missed a day to see the fountains, Samson and the Lion, the Sugar Loaf, the Chess-board, Niobe, Adam and Eve, and many others.

Almost the entire Romanov clan lived either at Peterhof or in its neighborhood, at Krasnoe Selo, Strelna, Ropsha, and Pavlovsk, and the guest rooms at Alexandria were always full, one of the most regular visitors being the Duchess of Edinburgh, Alexander III's only sister.

"She came often, but I remember there were always difficulties with her mother-in-law. To my father, Queen Victoria was 'that nasty, interfering old woman,' and she thought him a boor. I liked my Aunt Marie, but I don't think she was very happy. She relaxed at Peterhof, though."

By far the most exciting visitors came from Greece—"the Greek crowd," as they were known—headed by Queen Olga, the Emperor's favorite first cousin. She usually went to her mother's little palace at Strelna, but some of her sons came to Alexandria and their presence certainly heightened the pleasure of the holidays.

"Aunt Olga[4] looked a saint and her serenity did us all much good. She usually had masses of exquisite Greek embroideries in her luggage. She brought them to Russia so as to raise money for one or another of her many philanthropic activities in Greece. Her enthusiasm was infectious, though I am afraid that few, if any, of her plans ever came to anything."

It was in Peterhof that a close friendship developed between the Tsarevich Nicholas and the second oldest son of Queen Olga, Prince George of Greece ("Greek Georgie").[5]

"Georgie, who was tall and had laughing blue eyes, wore a thin moustache which gave him quite a dashing air. We all loved him, but I was always in awe of him. Although at the time he could not have been much older than fourteen, it was whispered, through the palace grapevine as usual, that he had had an affair with Photini, one of the Greek nursery maids. Being very young, I could not understand what the fuss really was about, but I was certain that the whole thing sounded terrible."

June and July were spent in Peterhof and when August came they went to Kronstadt and boarded the Emperor's yacht *Derzhava* to go to Denmark and stay with "Apapa" and "Amama" at Fredensborg.

Apapa and Amama were Olga's grandparents, and King Christian IX was known as "Europe's father-in-law." The great family gatherings at Fredensborg were called "the whispering gallery" by those who were not invited to join them. Bismarck, in particular, insisted that political schemes were hatched at the castle. Queen Victoria said that she would never have enjoyed "such terrible noise."

"Yes, all the young were certainly noisy," Grand Duchess Olga said to me, "but my grandfather strictly forbade all political discussion. If anything, the Fredensborg reunions were a wedding market!"

The Romanovs' departure for Denmark was a fearful business. More than twenty freight cars were needed to carry the luggage from Peterhof to St. Petersburg and from there by barges on to Kronstadt, but the route, once mapped out by Nicholas I, was never altered in a single particular. More than one hundred people accompanied the family, and camp beds were part of the luggage—again in accordance with the tradition started by Peter the Great.

"We were allowed to have some of our pets with us, but not Kuku the hare or my wolf cub—they would have been too wild. Altogether the yacht looked rather like Noah's ark. Even a cow was taken on board. The voyage took precisely three days, and my mother thought that fresh milk was essential."

It was indeed a gathering of the clans: the Prince and Princess of Wales, and the Duke of York, King George and Queen Olga of Greece, and their seven extremely lively children, the Duke and Duchess of Cumberland, and numbers of relations from all parts of Germany, from Sweden and Austria, all accompanied by children and retinues. Many guests slept in huts scattered all over the great park.

"My brothers, Nicky and George, always shared a tiny hut in the rose garden, and people were cramped even in the palace, some of the men having to sleep on sofas, but nobody minded such petty discomforts. My grandfather's affection made up for everything, though some people grumbled at the food. I remember Sir Frederick Ponsonby, my Uncle Bertie's secretary, complaining about the endless rich sauces."

At times more than eighty of Europe's greatest royal figures of the day would sit down to dinner at Fredensborg. The Grand Duchess and Michael, both immaculately dressed by their nurse, would come to the dining room before dinner to say good night to their grandparents and the assembled relatives. Later, they would tiptoe from their bedrooms upstairs to the railing of the upper rotunda to gaze down at the splendid sight of Europe's assembled royalty. Pheasant was the favorite dish on these occasions, and the Grand Duchess recalled that the smell of the roasted birds seemed to fill the entire palace.

"How did you spend the time?" I asked.

"Enjoying our freedom," the Grand Duchess replied. "And it was freedom in the true sense of the word. No member of the Okhrana was there to guard us from dangers which did not exist. Nana and I drove into Copenhagen, left the carriage somewhere on the outskirts, and wandered about on foot, and went into shops. I shall never forget the thrill of walking down a street for the first time, of seeing something I liked in a shop window and knowing that I could go in and buy anything I pleased! It was more than fun! It was an education! At home, not a drive could be taken but it involved most elaborate security measures. In Copenhagen, we felt we were just human beings and Nicky and Michael were so happy."

Fredensborg itself was something of a school.

"It was such a cosmopolitan crowd. Michael and I learned to distinguish them by smell. The English royalty smelled of fog and smoke, our Danish cousins reminded us of damp, newly washed linen, and we ourselves smelled of well-polished leather."

The Greek princes would easily have been leaders in all pranks if it had not been for Olga's father, who, when wearying of his contemporaries' company, joined the children in their lawful and unlawful adventures: "He loved getting into mischief. He'd lead us into muddy ponds to look for tadpoles, and into orchards to steal Apapa's apples. Once he stumbled on a hose and turned it on the King of Sweden, whom we all disliked. My father joined us in all the games and made us late for meals, and nobody seemed to mind. I remember that couriers sometimes came with dispatches, but there was no telephone to St. Petersburg, and the three weeks in Denmark meant such a refreshment to him. I always felt that the boy had never really died in the man."

The Grand Duchess did not often smile, and her laughter came even more seldom, but I shall always remember her laughing like a girl the day she told me of an adventure at the Copenhagen Zoo.

"Several of us went together with my mother and Aunt Alix.[6] That afternoon my mother wore a big hat, its broad brim trimmed with very bright red cherries...."

The Empress and her sister stopped to look at a chimpanzee. The ape liked the look of the cherries. He pushed his arms through the bars and snatched at the hat, but an elastic held it secure to the Empress's head. The ape yelled and pulled harder. The Empress screamed and pulled in her turn. The Princess of Wales seized her by the waist and began pulling in her turn. In the end, the chimpanzee, deciding that a handful of cherries was hardly worth such a lot of trouble, let go the hat so violently that the elastic snapped, the hat flew off the Empress's head and settled on the cap of a passer-by.

"And everybody laughed," ended the Grand Duchess. "That might give you an idea of the glorious liberty we enjoyed in Denmark. In Russia my mother would never have dreamt of paying a visit to a zoo, but if she had and if anything of the kind had happened there would have been an immediate and tedious inquiry, someone suggesting that the keeper in charge of the chimpanzee was responsible for its behavior! And yet such conditions in Russia were unavoidable."

It was at Fredensborg that the Grand Duchess came to know her English relations.

"I grew very fond of Uncle Bertie and Aunt Alix, but I felt so very sorry for their daughter, Princess Victoria. Poor Toria was just a glorified maid to her mother! Many a time a talk or a game would be broken off by a message from Aunt Alix, and Toria would run like lightning—often to discover that her mother could not remember why she had sent for her. And it puzzled me because Aunt Alix was so good. My own mother was inclined to treat me the same way, but I'd something of a rebel in me. Toria had not. No wonder she never married."

The Empress Marie and her sister were very much alike. Both loved fine clothes, jewelry, gaiety. Neither was clever. Neither understood politics or a way of life different from their own. And neither was punctual by nature.

At Fredensborg her brother Nicholas and the young Duke of York, later George V, became close friends.

"They resembled each other so much that my grandfather's servants often mistook one for the other. The resemblance was more than physical. Both were honest, shy, and modest."

The youthful Duke of York took a great liking to his young cousin Olga from the time they met at Fredensborg. He would laugh at her and teasingly invite her to "come and roll with me on the ottoman."

"This became a secret joke between us," the Grand Duchess laughed. "And later, when we were both grown up and would attend the same official functions, his eyes would twinkle and he would whisper in my ear, 'Come and roll with me on the ottoman,' to which I would blush and look 'round us to be sure nobody had heard the future King of England making such a scandalous suggestion to an imperial Grand Duchess of Russia!"

All of them disliked the Kaiser. "My father thought him an exhibitionist and a nuisance. My grandfather took care not to invite him, but once he turned up because he said he wanted to. I remember how he went about, slapping everybody on the back and pretending that he was very fond of us all, and weren't we relieved when he left!"

"Did Queen Victoria ever come to Fredensborg?"

"Never!" The Grand Duchess paused. "I may be wrong, but she wasn't really fond of anyone except her German relations. She certainly did not like us. She loathed my grandfather and did not really want her son Alfred to marry my Aunt Marie, nor did my aunt have a very happy time in England. Victoria was always contemptuous of us. She said that we possessed a 'bourgeoiserie,' as she called it, which she disliked intensely—but, come to think of it, the boot was on the other foot. My father could not stand her. He said that she was a pampered, sentimental, selfish old woman. Nobody felt sad because Victoria did not come to Fredensborg."[7]

The family gathering lasted precisely three weeks, and the Emperor's children felt sad when they boarded the yacht for the return voyage to Russia. It was their dearly loved home country and they were happy there, but something in them had been teased into subconscious discontent because of all the varied little freedoms they had enjoyed in Denmark.

The First Great Sorrow

*I*n such a way the yearly round continued. The holiday in Denmark was followed by a short stay at Livadia, in the Crimea, where Alexander III had built a white, Moorish-looking palace on the estate stretching from the wooded hill of Ai Petri to the shore of the Black Sea. All along the Crimean coastline, between Yalta and Sebastopol, beautiful summer villas nestled in gardens teeming with wistarias, oleanders, Judas and cypress trees, and thousands of roses. Several of the Grand Dukes, Nicholas and Peter Nicholaevich, Alexander and George Michailovich, and Dimitri Constantinovich, owned sumptuous properties along the coast. So did some of the leading princely families, the Yusupoffs, Bariatinskys, and Worontzoffs, all of whom were anxious to entertain the imperial family. These were gentle days of picnics, tennis, sailing, and swimming, and evenings of outdoor dances and dinners, for which the imperial yacht orchestra provided soft music. By September the family was back in the North, Olga's elder brothers taking up their military duties and she herself struggling once again with geography and French irregular verbs.

And so Olga's life passed until the autumn of 1893 when she celebrated her eleventh birthday. She had no governess. Mrs. Franklin, her duties slightly less onerous, stayed on. The Grand Duchess's immediate world seemed small enough: her father, her brothers Michael and Nicholas. Then came a never-ending procession of servants, pets, and relations, in that order. Somewhere on the fringe were members of the court and the brilliant ranks of society. There were banquets and balls. Her sister, Grand

Antichkov Palace.

Duchess Xenia, was by then fully "out," but to Olga all the activities seemed rather boring.

There was no doubt of her being a tomboy. But she was much more than that. Indifferent to compulsory lessons, she came to life, as it were, when alone with her father, her paint box, her violin. Trees and running water had much more to say to her than the walls of any palace. The peasant accents of a private in the guards or a gardener stirred her more than the polished conversation of people at court. All her preferences, however clumsily she would have expressed them at the time, lay with the uncontrived simplicities of life.

The winter of 1893–94 sped by on wings. Administrative matters kept her father busier than ever. Social duties absorbed her mother. The imperial train plied continuously between Gatchina and St. Petersburg, to the undisguised distress of the Emperor and the equally candid delight of the Empress.

The season proper began, as usual, with the great entrée on New Year's Day. The family never stayed at the Winter Palace where all the important functions were held. Anitchkov Palace on the Nevsky Prospect was their home during their stay in the capital, and once or twice that winter Olga happened to be in the Empress's rooms when her ladies were getting their mistress ready for a hall or a banquet.

"It was an absolute beehive—with no fewer than five maids bustling in and out under the severe scrutiny of 'the fabulous Kotchoubey.'[1] Certainly my mother looked lovely when she wore what we used to call her 'imperial panoply,' a silver brocade gown, her diamond tiara, and pearls—pearls everywhere! She had quite a weakness for them, and sometimes I saw her wearing ten rows of them, some reaching down to her waist. Frankly, I did not envy her a bit."

And there Olga was wholly her father's daughter: he never looked happy at a ball.

This often created amusing situations. While the Empress was anxious to leave Gatchina as soon as possible after Christmas and move into the gay society of St. Petersburg, the Emperor did his best to find convincing excuses to delay the departure. During palace balls it was the Empress who was the center of attention on the dance floor while the Emperor stood silently to one side, frowning and obviously unhappy. Sometimes, when the ball had lasted too long to suit him, he would impatiently begin ordering the musicians, one by one, out of the ballroom. Finally only a solitary drummer would remain on the orchestra stand, too frightened to leave, too frightened to stop playing. If the guests continued to dance, the Emperor would turn off the lights and the Empress would bow to the inevitable, graciously taking leave of her guests by saying with a smile: "Well, I suppose the Emperor wants us all to go home."

"My parents had so little in common, and yet their marriage could not have been happier," was the Grand Duchess's answer to my suggestion that such dissimilarities might well have led to friction in the family. "They complemented each other perfectly. Court life had to run in splendor, and there my mother played her part without a single false step. She proved herself immensely tactful with her in-laws, and that," sighed Olga, "was no easy task."

Her father certainly held the great clan together, but even his firmness could not prevent certain factions and rivalries. The center of them all was under the roof of his younger brother, Grand Duke Vladimir, married to a Mecklenburg-Schwerin princess, whose people were excessively friendly with the Kaiser and Bismarck. Vladimir and his wife were clever, artistic, wealthy, and insatiably ambitious. The Grand Duchess's balls all but eclipsed the splendor of the Winter Palace. The parties they gave at their country place at Ropsha near Peterhof were almost oriental. Both patronized the arts and were known to consider Gatchina as something of a provincial manor.

The only link between the brothers was their anglophobia. Otherwise, there was deep-seated jealousy on Vladimir's part and something like rough contempt on Alexander's, who is supposed to have said immediately after the Borki catastrophe: "Imagine Vladimir's disappointment when he hears that we all escaped alive!"[2]

But the Empress Marie helped to keep up at least a semblance of good will between the two families.

"I know that my mother did not care for Vladimir or his wife any more than the rest of us did, but I never heard her say a single unkind word about them," Olga mused.[3]

But during that winter of 1893–94 the imperial family had not much leisure to consider any rivalries. The Tsarevich had not yet won the hand of Princess Alix of Hesse, but Grand Duchess Xenia was betrothed to a very handsome young cousin, Grand Duke Alexander, known to them as Sandro, one of the six sons of Grand Duke Michael, the Emperor's uncle. A great many difficulties had to be overcome before the engagement could be announced. The close blood tie meant a special dispensation from the Holy Synod, and the Empress opposed it rather vehemently, saying that her daughter was far too young.

"Which was nonsense," said the Grand Duchess. "Romanov girls have been known to get married even at sixteen. My mother just did not want to lose all control over Xenia. She meant her to stay on as a companion to herself. But everybody knew that something of the kind would happen, one day. Xenia and Sandro had known each other since childhood. In the end my father and my Great-uncle Michael carried the day and then, as usual, my mother made the best of it."

The wedding was to have taken place in July, 1894. At the beginning of spring they were at Gatchina, and one afternoon the Emperor and Olga went out for their usual ramble in the woods. She ran some distance ahead to a spot where she hoped to find violets. He caught up with her and in a few moments she realized that, instead of outpacing her with his long strides, the Emperor was making an effort to keep up with her. She stopped and her hands went cold. He looked at her with a little smile.

"Baby, you will keep my secret, won't you? I feel tired and we had better go home."

They turned towards the palace, Olga walking, her eyes blind to the matchless spring day. But she kept looking at her father. Never before had she known him to admit the least weariness. Now she realized that he looked exhausted. It seemed as though the words he spoke had aged him. She fought back her tears and she promised that she would keep his secret.

Grand Duchess Xenia's wedding took place in July at Peterhof. It took six months for dressmakers and jewelers to prepare the trousseau. Wedding

presents arrived from all over the world in such quantity that several huge halls in the Winter Palace had to be used for the usual exhibition.

There were enormous amounts of useless trinkets but there were also beautiful things. There was silver plate for at least a hundred persons, a solid gold toilette set of over one hundred articles, dozens of gold-rimmed glasses, cups and dishes emblazoned with the imperial monograms, every kind of coat and wrap of ermine, chinchilla, mink, beaver, and astrakhan, and endless tables loaded with linen, china, and household articles. The jewelry was superb. There were pearl necklaces, some with five strings, each holding more than a hundred pearls and, of course, necklaces of diamonds, rubies, emeralds, and sapphires, with tiaras and earrings to match.

Grand Duchess Olga and two of her cousins at Gatchina Palace the spring before Xenia's wedding, 1894.

"My father's present to the groom was, according to custom, clothing. Also on display with the trousseau were the embroidered silver nightgowns, each weighing well over fifteen pounds that by Romanov tradition an imperial Grand Duke and Grand Duchess had to wear on their wedding night."

The great palace teemed with royal visitors from all corners of Europe. It was the first occasion on which Olga appeared in public. She was to entertain the children of the guests. There was no leisure left for brooding over that frightening experience in the woods of Gatchina. The Emperor seemed well enough and able to enter into all the festivities.

"At the wedding I was all excitement," said the Grand Duchess. Wearing a full-length court dress for the first time, she walked in the procession of the bride and bridegroom on their way from the chapel to the banqueting hall. The Emperor looked happy—"Never again was I to see him like that."

When the guests had dispersed to their several homes, the great palace was shuttered once again and the imperial family returned to Alexandria—but that summer there were no afternoon rambles for the Emperor. He took to sleeping very badly and lost all appetite. The Empress at once summoned the court physicians who had nothing to say except that His Imperial Majesty had been working too hard. They advised a long rest and a change of air. The former was out of all question for a Tsar of Russia. The latter seemed reasonable enough.

The yearly trip to Denmark was canceled. They all thought that the forest air of Bieloviecz in Poland, where Alexander had a hunting lodge, would prove beneficial, and in September the family got ready to leave the North.

Yet before leaving, the Emperor had one last duty to carry out—that of reviewing his troops at Krasnoe Selo. For the first time, Olga was allowed to be present at the annual review.

She took her place behind the Empress on the immense gold-and-red draped imperial stand. The enormous parade ground stretched below, and all the guards regiments were drawn in endless regular lines, a sea of white plumes, gleaming helmets, red, white, green, and yellow tunics. To the left and the right of the foot guards, the cavalry regiments sat their gleaming, beautifully accoutered horses. There was not a hint of movement anywhere; the Grand Duchess might have been looking at some gigantic piece of painted statuary.

Then, very slowly, mounted on a superb gray, and wearing the green tunic of the Preobrazhensky Guards, the oldest regiment of all, the Emperor rode past the stand. He rode alone, no equerry accompanied him; in a minute, the Commander-in-Chief, Grand Duke Nicholas, Alexander's uncle, was seen, mounted on another gray, riding toward the Emperor. The Grand Duke saluted, raised one white-gauntleted hand, and presented his report to his nephew, who took it and saluted in his turn.

"Even now I can remember how proud I felt of my father, my whole family, all those thousands of men—and when the massed bands broke into 'God Save the Tsar' I knew what its tune meant, not only to those thousands but to millions. That tune entered our very hearts."

His equerries and a group of staff officers riding behind him, the Emperor rode slowly along each of those numberless lines, and still the bands played on. It was almost an hour later that Alexander returned and took his place on the stand for the march past.

"My heart nearly missed a beat. I could see how pale and tired he was and as I looked at that dear, dear face I had a dreadful feeling that the great review was also my father's farewell to his guards."

It was a hot day. The giant Tsar stood very erect, his right hand raised in salute. The march past began to the strains of "How Glorious Is Our Lord in Sion." From time to time the Emperor would shout to the men:

"*Khorosho, rebiata!*" (Well done, children!)

And the thunder of their choral reply rolled all over the great parade ground:

"*Rady staratza Vashe Imperatoraskoe Velichestvo!*" (We are happy to serve Your Imperial Majesty!)

"Had you been there with us," the Grand Duchess told me, "you would have known that the men meant every word of it. It was not a dry formality ordered by tradition. The look of love and dedication in all those upturned faces was unforgettable. It is all but forgotten today that to the Russian masses of my youth the Tsar was chosen by God to rule the country. Their devotion to him embraced their feeling for God and their country. Believe me, I have seen many examples of that truly dedicated affection. It was the main support of the Romanov sovereigns in their unrewarding task of wielding absolute power. Between the crown and the people was a relationship hardly ever understood in the West. That relationship had nothing to do with government or with petty officialdom. The Tsar and the people were bound together by the solemn vows of the Tsar's coronation oath when he pledged himself to rule, judge, and serve his people. In a Tsar, the people and the office were joined together."

Alexander was so exhausted after the review that the journey to Bieloviecz had to be put off for a few days.

"It was hardly a wise choice of place," said the Grand Duchess.[4] "There was no railway station for miles and miles, and I remember the interminable ride across the gloomy drives. The hunting lodge, built of wood, had enormous trees girdling it all 'round. It was terrible. I could not see how such a place came to be chosen."

At first, Alexander joined the others for the shooting, but he seemed to have lost all zest for the sport. He lost his appetite, would not go into the dining room, and on occasion had food brought to the study, and Olga alone was allowed to be present. A foreboding none of them dared utter deepened over the hunting lodge. At last, the Empress summoned Dr. Zacharin, a specialist from Moscow.

"I still remember him," the Grand Duchess said to me. "That famous specialist was a stubby little man who wandered about the place all night, complaining that he could not sleep because of the ticking of the tower clock. He begged my father to have it stopped. I don't think his coming did any good. Certainly my father did not think much of a doctor who seemed mostly concerned about his own health."

In less than a fortnight they left Bieloviecz for Spala, a hunting box near Warsaw. The Emperor's condition worsened. His legs began to swell. The Berlin specialist, Dr. Leyden, was sent for. He would have kept his diagnosis from the Emperor, but Alexander insisted on being told the truth. It was virulent dropsy, said Dr. Leyden, reluctantly admitting that he saw no hope of a cure.

The Emperor's immediate reaction was to telegraph his second son to come to Spala. Grand Duke George had contracted tuberculosis in 1890 and he lived at Abbas Tuman in the foothills of the Caucasus. "I think now that he knew he was dying, my father wished to see him for the last time. I remember how happy he looked the day George arrived at Spala, but poor George looked so ill—and, believe it or not, my father spent whole hours watching by his bedside at night."

Meanwhile, all the members of the family had been told the truth. Queen Olga of Greece at once offered her villa, "*Mon Repos*," on the island of Corfu, and Dr. Leyden agreed that a warm climate might do some good to this patient. So they all made for the Crimea to stop at Livadia for a few days before going on to Corfu. But when they reached Livadia, they knew they could go no further. The Emperor's condition was pitiful.

"Every movement became an agony. He could not even lie in bed. He felt slightly more comfortable when they wheeled his chair to an open window and he could see the oleanders sloping toward the sea shore...."

It was early October. The air was grape-scented. The sun felt warm. But nobody at Livadia had thought about either the weather or the landscape. Alexander III was dying, and the doctors could do nothing except continue to vary his diet from day to day. Always suspicious of drugs, the Emperor refused to have his pain alleviated in any way.

"There was a day," the Grand Duchess said, her voice none too steady, "when I sat on a stool by his chair and he whispered suddenly, 'Baby dear, I know there is some ice-cream in the next room. Bring it here—but make sure nobody sees you....'"

His daughter nodded and tiptoed out of the room. She knew the doctors had forbidden him to eat ice-cream. She also knew that he longed for it. She ran to Mrs. Franklin for advice.

"'Of course, give it him,' Nana replied instantly. 'His having a little ice-cream would not make any difference now. There are few enough pleasures left for him.' So I smuggled the plate into my father's room. It was a delight to see him enjoy it. Nobody knew except Nana and me, and it didn't hurt him...."

Days went on. By mid-October the Emperor became weaker, and his

Alexandra, "Alicky," the last empress of Russia, who died with her family at Ekaterinburg in 1918. Grand Duchess Olga was very fond of this portrait.

confessor, the saintly John of Kronstadt, arrived from the North. That same day Alexander was closeted alone with his eldest son, and a telegram was sent to Darmstadt to summon Nicholas's fiancée, Princess Alicky, to the Crimea. He had overcome her hesitation, and they had become engaged earlier in the year at Coburg after the wedding of Princess Victoria of Edinburgh to the Grand Duke of Hesse.[5]

"I loved her from the beginning," the Grand Duchess said very firmly, "and what a joy it was to my father when she came. I remember that he kept her for a long time in his room...."

By October twenty-ninth, the Emperor's condition was so bad that his wife wired to Sandringham and the Prince and Princess of Wales left for Russia at once. November first came, all shrouded in damp mist.[6] Father John was called to the Emperor before noon. Nobody thought of meals. By the early afternoon the entire family was gathered in the room. Father John, standing by Alexander's armchair, put both hands on his head, which was resting on the Empress's shoulder.

"How good," whispered the Emperor.

They were all kneeling in the room. Outside, the fog kept thickening. Somewhere a clock struck three, Alexander's head dropped on his wife's breast, and the first prayer for the rest of his soul was heard in the room.

"Then everything seemed hushed. Nobody sobbed. My mother still held him in her arms. We all rose as quietly as we could, crossed the room, and kissed my father's forehead and hand. Then we kissed my mother. It seemed as though the fog outside had entered the room. All of us turned to Nicky and kissed his hand for the first time." Here again the Grand Duchess's voice began to tremble.

She must have been utterly alone that day, although the palace was crowded with relations. Nobody dared intrude upon the Empress's grief. The young Emperor had his fiancée; her sister Xenia had her husband; her brother, Grand Duke George, was far too spent to be troubled by a much younger sister. Grand Duke Michael, aged sixteen, had his own duties. The rest, the first hours behind them, cried bitterly, discussed their mourning, and wondered how the court climate would change. The young Emperor, overwhelmed with grief, was surrounded by his uncles and his father's ministers.

There was nobody for Olga except her faithful Nana, and Mrs. Franklin alone must have understood that for that child of twelve childhood was over. Devotion to her father had been the very root of her entire existence. Innocent pranks, wild griefs, pleasure and achievement, her inarticulate love for her motherland and her affection for its common folk, her pride in its past and her hope in its future, everything had been shared with her father, at once sovereign, counselor, and friend.

Faith, rather than the strict training Olga had received, enabled her to get through those days.

Having shared those memories with me, the Grand Duchess began speaking of her father, her voice much steadier:

"How much unkind and unjust nonsense has been written about him! In a recent book he was described as a blockhead and a man always governed by petty prejudices. People forget that not since the days of Alexander I had Russia enjoyed such respect in the world. His was the only Romanov reign unmarred by war. He meticulously avoided any entanglements. Not for nothing was he known as 'the Peacemaker.' Ambiguity and expediency were two words he abhorred. He preferred a direct approach to every problem. He met threats by bluntness or by mockery. Once, at a banquet, the Austrian ambassador began discussing the Balkan question and hinted that Austria could immediately mobilize two or three army corps if Russia decided to intervene in a current minor dispute in the Balkans. The Emperor picked up a heavy silver spoon, twisted it out of shape, laid it by the ambassador's plate, and said, 'That is what I would do to your two or three corps.' I also remember that the Kaiser once made an asinine suggestion that Germany and Russia should divide all Europe between them, and my father instantly replied, 'Don't behave like a whirling dervish, Willy. Look at yourself in the mirror.'"

There was a question I had long since wanted to ask her. "The Emperor's interior policy—" I began, and the Grand Duchess broke in:

"Yes, yes, I know what you are going to say. My father was considered a reactionary, and I suppose he was—in a sense. But consider the circumstances in which he came to the throne. What choice had he but to suppress the terrorists? He was opposed to irresponsible liberalism and he refused to placate people who wanted to introduce the governmental reforms of Great Britain and France. Remember—our intellectuals were a minority. The majority, the masses, what could they have made of a democratic government? My grandfather had started many reforms. I know that my father was deeply concerned about improvements in education and the standard of living—but a mere thirteen years was not enough—especially when you remember the conditions at the beginning of the reign. And he died at forty-nine! I am convinced that if he and Uncle Bertie had been alive in 1914, there would have been no war. The Kaiser was terrified of them both."

The Grand Duchess paused, and her face became shadowed.

"I want you to give a true story to the world, and nothing of the truth must be concealed. My father was everything to me—but, as I grew older, I knew he had made mistakes and one of them was a most grievous one."

Once again she was back in those sorrowful days at Livadia and in her memory she stood again on a verandah as Nicholas came up to her, put his arms 'round her shoulders, and sobbed. . . .

"Even Alicky could not help him. He was in despair. He kept saying that he did not know what would become of us all, that he was wholly unfit to reign. Even at that time I felt instinctively that sensitivity and kindness on their own were not enough for a sovereign to have. And yet Nicky's unfitness was by no means his fault. He had intelligence, he had faith and courage—and he was wholly ignorant about governmental matters. Nicky had been trained as a soldier. He should have been taught statesmanship, and he was not."

She paused.

"It was my father's fault. He would not even have Nicky sit in Council of State until 1893. I can't tell you why. The mistake was there. I know how my father disliked the mere idea of state matters encroaching on our family life—but, after all, Nicky was his heir. And what a ghastly price was later paid for the mistake. Of course, my father, who had always enjoyed an athlete's health, could not have foreseen such an early end to his life. . . . But the mistake was there."

The last days at Livadia would have been beyond anyone's endurance were it not for the presence of the Prince of Wales. He and his wife reached the Crimea two days after Alexander's death. The Princess of Wales at once took care of her disconsolate sister. Uncle Bertie quietly began calming down the tumult that met them on their arrival.

The young Emperor was constantly bullied by his uncles, Vladimir and Serge. His father's ministers kept harassing him with their demands and contradictory suggestions. His fiancée, ignored by all except Grand Duchess Serge, tried not to interfere, kept herself aloof, and was criticized by the whole household for her reserved manner. The court officials lost their heads, and the crowd of servants seemed to spend their time in weeping for their dead master. The Empress, prostrate with grief, gave no orders and apparently did not wish that anyone else should give them, and nobody had a clear idea about the funeral arrangements except that Alexander's body must be taken to St. Petersburg.

The Prince of Wales put an immediate stop to grand-ducal truculence, tried to hearten his nephew, succeeded in making the senior court officials return to their senses, and spent hours giving his help and advice about the extremely complicated funeral arrangements.

"I wonder," the Grand Duchess said musingly, "what his tiresome old mother would have said if she had seen everybody accept Uncle Bertie's authority! In Russia of all places! I still remember those dreadful days. They went in a fog!"

The cruiser *Pamiat Mercuria*, escorted by six ships of the Black Sea Fleet, carried the Emperor's body to Sebastopol where the imperial train was waiting to start its 1,400-mile journey to St. Petersburg. At every station along the route, a halt was made for a panikhida to be chanted by local clergy and choir. A three-day stop was made in Moscow where the purple-draped coffin lay in state in the Archangel Cathedral within the Kremlin walls. By order of the young Emperor, "memorial dinners" were given to the poor both in Moscow and in St. Petersburg.

The capital was reached at last. The lying-in-state at the Cathedral of SS. Peter and Paul in the fortress lasted an entire week, and every morning members of the imperial family, including young Olga, drove across the Neva for yet another solemn *panikhida*.

"I accompanied Uncle Bertie and Aunt Alix. We always went in a closed carriage. I was past tears. . . ."

The funeral, attended by nearly all the kings and queens of Europe, took place on November nineteenth. In that crowded cathedral, lit by thousands of candles, the last Romanov sovereign ever to be buried there was laid to rest in the ancestral vault.

"We all knelt at the first words of 'Eternal Memory.' The Grenadiers began lowering the coffin. I could see nothing. I felt numb. I daresay I was far too imaginative at twelve, but a sense of doom weighed me down, and I felt that doom concerned the future. I could talk to nobody about those things. I saw nothing of my mother in those days. She spent them with Aunt Alix and did not seem to want anyone else. I did not know Alicky well enough. I was just alone at that gloomy Anitchkov Palace. There was not even a park to lose myself in. We were in deep mourning and so I could not even play my violin. There were no lessons. But in deep mourning though we were, there was no quiet! Such a bustle going on—I felt like screaming sometimes. I would have screamed if I had not my dear Nana to steady me."

"What was the bustle about?" I asked in amazement.

"Getting ready for Nicky's wedding," she replied. "He did not want Alicky to return to Darmstadt. He needed her so badly. So mourning was relaxed on the twenty-sixth of November—my mother's feast day. I must say I felt glad for Nicky and Alicky—but it was a very strange wedding. There was no reception. They had no honeymoon. They had not even got a home. They came to live in six poky rooms at the Anitchkov Palace."

"And what did you do?"

"Well, lessons began again. I can't remember how long we stayed in St. Petersburg. Of course, there was no season that winter—not that it mattered to me."

All that I have recounted happened in 1894. I heard it from the Grand Duchess in 1958. The look on her face, the timbre of her voice, the occasional trembling of her hands, were proof enough of what she had endured in the days which saw her childhood come to its end.

A New Era

The winter following her father's death was a shrouded season for the twelve-year-old Grand Duchess and that in more senses than one. To begin with, she became, as it were, the "odd man out" in the family. She hardly saw her eldest brother except at meals. She would have liked to draw nearer to her sister-in-law, but their mutual shyness stood between them at the beginning. Grand Duke George, whose condition forbade living in the North, went back to the foothills of the Caucasus immediately after the wedding. Grand Duchess Xenia, a married woman, had not much leisure to spare for a schoolroom sister, and "Floppy," now in his seventeenth year, had duties both as Grand Duke and as soldier in which Olga could not share. Outside the immediate family circle, uncles, aunts, and cousins spared her a moment's thought and no more.

It is doubtful that anyone, except Mrs. Franklin, realized the girl's loneliness. The rigid training she had received barred the way to the least emotional outburst outside the walls of the schoolroom. The taboo catalogue was heartbreakingly long, but even a million taboos would not have succeeded in killing her hunger for warmth, for someone's response to her affection, her curiosity and wonder, and her deep-seated naturalness.

Life was indeed a burden for those very young shoulders.

To begin with, as the Grand Duchess said to me, they were "terribly overcrowded" at the Anitchkov Palace. Such a statement, the size of the building considered, seems an absurdity. It was not. Both "the old court" and "the young court" were housed under the Anitchkov roof. It was indeed grotesque that it should have been so. The young Emperor's

Olga with her beloved "Nana," the faithful Mrs. Franklin.

Grand Duchess Olga in the park back at Gatchina Palace, age eighteen.

engagement dated back to the spring of 1894. His marriage had been hurried on, but even so, arrangements might have been made for some apartments at the Winter Palace to be in readiness for the young couple. But the Dowager Empress considered all such arrangements unnecessary. She preferred them all under her roof. The Anitchkov Palace became exclusively her own on her husband's death. So Nicholas and his bride, Xenia and her young husband all lived there, none having a voice in the smallest household matter.

"Nicky and Alicky spent their first months together in Nicky's old rooms which he and Georgie had once shared. There were six of them; they were downstairs—separated from mine by a long corridor. At first, I felt too shy to go and see them—but that, I am thankful to say, did not last very long in spite of Alicky's little terrier who had a habit of making for the ankles of any visitor. . . ."

The young Emperor and his bride had not even a dining room of their own. They lunched and dined together with the rest in the great room with the Empress Marie at the head of the table. The dowager, however, permitted them to have breakfast and tea in privacy.

"Their sitting room was small but cozy, and Alicky often invited me to tea. A pianola stood in the corner and I played on it. Little by little, I grew deeply attached to my sister-in-law. And there was still another link between their rooms and mine. Alicky's Nana, Mrs. Orchard, or Orchie, as we all called her, made great friends with Nana. Orchie often crossed the long corridor to sit with Nana and me. She told us lots about Alicky's childhood in Darmstadt. . . ."

That winter, however, had one bright side to it. The Dowager Empress postponed her leaving for Gatchina time and again, and Olga began to get to know St. Petersburg. Of free and unplanned walks there could be no question as yet, but even the drives, with Mrs. Franklin for a faithful companion, were enough to lay the foundation of a lifelong affection and loyalty. The lovely city, with its unrivaled waterfront, its hundred and fifty bridges linking the nineteen islands one to another, its vast pleasances tranquil under the snow, its whimsical skies and winds, all of it captured Olga's heart and set her imagination on fire. Back at the Anitchkov Palace, she drew and painted harder than ever before.

She had matured that year, and little by little the atmosphere at the Anitchkov came to be understood by her. The tension between the Dowager Empress and her daughter-in-law never came to an open rupture but often enough it reached a dangerous edge.

"I still believe that they had tried to understand each other and failed. They were utterly different in character, habits, and outlook. My mother, the first shock overcome, returned to her public functions, her self-confidence stronger than ever. She was inherently gay; she loved clothes, jewelry, brilliant lights 'round about her. In a word, she was made for court life. All the things which had so bored my father were meat and drink to her. Now that he was no longer with us, my mother was absolute mistress. She had great influence over Nicky and began giving him advice on state matters. She had never before taken the least interest in them. Now she felt it was her duty. And at the Anitchkov her will was law to us all. And poor Alicky was shy, retiring, sometimes moody, never at her ease among people."

"The atmosphere must have been rather electric," I suggested, but the Grand Duchess shook her head.

"Not quite—at least, there were no explosions. But my mother did like gossip. Her ladies did not take kindly to Alicky from the very beginning.

There was such a lot of tittle-tattle—particularly about Alicky's jealousy over my mother's precedence. I happen to know that far from being jealous, Alicky was actually relieved at not taking the first place."

"But surely," I broke in, "your sister-in-law was the reigning Empress. How could the dowager claim precedence?"

"By law," the Grand Duchess explained. "The Emperor Paul I passed that act in 1796. They said he did not care for his daughter-in-law. I don't know if that was true. But according to that law, my mother came first. At public functions she would appear, her arm in Nicky's, Alicky following behind with the senior Grand Duke. George was ill and away, Michael could not always appear, and it would usually fall to my Great-uncle Vladimir, whose anglophobia was a by-word and who had opposed Nicky's marriage to the last. So poor Alicky could not have been very happy! But I never heard her complain. Again the same law laid down that the Dowager Empress had the use of heirlooms and other crown jewels. Alicky, as I know, did not care a bit about anything except pearls, and she had plenty of her own, but the court gossip preferred to imagine that she resented not being able to wear all the rubies, pink diamonds, emeralds, and sapphires which were in my mother's keeping."

The Grand Duchess, however, admitted that there was a certain friction between the two ladies from the beginning. The Empress insisted on choosing all the ladies-in-waiting and maids-of-honor for her daughter-in-law. The Mistress of the Robes was Princess Marie Galitzine, known to inspire awe even in Grand Dukes.

"Her brusqueness hardly helped Alicky," said the Grand Duchess. "And then there was the matter of clothes. My mother liked fussiness, trimming, and certain colors. She never allowed for Alicky's own taste. My mother would order dresses and Alicky did not wear them. She knew but too well that severity suited her best. The contents of my own wardrobe often infuriated me, though I did not really care what I had on; but I, of course, had no voice whatever in the choosing of anything. How I hated all that trimming! I felt happiest in the linen smock I wore when I painted!"

There were thus no open quarrels at the Anitchkov. But many seeds of mutual bitterness were sown at the time.

"She is the most maligned Romanov of us all. She has gone down in history so calumnied that I cannot bear reading any more of the lies and insinuations people have written about her," the Grand Duchess said of the Empress Alexandra. "Nobody even in our own family tried to understand her except myself and my sister Xenia and Great Aunt Olga. Even as a girl in my teens, I remember things which set my teeth on edge. She could do nothing right so far as my mother's court was concerned. Once I knew she had a dreadful headache; she looked pale when she appeared at dinner, and I heard them say that she was in a bad humor because my mother happened to talk to Nicky about some ministerial appointments. Even in that first year—I remember so well—if Alicky smiled, they called it mockery. If she looked grave, they said she was angry...."

Nobody except two or three people, including Grand Duchess Olga, knew what help the young Empress gave her husband at the time.

"She was absolutely wonderful to Nicky, especially in those first days when he was crushed by his responsibilities. Her courage undoubtedly saved him. No wonder Nicky always called her Sunny, her childhood name. She undoubtedly remained the only sunshine in the ever-growing darkness of his life. I had tea with them often enough. I remember Nicky coming in—tired, sometimes irritable, his mind in a maze after a day crowded with audiences. Alicky never said a wrong word or did a wrong thing. I loved to watch her tranquil movements. She never resented my being there."

The Anitchkov interlude came to an end in the spring of 1895 when the young Emperor took his wife to the Alexander Palace at Tsarskoe Selo.

In May, 1896, the Grand Duchess, accompanied by Mrs. Franklin, left for Moscow for the last coronation ever to be held in Russia. They joined the rest of the imperial family at the old red-stone Petrovsky Palace just outside the walls of the ancient Russian capital. Olga and her Nana were given one room in a tower of the palace which was built on a hill—so that from her windows the young Grand Duchess could look at the numbers of cupolas and belfries in the city and the tall white walls of the Kremlin.

The Emperor's younger sister was of no particular importance in that glittering assembly of royalty and nobility. She had no duties to carry out and did not appear at any of the banquets. But she went to the Assumption

Cathedral on the morning of the great day, and its memories were indelibly engraved on her mind.

"I was so excited that I could hardly sleep the night before. I was up long before Nana stirred. I suppose we had breakfast. I wore a full-length court dress of silver tissue, and for the first time I had the wide red ribbon of St. Catherine's order across my shoulder. They put a white *kokoshnik*, embroidered with silver, on my head. The dress had a mantle with a train falling down—pinned to the left shoulder. It was my first experience of wearing the 'armor,' as we called it, and I found it heavy and wearisome. I had a single string of pearls and no other jewelry. And it was such a hot day!"

She rode in the procession in one of the beautiful gilded coaches which looked enchanting, but they were torture chambers inside. Any bump on the road made the passengers feel as though their bones had cracked. Those coaches were used very seldom. Their gilt handles and velvet upholstery would have been furbished up before a coronation, but apparently nobody thought of airing them because, according to the Grand Duchess, the three of them felt nearly faint from the stuffiness. She was squeezed in between her great-aunt, Queen Olga of Greece, and her cousin, Crown Princess Marie of Roumania.

The coaches moved at a snail's pace, forging their way toward the gates of the Kremlin. Olga, looking right and left, saw a sea of bared heads, upraised arms, eyes full of enthusiasm and affection. Even through the thick glass windows she could hear the cheers, mingling with the peals from Moscow's sixteen hundred belfries. Little by little, she grew unaware of the stuffiness and the discomfort of her "armor." The ceremony to start so soon ceased to be a mere pageant—however glorious. She remembered the purpose behind it and she prayed for her brother, riding all alone at the very head of the procession.

Once within the Cathedral of the Assumption the young girl felt "completely lost and forgotten." The cathedral being rather small, special wooden stands had had to be built along the frescoed walls to accommodate those few thousands who had been invited. But apparently no special place was reserved for Olga. She considered herself lucky to be squeezed between a stand and one of the pillars, which gave her support during the five hours of the solemnity. To her, the most important moment of all came when the Emperor, his coronation oath spoken, accepted the crown from the hands of the Metropolitan of Moscow and put it on his head.

"It looked a simple enough gesture," the Grand Duchess said gravely, "but from that very moment Nicky's responsibility was to God only. I admit that the very idea may sound unreal today, when the absolute power of sovereigns has been so discredited. Yet it will always retain its place in history. The coronation of a Tsar of Russia was a most solemn and binding contrast between God and the sovereign, His servant. That is why, after sixty-four years, the memory of it has a special sanctity for me."

She paused, and in my imagination I saw the frescoed walls of that ancient cathedral, where so many Tsars of Muscovy lay in their last sleep, a congregation assembled from the four corners of Europe and even beyond, the pomp, the glory, and also the hush of those moments. The Grand Duchess was telling her story in a humbly furnished cottage in a land thousands of miles away from her country. The pomp and the glory had long since fallen into dust. Not so the hush, and I felt deeply moved by the words of a woman whose own world had been shattered in the wreck that followed. And now, near to her own midnight, she still retained her hold on despised ideals and ancient sanctities, although her country, in place of an autocracy bestowed by an act of God, had a dictatorship, its holders denying the very existence of God, and wielding their power in the hollow name of an ideology where the interests of an individual were as nothing compared with those of a state.

The Grand Duchess spoke again. "The ceremony ended with a very gentle and human climax. Alicky knelt before Nicky. I shall never forget how carefully he put the crown on her head, how tenderly he kissed her and helped her to rise. And then all of us began filing past them, and I had to leave my corner. I was just behind the Duke and Duchess of Connaught who represented Queen Victoria. I swept a deep curtsey, raised my head, and saw Nicky's blue eyes looking at me with such affection that my heart was all aglow. I still remember how passionately I vowed to dedicate myself to my country and her sovereign...."

Now they were out of the Uspensky Cathedral, crossing the Red Square towards the ancient Granovitaya Palata, where Tsars of Muscovy used to hold their councils and give audiences. There, on a dais, a long table, draped in a snow-white cloth, was laid for the coronation dinner, a golden canopy above it. According to tradition, the Emperor and his wife dined alone, and during the meal all the members of the diplomatic corps came in one by one, went up the steps of the dais, and toasted the imperial couple.

"I think I was supposed to return to the Petrovsky Palace immediately after the coronation, but I did not. I managed to follow that crowd of royal guests into the gallery of the Palata. I felt so sorry for Nicky and Alicky. They still wore their crowns and their purple mantles edged with ermine. They must have been exhausted. They looked so lonely—just like two birds in a golden cage."

Then, at the sight of so much food, served on gold, and barely touched by them, Olga realized how ravenously hungry she was.

"I had been up for hours. Now it was afternoon and my stomach was achingly empty. I stared at all that food being brought up to the table and then carried away, and I remember how desperately I wished I could run down the gallery stairs, find my way into the kitchens, and gorge myself!"

But in the end a carriage came for her and she was taken back to the Petrovsky Palace, her Nana, and a meal. Moscow streets were so crowded that at times her carriage had to inch its way through. Cannon booming, church bells ringing, crowds cheering, singing and shouting—the entire world seemed mad with joy that day—and the young girl, however exhausted and hungry she was, could hardly eat for her excitement.

On the evening of the coronation, vast illuminations and fireworks lit up Moscow like a fairy town, its golden domes and cupolas shining mistily against the flickering lights. "Just before being tucked into bed, Nana let me have one last look from the big window at the distant scene. And for those fleeting seconds I was as absorbed in the spectacle as Napoleon must have been eighty years earlier when gazing, probably from the same window, at the burning of Moscow."

The great day was followed by others—filled with banquets, fêtes, and balls. None of those were for the Tsar's younger sister to enjoy. Yet there was one festivity they permitted her to attend—the distribution of the imperial largesse on the Khodynka Meadow just outside the city walls, an enormous field where gunners and sappers usually held their exercises. The Khodynka festival meant the inclusion of the peasantry. They came to Moscow in their thousands, went to the Khodynka to receive a souvenir of the coronation, an enameled mug filled with sweets, to eat a large meal as guests of the Emperor, and to spend the rest of the day dancing and singing on the meadow. The wooden stands were in the middle, the brightly enameled mugs piled high on them. The Tsar and the rest of his family were to come at noon—but about half a million people had gathered together long before dawn. Some Cossacks and policemen were on duty. The field was cordoned off.

Nobody knew the real cause of the disaster. Some said one thing, some another. It was generally attributed to a rumor spread in the crowd that there would not be enough gifts for them all. Whatever was the cause, those nearest to the cordon moved toward the stands. The Cossacks tried to stop them, but what could a mere hundred men do against five hundred thousand? Within a few instants the first furtive movement became a savage stampede. Pressed by those in the rear, the crowd surged so wildly that a great many were at once trampled to death by those behind. The exact number of the casualties never came to light, but it ran into thousands. The May sun shone upon a scene of ghastly carnage.

The authorities lost their heads completely. They also wasted time. In the end it was decided not to send an immediate message to the Kremlin palace. Wagons and carts were mustered from all over Moscow to take the wounded to the hospitals and the bodies to the mortuaries in the city.

"The authorities had muddled everything and so had the court officials. Our carriages were ordered too early. It was a perfect morning and I remember how gay we all were when we drove out of the city gates, and how short-lived was that lightness of heart...."

They saw a procession of carts coming nearer. Pieces of tarpaulin were thrown roughly over them, and they could see many dangling hands.

"At first I thought that people were waving to us. Then my blood froze.

I felt sick. Yet I still stared on. Those carts carried the dead mangled out of all recognition. . . ."

The catastrophe plunged Moscow into mourning. It had many repercussions. The enemies of the crown used it for their propaganda. The police were blamed. So were the hospital authorities and the municipality. "And it brought to light many bitter family dissensions. The younger Grand Dukes, particularly Sandro, Xenia's husband, laid the tragedy at the door of Uncle Serge, governor of Moscow at the time. I felt that my cousins were unjust to him. What is more, Uncle Serge himself was in such despair and offered to resign at once. But Nicky did not accept it. By their efforts to throw the entire blame on one of their own kin, my cousins actually incriminated the entire family and that at a time when solidarity among them was so essential. When Nicky refused to dismiss Uncle Serge, they turned on him. . . ."

The Russian socialists, then living in Switzerland, accused the Emperor of callous indifference to his subjects' suffering because that very evening he and his wife had gone to a ball given by Marquis de Montebello, the French ambassador.

"I know for a fact that neither of them wanted to go. It was done under great pressure from his advisers. The French government had gone to immense expense and trouble to arrange the ball. Tapestries and plate were brought over from Versailles and Fontainebleau and one hundred thousand roses from the South of France. Nicky's ministers insisted that he must go as a gesture of friendship to France. I know that both Nicky and Alicky spent the whole of that day visiting one hospital after another. So did my mother, Aunt Ella, Uncle Serge's wife, and several others. How many people know or care today that Nicky spent thousands and thousands of rubles to provide pensions for those disabled at Khodynka and for the widows and orphans? Later I learned from him that it was not very easy to do at the time—he did not want to embarrass the Treasury, and all the coronation expenses were paid out of the privy purse. He had it done so unobtrusively that none of us knew of it at the time—except for Alicky, of course."

"Did you stay long in Moscow?" I asked the Grand Duchess. "Oh, no! All the foreign guests left for home. Nicky and Alicky went on one of their first tours of the country."

"And what did you do?"

"My mother returned to Gatchina. I followed her."

It was fortunate for Olga that the Dowager Empress grew ever busier and busier during the years following her husband's death. Girls' education and hospitals had always interested her, but now she turned to politics and diplomacy. Her eldest son's total lack of experience provided the Empress Marie with an excuse. To give her justice, she did not meddle. She gave advice, she studied the drifts of international affairs, and greatly profited by her conversations with ambassadors and with the Emperor's ministers.

Grand Duchess Olga at her St. Petersburg residence shortly after her first marriage to Prince Peter of Oldenburg.

"It was an absolute revelation to me to see my mother's shrewdness in handling such matters," said the Grand Duchess, "and she became ruthless too. I happened to be in her rooms during the audience she gave to a prince, then the Director-General of all the girls' schools in the Empire, a fussy, bad-tempered man who always made muddles and laid the blame on his underlings. He was disliked by everybody. That day my mother had him summoned to the Anitchkov Palace to dismiss him. She offered no explanations. She just said in her iciest voice: 'Prince, I have decided that you must go.' The man was so taken aback that he stammered: 'But ... but I could never leave Your Majesty.' 'And I am telling you that you are—' she answered and swept out of the room. I followed her; I did not dare look at the man. . . ."

Olga had reached her late teens. The Empress Marie decided to have Mrs. Franklin replaced by a properly appointed lady-in-waiting. The news reached the Grand Duchess in a devious way. She said nothing to Mrs. Franklin. Her brother and his wife were at Tsarskoe Selo, and Olga felt pretty sure of the Emperor's support. She knew she could not be parted from Nana, who alone understood everything about her. So Olga went to her mother and, etiquette and training thrown to the winds, made a scene.

"Alicky had her Mrs. Orchard brought to Russia. What shall I do without Nana? If you send her away, I will run away myself—I will elope with a palace sweep, I will go and peel potatoes in someone's kitchen, or offer myself as a kennel maid to one of the society ladies in St. Petersburg! And I am sure that Nicky will be on my side!"

"You have always been wilful. Now you are mad! Leave the room," her mother told Olga.

Mrs. Franklin stayed on. No lady-in-waiting came to the Grand Duchess's apartments.[1] Nana ruled supreme—in spite of the difficulties. Nicholas having indeed taken his sister's side in the matter, the Dowager Empress regarded Mrs. Franklin as the usurper of affection which should have been hers. The lavish Christmas presents and other tokens of imperial favor dwindled in value and in number. Nana became "that odious woman" to the Empress Marie.

It was indeed a healthy spirit of independence on the part of the Grand Duchess, but it looked as though victory had sapped the rebellious energy in her—at least for a time. With no courtiers in her own rooms, the Grand Duchess observed her mother's entourage rather mockingly. The Empress Marie liked familiar faces. There were many at her court who were long past all usefulness but could not be dismissed. There was Mademoiselle de l'Escaille, a Belgian, so old that nobody could remember her even middle-aged, who had been the Empress's nursery governess. She moved from Gatchina to St. Petersburg and back again, always immaculately gowned and mittened, very fond of food and solitaire, and having little to say to anyone. There were the maiden Countesses Kutuzov, two sisters, descendants of the great field-marshal, appointed as ladies-in-waiting in 1865. They too were long past carrying out any official duties, but they were kept very busy looking after each other and fussing over their health. There was a very old gentleman, who wore a white wig and was the son of the poet Zhukovsky. His father's long-since-faded laurels alone assured him comfortable rooms at the Gatchina Palace—with sumptuous free board thrown in for good measure. There was also the Empress Marie's favorite lady, Countess Elizabeth Voronzov, who had a family of eight, but neither husband nor children interfered with her attendance at court.

"Her capacity for gossip was incredible. She could smell scandal for miles. And I am afraid my mother liked listening to her," said the Grand

Duchess. "Newspapers in those days did not print idle tittle-tattle, certainly not the Russian newspapers. And Lili Voronzov had the art of building a story out of someone's imprudent hint. I disliked her, though I had to be very polite to her—for the sake of peace. Still, I became rather fond of Sandra, her eldest daughter...."

Time and again, when the Grand Duchess mentioned names, I heard of her "being friendly with" or "becoming fond of" now one, now another person at court. Yet few among them were young. She still had her Sunday afternoons when she and Grand Duke Michael played host and hostess to a carefully selected few from among the sons and daughters of the nobility, but no single abiding friendship seems to have blossomed out of those gatherings. And yet Olga's vivaciousness and her hunger for affection and spontaneity were always there.

When the Dowager Empress interfered with the daily routine, or dropped delicate hints about the young Empress refusing to take her place in society, the rebel in Olga would leap forward and offer battle in defiance of her upbringing, or precedent and tradition. But when the young Grand Duchess found herself standing at a distance, she quite sincerely admired her mother.

"As a sovereign lady, she was perfect. Her personality was magnetic and her zest for activity incredible. She had her finger on every educational pulse in the Empire. She would work her secretaries to shreds; but she did not spare herself. Even when bored in committee, she never looked bored. Her manner and, above all, her tact conquered everybody. And quite openly, my mother enjoyed being the first lady in the Empire. People who served her, as for instance the Sheremetevs, the Obolenskys, the Galitzins, looked upon their service as a dedication. In Russia, as in Denmark, it was always the same—now one person, now another would come and share their problems and troubles with her. And," added the Grand Duchess, "I did always try to remember how deeply my father had loved her...."

Top: Grand Duchess Olga's beloved brother Grand Duke Michael at Gatchina Palace playing with a bear cub presented to him by an army regiment.
Bottom: A footman with a plate of food for the cub. The bear in these picture is indicative of the grandeur of Gatchina Palace.

She was seventeen; she had her Nana, her violin,[2] her painting. And then an anxiety attacked her. Xenia, her elder sister, married to a Russian Grand Duke, had stayed at home, but would there be another Romanov for her, Olga, to marry? She knew that it would be torture for her to leave her beloved country. Fredensborg had satisfied her during an annual holiday, but she could never make her home in Denmark. There remained the German courts, and Olga remembered her father's fierce contempt for these.

"I had nightmares about being in exile, and Nana would get up and make me feel all secure and safe again. Of course I would not have dared to speak of such things to my mother."

The young Emperor would often come to Gatchina from Tsarskoe Selo. ". . . And sometimes I had permission to drive over and see Alicky. Countess Voronzov would come to Gatchina and tell my mother that society grumbled about Alicky's aloofness. I thought it was so unfair. Alicky's health grew poorer and poorer. Her heart was none too good. She suffered from sciatica. Her pregnancies were difficult."[3]

Early in 1899 the Empress Marie told her daughter that she would come out officially in the summer. Olga's heart sank. Among other things, that would mean an end to a host of small but delightful freedoms: an hour snatched for the violin, rambles in the park, the happy sessions in her studio. To be "out" would mean a never-ending sequence of public appearances, drives with her mother, receptions, banquets, audiences. But the Grand Duchess was granted a year's reprieve—for a very sad reason.

In July, 1899, Grand Duke George died of tuberculosis at Abbas Tuman. Nicholas received word of his brother's death by telegram and broke the sad news to his mother.

"Mother, Georgie is gone," he said quietly, and the Empress burst into tears. He was twenty-seven, and his death, as the Grand Duchess said, was an irreparable loss. Intelligent, generous, with a winning personality, the Grand Duke might have given great support to Nicholas. Olga believed he was the best-suited of her brothers to become a strong and popular Tsar. She was convinced that had he lived he would have readily accepted the burden of the crown that Nicholas meekly resigned in 1917, thus probably saving Russia from the Communist Revolution.

"And George need not have died. The doctors had muddled everything from the start. They kept sending him from one place to another. They would not admit it was tuberculosis. They kept referring to George's 'weak chest.'" Olga revealed that her brother was found by a peasant woman at the side of a road, lying beside his overturned motorcycle. He died in her arms, bleeding at the mouth and coughing and gasping for air. The woman, a member of the religious sect of the Malakani, was brought to Peterhof to describe to the distraught Empress the last agonizing moments of her beloved son.

"I remember the tall, black-robed woman from the Caucasus, with her flowing black and white veils, silently gliding by the fountains of Peterhof; she was a figure from a Greek tragedy. Mother was closeted with her for hours."

Grand Duke George shortly before his death in 1899 at a sanitarium. The family was certain he would recover from tuberculosis.

At the time, sinister rumors about his death circulated in Russia, but the Grand Duchess always believed that her brother had died from a hemorrhage caused by the vibrations of the motorcycle he had been strictly forbidden to ride.

The death of the Grand Duke George also brought to an end the family pilgrimages, in early spring or late autumn, to visit him in distant Abbas Tuman, a trip that always created much excitement among the younger imperial children. Amid the serenity of the Caucasian mountains the imperial family relaxed completely, leading a carefree existence of rustic simplicity. How rustic and truly simple this existence was is indicated by a surprising story told by the Grand Duchess.

"The food we ate, cooked and served by the local Caucasian staff was always Caucasian except for the big Danish cheese which was the favorite of Mother's. And every time the cheese was brought in, there were several tiny mice playing hide and seek in its large holes. For the sturdy Caucasians the sight was quite normal and not alarming in the least. We even became so used to the merry occupants of the cheese that the few times they were absent gave us quite a disappointment."

The Caucasian countryside was teeming with robbers because of its proximity to the Turkish border. All Caucasians carried arms, and every time the Dowager Empress stepped out she was escorted by a special Caucasian bodyguard. Among them, according to Grand Duchess Olga, was Omar, a particularly handsome and strapping Caucasian with fiery black eyes, who was a favorite of her mother. "Mother was always asking him about robbers and would teasingly say: 'Omar, when I look into your eyes I am sure you were once a robber yourself!' Omar avoided looking at her but always denied the story. One day, however, he broke down completely. Falling on his knees, he admitted he indeed had been a robber and asked Mama's forgiveness. Mama not only forgave him but made him a member of her permanent bodyguard. From that time onwards, Omar followed her like a pet. I can imagine the uproar in St. Petersburg if it had been known that a member of the imperial bodyguard had once been a common highway robber!"

Grand Duke George being the heir presumptive, the court mourning lasted a year. At last, in the summer of 1900, the Empress Marie gave a mammoth reception in honor of her younger daughter.

"It was a nightmare. It fell on a particularly hot day. In full court dress, with an unwanted lady-in-waiting hovering behind me, I felt as though I were an animal in a cage—exhibited to the public for the first time. And, do you know, that feeling never left me later? I always imagined myself caged and chained whenever I had to appear in public. I would see a crowd and that crowd had no face. It was horrible. I should have remembered who I was and done my duty without any such feelings—but I couldn't help myself. And it is something of a riddle because I was immensely proud of the name I bore and all the tradition—but there lived an imp somewhere inside me...."

On a day in May, 1901, a terse announcement came simultaneously from the Alexander Palace at Tsarskoe Selo and from the Gatchina Palace. It told the country that Her Imperial Highness Grand Duchess Olga Alexandrovna was, with the joint consent of the Emperor and the Dowager Empress, betrothed to His Highness Prince Peter of Oldenburg.

The news rather shook St. Petersburg and Moscow, and nobody believed it to be a love match. Olga was nineteen, Prince Peter thirty-three, and St. Petersburg knew that he never showed much interest in women. Most people took it for granted that the Dowager Empress, her elder daughter busily producing one baby after another, had sacrificed the younger sister's happiness to ensure that Olga would always remain "on call" both at Gatchina and the Anitchkov Palace. The Grand Duchess's own idea was that her mother had been argued into the match by Prince Peter's parents, particularly by his ambitious mother, Princess Eugénie, who was an intimate friend of the Empress Marie.[4]

The Grand Duchess had no knowledge of any such machinations. She used to meet her cousin at most family gatherings and always thought him too old for his years. He was very fussy about his health. His only other interest lay in gambling. He loathed pets about the house, open windows, and walks. Apart from family gatherings, he either stayed at home or spent whole nights at a gambling club in St. Petersburg. Music made him yawn. Painting left him dumb.

"To tell you the truth, I was just tricked into it," the Grand Duchess said. "I was asked to a party at the Voronzovs'. I remember I did not want to go but I thought it would be unwise to refuse. Hardly had I got there than Sandra took me to her sitting room upstairs, stood back, let me go in, and then closed the door on me. And imagine my amazement when I saw old Cousin Peter standing there, looking extremely ill at ease. I can't remember what I said. I do remember that he did not look at me. I heard him stammer through a proposal. I was so taken aback that all I could say was 'thank you,' when the door flew open, Countess Voronzov ran in, embraced me, and cried, 'All my congratulations!' I can't remember anything of what followed. That evening at the Anitchkov, I went to Michael's rooms and we wept together."

The Grand Duchess added nothing to that narrative. I longed to ask so many questions. I did not dare to do so. Even if her mother could be ruthless, surely her brother, the Emperor, should have withheld his consent. The Grand Duchess never mentioned him in connection with her betrothal. Probably her loyalty forbade her. Yet it remains obvious that the young Emperor must have allowed himself to be overruled by his mother.

Olga had fought like a tigress over Mrs. Franklin's dismissal. On this occasion she offered no battle at all. Her future seemed doomed in one sense—but she would not have to leave her country. I can only suppose that that alone reconciled her to a mockery of marriage. But even that could hardly have satisfied a heart always hungering after affection.

The Empress Marie hurried on with the wedding. It took place at the end of July, 1901, none but the immediate members of the family being invited. There was hardly any gaiety. The bride having changed her dress, the couple left for the Oldenburg Palace in St. Petersburg where the young Grand Duchess spent her wedding night alone, having cried herself to sleep. Prince Peter went to meet his cronies at the club. He returned in the morning.

"I shared his roof for nearly fifteen years," Olga said frankly, "and never once were we husband and wife."

Princess Eugénie of Oldenburg, whose son was now brother-in-law of the Emperor, began lavishing magnificent jewels on Olga, among them a diamond necklace of twenty-five stones, each the size of an almond, a ruby tiara given by Napoleon to Empress Josephine, and a fabulous sapphire parure. "The necklace was so heavy that I could not wear it more than a few hours at a time. I used to carry it in my bag and put it on just before appearing in public so that I could avoid for a few moments longer its uncomfortable weight. . . ."[5]

There was some vague talk about their going to the South of France, but there was no honeymoon and, presently, the Grand Duchess had an acute attack of melancholia. It passed, but she began losing her hair and in the end a wig had to be made for her. She never learned how to wear it, and once, driving in an open carriage with the Emperor and her sister-in-law, Olga realized that the wig was slipping down under her hat.

"I clutched it hard—I kept my hands on it. Since my illness had not been made public, people must have thought me deranged. . . ."

In the autumn of 1901, Prince Peter reluctantly consented to give up his gambling parties in St. Petersburg, and they went to Biarritz, Dina and Mrs. Franklin accompanying Olga.

"We went to the Hotel du Palais. One evening we gave a party. I was dancing a fox-trot when someone bumped into me and my wig flew off and landed in the middle of the floor. In the silence that followed, even the orchestra stopped playing. I turned green with horror. I can't remember who picked up my wig, but I never had the courage to dance until my own hair began growing again. By the beginning of 1903 the wig had done its service."

One evening at the Hotel du Palais, they were having dinner when the restaurant filled with smoke. "There is a small fire in one of the wings, but Your Imperial Highness has nothing to worry about," said the maître d'hôtel in his most reassuring French. An instant later everybody was scrambling for their lives.

The Grand Duchess ran up to her suite to try to save some of her belongings. When she reappeared on the front lawn, panting and disheveled, she found that all she was holding was a clothes pin. "It was the only thing I managed to grab in my excitement." To her immense relief, a corpulent Greek gentleman, occupying a room on her floor, arrived out of breath and carrying her entire jewel box. "I later found out that he had a daughter married to Prince Orlov-Davadov, hence his interest in the welfare of Russian Grand Duchesses." Prince Peter of Oldenburg was not so lucky as his wife. He lost his entire wardrobe, including all his uniforms and decorations, among them the famous Danish Order of the White Elephant made expressly for him by Fabergé.

Grand Duchess Olga at her St. Petersburg residence shortly after her first marriage to Prince Peter of Oldenburg.

Later they went to Carlsbad to stay with Uncle Bertie. Carlsbad had been selected by Edward VII and his cronies as the place where, under the pretense of taking the cure, they could pursue those pleasures which helped establish the notoriety of the Edwardian Era.

"I can still remember Uncle Bertie sitting unperturbed in front of his hotel, puffing a cigar while hordes of Germans stood outside staring at him with awe and curiosity.

"'How can you stand it, Uncle Bertie?' I asked him one day.

"'Why, it's as much entertainment for me to stare at them as it is for them to stare at me,' the King replied."

The Grand Duchess said nothing about King Edward VII's reaction to her marriage. But he was kind, and placed a small yacht at her disposal to take her on a cruise along the Mediterranean coast of Italy.

"At Sorrento we went ashore and gave a buffet party on the verandah of a hotel. Suddenly I saw a young British naval officer with a shock of red hair. He stood and stared at the sea. We began pelting him with grapes and in the end I asked him to join our party. He did." This young naval officer, soon known as "Jimmie," then a lieutenant in the Royal Navy, became Vice-Admiral T. V. James, and one of the Grand Duchess's closest friends. His courage and resourcefulness during the Revolution were to prove of inestimable help to her.

"Oh, yes," she replied to a question of mine, "we were gay enough at Sorrento. The first great shock was over. I still had hope for the future—but unfortunately there were complications during our stay there. My brother Michael joined us. He had already fallen in love with Dina, my first lady-in-waiting, and now they planned an elopement, but someone gave them away. Dina, of course, was dismissed summarily. My brother was disconsolate. He blamed my mother and Nicky. I felt powerless to help him. I sometimes wondered if it had been better for all of us Romanovs to be born without hearts. Mine was untouched, but I was bound to a man to whom I was just an imperial cipher. To please his ambitious mother, he had become the Emperor's brother-in-law in name. If I had talked to him about my starved heart, Cousin Peter would have thought me mad. . . ."

They returned to Russia shortly before Christmas. There followed a few weary months at St. Petersburg and then, to Olga's joy, they left for the country south of Moscow—Ramogne, the huge estate of her mother-in-law. And there, for the first time in her life, Olga came into close contact with the peasantry.

"I went from village to village, nobody interfering with me. I went into their huts, I talked to them and felt at my ease among them. There were hardships and I saw penury too, of a kind I had never imagined to exist. But there was also kindness, magnanimity, and an unbreakable faith in God. As I saw it, those peasants were rich for all their poverty, and I had the sense of being a genuine human being when I was among them."

But those frequent visits to the villages were not enough for Olga. The tedious manner of life as lived in the ugly Oldenburg house soon palled on her, and she decided to assert her independence. First, she began going daily to the hospital on the estate, watching the work of doctors and nurses, learning something every day. Next she decided to build a small white villa at some distance from Ramogne.

The Oldenburgs raised no objections. The villa came to be built. It was called "Olgino." I cannot tell if Prince Peter followed the Grand Duchess to the new home. He may well have found it more comfortable to stay on at Ramogne.

"I had Olgino built on a hill overlooking the little Veronecz which ran into the Don. The view was superb. Fields ran into woods, and beyond gleamed the golden spires of the ancient monastery dedicated to St. Tikhon, a place of numerous pilgrimages. I remember one summer evening I sat on the balcony and watched the sunset, and the peace of Olgino was so soothing that then and there I vowed that if God would ever grant me happiness, I would have my first-born son christened after St. Tikhon."

The Grand Duchess so loved Olgino and her peasants in the neighborhood that it was a wrench to leave them in the autumn. But, for all her spurts of independence, she was not her own mistress. She had to return to the North. Her first winter was spent at the enormous Oldenburg Palace on the Palace Quay.

"It was ghastly being there," she said. "There were endless scenes at table between my husband and his parents. They accused Prince Peter of wasting his money on gambling. His defense was that he had never been taught anything useful. My mother-in-law's tongue was like a scorpion, my father-in-law's temper too frightful for words. I escaped whenever I could, but it was not always possible. Peter would sometimes rush away to his club before the end of dinner. So many people witnessed those scenes, including the servants, that St. Petersburg must have known everything about the happy family life led by the Oldenburgs. Still, I had affection for Prince Alexander, my father-in-law. Although he was notorious throughout Russia for his temper, he was a man and not a dressed-up dummy."

A Kind of Happiness

I t was a relief for the Grand Duchess to leave the Oldenburg palace after a year. Her brother had bought her a big house in Sergievskaya Street. Some alterations had to be carried out before the Grand Duchess could move in.

"You can have no idea what a pleasure it was to be in my own simple home—away from all those palaces," the Grand Duchess told me. Later I learned to my surprise that "the simple home" had more than one hundred rooms and had a staff of sixty-eight, not counting the seven chauffeurs for the seven cars, or the coachmen and grooms in charge of the great stables and enormous coach-houses. Still, it was Olga's first home where she might order a herring for her dinner if she felt like it, change the curtains in any of the rooms, and have her pets take possession of the sofas and armchairs without either the Empress Dowager or Princess Eugénie countermanding her orders and interfering with her habits. And Olga's own rooms were furnished so simply as to suggest austerity. Mrs. Franklin had her nook there, and next to her bedroom was a large studio.

Yet privacy came to be counted in precious moments. As the Emperor's sister, she had to receive all foreign royalty visiting Russia and give audiences to all the ambassadors. Those audiences always remained an ordeal because of their deadening formality.

"Thank heaven they did not last long. But I must have given many a *mauvais quart d'heure* to those diplomats...." Of such audiences, the one she enjoyed most was that of the tall and bearded Emir of Bokhara, absolute ruler of an autonomous state near the border of Afghanistan. Over his flowing robes he wore a Russian general's epaulettes made of diamonds.

Grand Duchess Olga, age 21, with her brother, Grand Duke Michael, age 23, at one of the many formal events she attended with her brother, rather than her husband. At this time Michael was an officer of the guards.

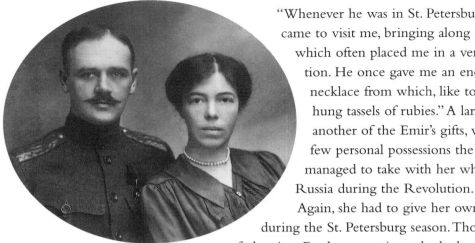

A formal portrait of Olga and her second husband, Colonel Nikolai Koulikovsky.

"Whenever he was in St. Petersburg the Emir always came to visit me, bringing along elaborate presents which often placed me in a very difficult position. He once gave me an enormous gold necklace from which, like tongues of flame, hung tassels of rubies." A large oriental carpet, another of the Emir's gifts, was one of the few personal possessions the Grand Duchess managed to take with her when she fled from Russia during the Revolution.

Again, she had to give her own receptions during the St. Petersburg season. Those meant weeks of planning. For her receptions, she had wild flowers shipped in a special railroad car all the way from the Caucasus to her florist who then descended upon the palace with his entire staff to arrange them. The Grand Duchess certainly had her ladies and gentlemen to help her. In the great house in Sergievskaya Street, Prince Peter led a life of his own. He never interfered with his wife, nor did he help her. They hardly ever appeared together.

Finally, there were interminable, tiresomely unavoidable calls on members of the family and on her friends. Those calls seemed to the Grand Duchess to be a sinful waste of time. Often enough she would be obliged to accompany her mother. Every morning, except in Lent, whether at Gatchina or at the Anitchkov, the Dowager Empress was presented with a large ornate sheet listing all the day's entertainments and parties in the capital.

"My mother often decided on the spur of the moment that she wanted to see a particular play or attend some gala party, and then I would get a message that she expected me to go with her. I had no choice. I shared my father's indifference to the theater, but Mother loved to attend because all eyes would be on her. . . ." As the Dowager Empress and Grand Duchess Olga took their seats in the imperial box, all the gentlemen in the audience would rise and bow respectfully. "During performances of the opera, especially *Aida*, Hussars from my own regiment or sailors from the imperial yacht *Standard* would often be called upon to play the parts of warriors. It was a riot to see those tall, husky men standing awkwardly on the stage, wearing helmets and sandals and showing their bare, hairy legs. Despite the frantic signals of the producer, they would stare up at us with broad grins.

"In the winter, I would often accompany Mama for an afternoon ride by sleigh along the broad and beautiful Nevski Prospect. On sunny days, especially Sunday, all fashionable St. Petersburg rode along the 'Quay.' There were some beautiful horses and sleighs." The Dowager Empress had a pair of shiny blacks and a blue net to protect her from the ice and snow that flew up from the horses' hoofs. As mother and daughter passed, gentlemen would raise their fur caps in salute.

To the despair of the Grand Duchess, her days in St. Petersburg grew more and more hectic. "Sometimes I found myself obliged to be in three different places on the same day. At Peterhof in the morning for some family matter, at Gatchina for luncheon with my mother, and then race back to St. Petersburg for an evening affair which I loathed and could not avoid."

On one occasion she and her brother, Grand Duke Michael, were driving to Gatchina to dine with their mother. "Poor Michael had an unfortunate habit of falling asleep at the wheel. That evening he was driving very fast—we were terrified of being late—and then quite suddenly he nodded, the car left the road and turned a complete somersault. We were both thrown out—miraculously unhurt. The car was not damaged. We just pushed it back on the road and drove on."

"The mad social whirl," as the Grand Duchess called it, meant clothes of the kind she detested. All the Romanov ladies at the time were dressed by a fashion dictator, Madame Brissac.

"She was tall and dark. When she came to supervise a fitting, I never missed an opportunity to complain about her prices. Brissac would first look hurt and then whisper importantly: 'Madame, I beg Your Imperial Highness not to mention these things at Tsarskoe Selo, but I always cut my prices for you.' And then Alicky told me how she too had complained about her prices, and Madame Brissac had replied, 'I beg Your Majesty not to mention it to anyone—but I always cut my prices for Your Majesty.'

"Alicky and I had a good laugh about it! The elegant old sinner! She did so well out of us all that she could afford to live in great style in a mansion in St. Petersburg."

For a Romanov lady to complain about a couturière's prices seems rather out of proportion, but the cost of her wardrobe was by no means the only financial problem for the Grand Duchess.

"My mother, Nicky, Xenia, Michael, and I were all embarrassed in this way," she told me. "I had an income of about one million dollars a year, but I never saw the money, nor did I really know how it was spent. Account books were kept, of course, but that did not help. I had twelve accountants and a very capable treasurer, Colonel Rodsevich, and between them the accounts were certainly kept in order, but the money melted like snow in spring. I had so much money—yet I never had enough to buy the things I wanted."

She remembered that once, at the end of a fiscal year, she wished to buy a small picture costing less than two hundred dollars, but her treasurer told her there was no money to meet the bill. It was an unwritten law that the Romanovs paid "on the nail" for all their purchases, and the men and women of the Grand Duchess's generation strictly observed it.

Her clothes, traveling expenses, the upkeep of the mansion in St. Petersburg and of Olgino, and a number of regular donations to charities did not exhaust the list of expenses. She was also expected to pay for the education of her servants' children.

"I had a staff of nearly seventy in St. Petersburg and that was considered quite a modest establishment for the Emperor's sister, and all of them had so many children, and all of them wanted their sons to be trained as doctors and engineers. So you can imagine that the expense was terrific. But I did not mind that item of the budget. That, at least, was worthwhile."

The root of all the troubles, however, lay in her husband's wild gambling habits. The Grand Duchess had a legacy of one million gold rubles from her brother George. Within a few years every penny of it was lost by Prince Peter.

Still the Romanov family was fabulously rich—particularly when one remembers the frozen assets. Besides the seven palaces crowded with art treasures, there was the jewelry acquired during the three centuries of

Romanov rule. Its conservatively estimated value ran into hundreds of millions. There was the Orlov diamond, weighing 194½ carats, bought by Count Alexis Orlov in Amsterdam in 1776 and presented by him to Catherine the Great; the great state diamond of 82 carats; the Mountain of the Moon, an uncut stone of 120 carats; and the Polar Star, a magnificent pale ruby of 40 carats. There was the great imperial crown made by Poisier, court jeweler to the Empress Anna. It was in the shape of a miter surmounted by a cross of five great diamonds held together by an enormous ruby. The band of the crown consisted of thirty-nine diamonds and thirty-eight pink pearls. A diadem, made during the reign of Alexander I, had five hundred diamonds, over a hundred pink pearls, and thirteen mammoth "ancient" pearls, the last named being taken from a fifteenth-century collar worn by a Tsarina of Muscovy. And over and above all these, there were necklaces and parures of pink diamonds, sapphires, emeralds, and rubies, a certain number of pieces being kept aside for family wedding presents.

"All of it represented fabulous capital which could never be touched, and I doubt if any of those treasures would have found a buyer," said the Grand Duchess—and I looked at the narrow gold bracelet she wore, set with a tiny ruby and a still-smaller sapphire. One of the revenues of the family came from the so-called Oudely—imperial manors scattered over the entire length and breadth of the Empire. Hundreds of thousands of acres were purchased by Catherine II as a prudent measure to assure the finances of the family. The Oudely consisted of farms, orchards, vast reaches of forest, valuable fisheries and vineyards. The most profitable Oudely were in the South, particularly in the Crimea. Their intrinsic value was astronomical. Owing to constant mismanagement and graft, they yielded little more than four million rubles a year. The civil list[1] of the Tsar and the entire Romanov clan came to twenty-two million gold rubles (today approximately $27,000,000).

"It sounds tremendous, but it was not. The fiscal year began on the first of January. Often enough Nicky would be broke by the autumn...."

The Emperor had the upkeep of two palaces at Tsarskoe Selo, two at Peterhof, one in St. Petersburg, one in Moscow, and one in the Crimea. He had to pay the wages of thousands of court officials and servants, all of whom were also given presents at Christmas and on Nicholas's saint's day. There was the upkeep of the imperial yachts and trains and all the traveling expenses. Three theaters in St. Petersburg and two in Moscow were kept out of the private income, as was the Imperial Ballet School. The Academy of Arts and the Academy of Science had their own endowments, but hardly a year went by but the Emperor had to assist them. Practically all the orphanages, institutions for the blind, almshouses, and many hospitals depended on him. And there was the family. Each Grand Duke received about eight hundred thousand gold rubles a year. Each Grand Duchess had a dowry of about three million gold rubles.

"And by the time Nicky came to the throne, there were so many of us. Xenia's husband Sandro alone had five brothers, my Uncle Constantine five sons and two daughters...."

In addition, the Tsar's private chancery was inundated with individual petitions for financial help. A policeman's widow asking to have her children educated, a brilliant university student requiring a grant to finish his course, a peasant asking for a cow, a fisherman needing a new boat, a clerk's widow asking for a sum needed to buy a pair of spectacles. The private chancery staff were strictly forbidden to leave a petition unanswered. Once certain inquiries were made and the case proved to be genuine, the petition was satisfied.

"Compared with some of the American magnates, my brother was a poor man."

The Grand Duchess, however, said that the Romanov difficulties were perpetually increased by the incredible mismanagement of the officials. The Emperor wanted to buy the hill of Ai Petri at the back of his estate of Livadia in the Crimea. Ai Petri and the land surrounding it belonged to a noble family. In the end, a vast sum was agreed upon and the property changed hands, but when the Emperor wished to build a small cottage on Ai Petri he discovered he had no right to do so: the price he had paid did not give him a full title to Ai Petri.

"I remember Nicky's anger," the Grand Duchess said, "but so many important people were involved in the scandal that he decided to drop the matter...."

The Grand Duchess told me another case of appalling mismanagement. Just before 1914, the accumulated yearly allowance of Nicholas's five children reached the sum of about one hundred million rubles. Against the Emperor's wishes, the Minister of Finance—together with one or two leading bankers—invested every penny of it in German stocks. Nicholas argued against it, but they kept assuring him that the investment was perfectly safe and very profitable. Needless to say, this fortune evaporated after World War I.

"And then there were the beggars," the Grand Duchess said contemptuously. "I don't mean the honest beggars from among the common people, but highly placed gentlemen-beggars—particularly officers of guards regiments—all living above their income and all expecting us to settle their debts...."

One afternoon an officer in the Cossack Guards, whom she had known since her childhood, came to her palace to beg her to give him about three hundred and fifty thousand gold rubles.

"I asked what he needed it for. He looked desperate. He said it was for a debt of honor. I gave him the money. Within a few days I learned that he had used it to buy a racing stable. I never spoke to him again...."

Then she remembered the handsome Prince Dadiani, also in the Cossack Guards, who found himself in genuine difficulties. To get out of them, said the Grand Duchess, the gentleman purloined some valuable paintings from a private art gallery and brought them to Olga's palace, begging her to ask the Emperor to buy the pictures for the Hermitage. The Prince said they were all treasured family possessions and it cost him dear to part with them, but he had no alternative. The Grand Duchess liked the pictures and had just persuaded her brother to agree to the purchase when the police, informed by the distracted owner, traced the provenance of "the Dadiani heirlooms."

"I am thankful to say that the man was dismissed from the service at once. All the same, the scandal was terrific. The men in the ranks were so much more honorable. They never cadged. Once only in all those years did a sailor, about to return to his home near the Caspian, ask me to help him buy a new fishing net. I gave him the money and he repaid every penny. In Russia, those men were called *nizhnye chini*, lower ranks. To me, they were noble with the true nobility of heart. One could be friends with them. None among them regarded a Grand Duchess in terms of loosened purse strings."

Had she been happily and truly married, the Grand Duchess would have made little of all those financial embarrassments. But she stood alone, with no man to advise or help her. She was far too conscientious to bother the Emperor with her own domestic problems. Grand Duke Michael, now a fully fledged officer in the guards, would have laughed at her difficulties. The only counsel she would have got from her husband, had she ever asked for it, would have been a suggestion that she should try her luck at the gaming table. And, as a result, those financial difficulties helped to deepen her loneliness and unhappiness.

She was lonely in St. Petersburg—even when she dutifully obeyed the social pattern. She went to many houses, she met many people. Sometimes her natural buoyancy conquered the boredom of the occasion. Yet, when she spoke of those years, I understood that not one lasting friendship was formed among all those acquaintances.

Not far from the Grand Duchess's home stood the great palace of Princess Yurievskaya, her step-grandmother. She had been Princess Catherine Dolgorukaya, first the mistress and then the second wife of the Emperor Alexander II. She was old, she lived in great style, and she thought of herself as the Dowager Empress, though Alexander II was killed before he could have her ambition realized. Olga grew fond of the old lady.

"She must have loved my grandfather dearly. Whenever I called on her, I felt I was stepping into a page of history. She lived entirely in the past. Time stopped for her on the day my grandfather was assassinated. She always talked about him. She kept all his uniforms and clothes, even his dressing-gown, in glass cases in her private chapel."

A house the Grand Duchess often had to visit with her mother was the Yusupoff Palace on the Moika Quay. Princess Yusupoff was an intimate friend of the Dowager Empress. It used to be said that the Yusupoff wealth far outshadowed that of the Romanovs. "And I can well believe it," the Grand Duchess said dryly. "I still remember their drawing rooms and tables crammed with crystal bowls filled with uncut sapphires, emeralds, and opals—all used as decorations. I think that all that fabulous wealth never spoiled Princess Yusupoff. She was kindly and generous and she could be a loyal friend. But, alas, she was a tragic mother—she spoiled her children far too much."

At no great distance from the Grand Duchess's home, in a huge house on the Fontanka Quay, lived the Count and Countess Orlov-Davidov. The Countess was reputed to be one of the best-dressed women in the world. Both were very popular, though he looked like a well-bred dog and was nicknamed *l'homme chien*. And then there were the two Netchaieff Malsteff sisters and their brother who entertained lavishly. "All three were unmarried, very eccentric, and very rich, and although many people laughed at them behind their backs the same people were the first to attend their famous receptions...."

The most famous hostess of the day was Countess Marie Kleinmichel, whose fancy-dress balls were the talk of the city all through the season. Rich, eccentric, somewhat of a cripple, the Countess hardly ever left her house and everybody who was anybody considered it an honor to come to her.

"A *grande dame* to the tips of her fingers," said the Grand Duchess, "but she was uncannily shrewd and clever. Somehow or other she succeeded in learning the intimate secrets of practically everyone in society. Her house was known to be a hotbed of gossip. She also dabbled in the occult, and I heard that on one occasion spirits got so mischievous that one of them pulled the wig off her head and revealed the secret of her baldness. I should not think there were many more séances after that evening."[2]

However short, the St. Petersburg season must have been torture for the Grand Duchess. From New Year's Day till the Carnival Sunday, society danced, drove about in decorated troikas, listened to concerts, went to opera and ballet, ate and drank, and danced again, each hostess trying to outrival the others in the ingenuity and originality of the entertainment she provided. There were the Bals Blancs for the débutantes and the Bals Roses for the newly married couples. Bands, such as Colombo's orchestra and Goulesko's Gipsies, were in great demand. No season was considered complete without the great ball given by Grand Duchess Vladimir, and the equally famous Bal Masqué of Countess Kleinmichel. By the evening of Carnival Sunday, the least pious hostess in St. Petersburg must have sighed with relief at the compulsory cessation of all merrymaking. None could be indulged in between the Pure Monday, following Carnival Sunday, and Easter Day.

The season opened in the morning of New Year's Day with the ceremonious *vykhod* (appearance) of the Emperor and Empress. From the chapel they made their way to the Nicholas Hall where some two or three thousand guests were presented to them, the gentlemen bowing three times, the ladies curtseying and kissing the hand of the Empress. About half an hour before the vykhod, all the Romanovs gathered together in one of the drawing rooms at the Winter Palace to take up their places in the solemn procession to the Nicholas Hall. That morning the masters of ceremonies and the court marshals had it all their way; not a movement could be made but it must accord with the rules of the most rigid etiquette in Europe.

"We made our entrance according to age rather than rank. I usually went with one of my cousins, either Grand Duke Boris or Grand Duke Andrew, the younger sons of Grand Duke Vladimir. Nicky, of course, stood at the head, with my mother on his arm, and Alicky was immediately behind with Michael.

"When all were in position, the doors into the Nicholas Hall were opened, the Grand Master of Ceremonies struck the floor three times with his ivory staff, and announced the entrance of Their Imperial Majesties. And we trooped in, two by two, just like a team of well-groomed, well-trained poodles to parade in front of a crowd at some fair."

Two or three balls were given during the season at the Winter Palace. The red-stone building stretched interminably along the river front. Within, it had an enfilade of halls, each vying with a cathedral in length and breadth, Nicholas Hall, St. George's Hall, White Hall, Malachite Hall, Throne Hall, all having two rows of windows. Away from those cavernous halls lay a vast cluster of private apartments, rooms for members of the household and servants. Much space was wasted in landings and passages which led nowhere. The palace fully justified its name; it could never acquire the warmth of a real home. For balls, it would be decorated with thousands of palm trees, exotic plants from the Crimea, masses of roses, tulips, and lilacs from the Tsarskoe Selo hothouses. But none of it could do away with the chilly, forbidding vastness of the place.

There was a riot of color. At every entrance and along all the staircases stood the giant troopers of the Chevalier Guards, all white, silver, and gold, and Cossack Life Guards in their crimson and blue cherkeskas. Negro footmen were in scarlet from head to foot. Court messengers wore caps trimmed with feathers. The palace footmen wore a livery whose color could hardly be distinguished for the wealth of gold braid. The balls followed the procedure of the New Year's *vykhod*.

"Oh, the color of it all!" said the Grand Duchess. "The guards officers in tunics of crimson, white, and blue, the senior court ladies in olive-green, the maids of honor in ruby-red velvet, and all of us in silver and gold brocade.... Rubies, pearls, diamonds and emeralds...and yet how I hated those balls at the Winter Palace which we all had to attend. Of our whole family, my mother alone liked them because she knew everybody had their eyes on her. She looked magnificent."

Every ball at the palace was opened by a polonaise, the Emperor leading.

"Nicky loved dancing and he was good at it—but unfortunately Alicky hated those occasions. She and Nicky stayed for supper, served rather early in the Malachite Hall, and then they vanished. So far as I was concerned, I would have escaped after the first polonaise but, of course, I could not do so."

On those occasions her husband was of use. He would arrive early to escort her home and take her through the palace guard rooms to a side entrance. As the Grand Duchess, a fur cloak thrown over her silver brocade dress, ran on tiptoe through those rooms, she heard the soldiers snoring.

"And how I wished I was in bed too. How I envied those men!"

The very last touch of the picturesque at the Winter Palace was the famous historical hall in January, 1903. The following year saw the outbreak of the war with Japan. There followed the years of unrest and worse. The Winter Palace had its windows shuttered. No flowers were ever massed again in its halls. No dance music was ever heard again under its exquisitely painted ceilings. It had known greatness. And once it had been a home. But that January evening of 1903 rang its knell in more than one sense.

And the Grand Duchess remembered it vividly.

"All of us appeared in seventeenth-century court dress. Nicky wore the dress of Alexis, the second Romanov Tsar, all raspberry, gold, and silver, and some of the things were brought specially from the Kremlin. Alicky was just stunning. She was Tsarina Maria Miloslavskaya, Alexis's first wife. She wore a sarafan of gold brocade trimmed with emeralds and silver thread, and her earrings were so heavy that she could not bend her head."

That Bal Masqué was in the nature of a swan song. The Emperor's guests, who danced the old national dances that night, were unaware that a curtain fell with the last bar played by the guards' orchestra. No other ball was ever given at the Winter Palace. An unfortunate incident in connection with the 1903 ball may almost be regarded as a premonition.

Grand Duke Michael had asked his mother to lend him a big diamond clip to wear as an aigrette in his fur cap. The clip was of fabulous value; it had belonged to Emperor Paul I, and the Dowager Empress wore it very seldom. She lent it to her son most reluctantly.

"And Michael lost it! It must have fallen off his cap while he was dancing. My mother and he were in despair—the clip being one of the crown jewels. All the halls at the palace were searched that very night. At dawn the detectives searched from basement to attic. The diamond clip was never found. As a matter of fact," said the Grand Duchess, "a great many valuables used to be lost at those balls, but I never heard of a single jewel being recovered."

Nobody was better pleased than Olga when the mad whirl of the season reached its end. She hated the noise, the glaring lights, the crowds, the inevitably rich food, that never absent feeling of her own self, all dressed up and bejeweled, being on show. With the beginning of Lent, theaters and other places of entertainment being closed, the Dowager Empress went to Gatchina. Her younger daughter stayed in St. Petersburg, receiving few people, eating plain, regular meals with Mrs. Franklin, spending hours in the studio, either playing the violin or painting.

And every morning she went out for a walk in the streets and along the quays of St. Petersburg. That habit of hers had no precedent among the Romanov ladies. No Grand Duchess had ever walked in the streets alone. Olga made a slight concession to the tradition: a lady-in-waiting followed behind at a distance, and still farther one of the chauffeurs drove a car at a snail's pace. But the Grand Duchess strode well ahead, accompanied by her borzoi, a poodle and a big husky. The weather made no difference. She walked when it snowed and sleeted. She would not give up her exercise even when the wind from the gulf buffeted her clothes and all but tore her hat off her head.

During that walk the Grand Duchess belonged solely to herself. That great and proud city, created by the will of an ancestor, spoke to her in a language she could understand. Its domes and spires, its granite and marble, its river, the sense of wind, water, and cloud, were to her all woven together into some imperishable covenant of strength, courage, and hope in the future. The dream of Peter the Great in building this new city had a permanent effect on the Russian people which should not be underestimated. Indeed, the dream could never have been realized had it not been for the ruthless determination of Peter; more than 125,000 men died in the treacherous marshes to build the city of St. Petersburg.

"But if ever the end justified the means, then it did in this case," said the Grand Duchess. She argued her point convincingly, asking me to explore the consequences of what might have happened to Russia and Europe if St. Petersburg had not been built. "If Peter had allowed Moscow to remain the capital, then Russia would probably have become steeped in Asiatic culture and would now be part and parcel of Asia. By ordering, however, the new capital built on the northern border of Europe, Russia instead was forced to join the cultural family of the Occidental nations and Europe was thus saved from having Asia at its very door. If, on the other hand, he had located his capital somewhere in the South, say the Crimea, than the Slav and Greek element would probably have joined forces against the Turks and thereby created a renewed Byzantine Empire with Constantinople as its center. It is also possible that under the temperate, lazy climate of the South, the Slavic leadership would have deteriorated, the northern Slavs falling under German domination while the South fell under the Turkish yoke...."

Often enough, reaching the great Senate Square, the Grand Duchess would halt and look at the bronze statue of Peter the Great.

"I often imagined him looking at me, his own descendant. I loved his story. I loved his city. I think it helped to keep my soul alive. There was so much courage and doggedness in it. There was not much happiness in my house in Sergievskaya Street. I often thought that my misery had no meaning at all. But that morning walk was good."

She had her Nana and no one else. She did not see her brother Michael as often as she used to: he was greatly occupied with military matters and affairs of the heart. Her sister Xenia and she had never been really intimate. Her conscience forbade her to bring all her problems to the Emperor, over-burdened as she knew him to be. Alicky was hardly ever in good health.

Conforming outwardly, the Grand Duchess was a rebel at heart. Her travesty of a marriage had not so much hardened as deepened her hunger for affection. Healthy and normal, she longed to be a wife and mother. Instead, she bore the name of a man who dutifully accompanied her to public functions, occasionally spent a half-hour in one of her drawing rooms, talked of little else than his recent good or bad fortune at cards, was extremely concerned about his own health, and regarded her numerous pets with open aversion.

On an April day in 1903 the Grand Duchess drove over from Gatchina to watch a military review at Pavlovsk. As she stood talking to some of the officers she saw a tall, fair man in the uniform of the Cuirassier Guards. She had never met him before. She knew nothing about him. Their eyes met.

"It was fate. It was also a shock. I suppose on that day I learned that love at first sight does exist."

She could hardly wait for the end of the review. She saw the tall officer speak to her brother Michael.

"They were friends. I learned the man's name—Nikolai Koulikovsky. I learned that he came from a prominent military family—not that such things mattered to me. I just told Michael I wanted to meet him. Michael understood. He arranged a luncheon party the very next day. I don't remember much about the luncheon. I was twenty-two years old and I loved for the first time in my life, and I knew that my love was accepted and returned."

What followed would have been incredible were it not for the Grand Duchess's own frank narrative.

She asked nobody's advice. She needed none. She went straight back to St. Petersburg, found her husband in his library, told him she had met a man she could love, and asked for an immediate divorce. No doubt she was greatly excited.

Prince Peter of Oldenburg did not show the least astonishment. He remained as calm as though the Grand Duchess had told him about having changed her mind about a party or a play. His wife's emotional state did not matter in the least. He heard her out and then replied that he cared deeply for his own dignity and the family name. An immediate divorce was out of the question, but he might consider the matter in about seven years.

Nikolai Koulikovsky.

Did the Grand Duchess hint at the possibility of an elopement, its consequences far more resounding than any divorce would have been? I cannot tell. She never mentioned it, but the next development certainly hints at some such weapon having been used by her.

Prince Peter of Oldenburg appointed young Koulikovsky as one of his personal aides-de-camp and told him that he could have his quarters at the house in Sergievskaya Street.

The extraordinary ménage à trois in the Oldenburg household, always remaining a well-kept secret and left undiscovered even by Countess Kleinmichel, continued until 1914 when the Grand Duchess left to nurse at the front and Koulikovsky followed his regiment. Prince Peter's promise to consider the matter in seven years was never kept, but their marriage was annulled in 1916 when the Grand Duchess became Koulikovsky's wife. After her death, I asked Vice-Admiral James, who had once stayed at Olgino, if he had ever had any idea of the relationship between the Grand Duchess and Koulikovsky, and he told me that never could he have dreamt that the Grand Duchess was in love with the man. Their relations seemed always correct and formal. "I was quite surprised when I learned of their marriage some years later," he said.

And through all those years the tall aide-de-camp, impeccably correct in carrying out his official duties, remained the only support of the Grand Duchess.

Olga was at once happy and unhappy. To be at last found desirable and loved was an attainment she had not sometimes dared to hope for. Yet all her honesty and her hatred of compromise warred against the ugly *mise en scène*. The absurd ménage à trois may have satisfied the perverted sense of honor in Prince Peter of Oldenburg. It depressed and shamed the Grand Duchess. Yet her misery would have deepened still further had Koulikovsky not been under that roof. And, at the very least, she can stand absolved of duplicity: the curious arrangement was made by her husband, not by herself. As to Koulikovsky, it is fairly evident that the Grand Duchess's persuasion made him accept the post on her husband's staff.

It is more than doubtful that they were lovers before their marriage in 1916. First and foremost, there was her religion. Her membership of the Orthodox church was insolubly bound with her origins, her way of life, her ancestry. She was neither a mystic nor a devotee. But her marriage having been contracted according to the Orthodox ordinance, there was no choice for her but to await its annulment by the same Church.

There must have also been another consideration. Olga had longed for children. To bear Koulikovsky's child at that time would have meant accepting the official paternity of Prince Peter. In the first place, nobody would have believed it. Secondly, the Grand Duchess differed from at least two of her famous ancestresses, Elizabeth and Catherine the Great, in that her rebellious spurts against the tyranny of deadening convention would never have carried her the length of betraying her inward truth. She was not an intellectual to reason out her problems. However bizarre her habits, she was not quite the eccentric some of her relations thought her to be. Excessive ambiguity in her personal life would, as she rightly guessed, have put out the only light she had to live by.

So she waited—all through those years of her youth. The waiting grew harder and more bitter. On occasions it must have been something of an agony to stay at the house in Sergievskaya Street.

It was just at that time when she found comfort at Tsarskoe Selo. We cannot tell if the Emperor knew her secret. He may well have done. The fact remains that from 1904 till 1906 Olga saw him and the Empress almost every day. Prince Peter having been given the command of a regiment stationed at Tsarskoe Selo, they moved there from St. Petersburg. By that time neither Nicholas nor Alexandra appeared much in society. In St. Petersburg there was already a faction, led by Grand Duchess Vladimir, who criticized the young Empress for all she did or all she did not do, and little by little the imperial family withdrew into their own circle. Olga became one of their intimates.

"It was a relief to be with them. Their love for each other was an inspiration, and I loved my four nieces. I think little Anastasia, then still a baby, was always my favorite. They were not as fortunate with their nurses as I was with my dear Nana. At the beginning, there was 'Orchie,' whom Queen Victoria had sent to Darmstadt to nurse Alicky and who followed her to Russia. She was most dictatorial and in the end left the palace in a huff. There followed spells of sheer chaos. My niece Olga's nurse was a rotter—fond of tippling. In the end, she was found in bed with a Cossack and dismissed on the spot. Then I remember a Miss Eager, Marie's nurse, who was mad on politics and would talk incessantly about the Dreyfus case. Once she even forgot that Marie was in her bath, and started discussing the case with a friend. Marie, naked and dripping, scrambled out of the tub and started running up and down the palace corridor. Fortunately I arrived just at that moment, picked her up, and carried her back to Miss Eager who was still talking about Dreyfus!"

Every day the Grand Duchess took her nieces for a walk in the park. "Sometimes Nicky joined us, but not Alicky, who was hardly ever strong enough for a walk. I must say I sometimes found it difficult to keep my nieces in order. They were so lively and full of energy, always running in different directions."

It was during those days of close association with her brother and his family that the Grand Duchess came to know the Emperor so well, to appreciate his character, and to guess at some of the burdens he carried. She admitted that he had faults, but she argued that his merits outweighed his defects, though it would have been impossible to make her see that the Emperor's good traits were those of a decent gentleman, not of a ruler. His habits were simple; his family life above reproach. He ate and drank sparingly, and his only indulgence was smoking, a result of nervous strain. He was careful with money where his personal needs were concerned. Yet his habitual calm and reserve led many people to believe that he was frigid and aloof and, unfortunately, such impressions, having once gained a foothold in the public mind, remained indelible. The Grand Duchess held that the Emperor's impassivity was a mask he wore to hide his feelings, and it is right that her opinion should be recorded. Her brother ruled over millions of subjects, and none of them knew that their Tsar felt everything so deeply that he was afraid he might break down in public. The Grand Duchess herself touched the root of the trouble when she said, "Perhaps only Alicky and I knew how deeply he suffered and worried. He was always handicapped by the dearth of experienced and disinterested ministers, and all the intellectuals could talk about was revolution and assassination. And didn't they pay for it?" And here she read me a passage out of an article "Revolution and Intelligentzia" by Rozanov, written soon after October, 1917:

> *Having thoroughly enjoyed the gorgeous spectacle of the revolution, our intelligentzia got ready to put on their fur-lined overcoats and to return to their comfortable houses, but the overcoats were stolen and the houses were burned down.*

Among the four nieces there was Anastasia, the youngest, born in June, 1901.

"A son had been expected," said the Grand Duchess, "but the arrival of a fourth baby girl did not make the family love her any less. Before she reached her first birthday she had won everybody's affection by her fun, her gaiety, and her laughter.

"My favorite god-daughter she was indeed! I liked her fearlessness. She never whimpered or cried, even when hurt. She was a fearful tomboy. Goodness only knows which of the young cousins had taught her how to climb trees, but climb them she did even when she was quite small. It was not generally known that she had a weak back and the doctors ordered massage. Anastasia or '*Shvipsik*,' as I used to call her, hated what she labeled 'fuss.' A hospital nurse, Tatiana Gromova, used to come to the palace twice a week, and my naughty little niece would hide in a cupboard or under her bed, just to put off the massage by another five minutes or so. I suppose the doctors were right about the defective muscle, but nobody, seeing Anastasia at play, would have believed it, so quick and energetic she was. And what a bundle of mischief!"

The Grand Duchess gave me one of her rare smiles, and, looking back at her own childhood, I felt that aunt and niece had indeed much in common, though the niece never had a brother to share in her pranks. The Grand Duchess's nephew, Alexis, suffered from a disease which forbade climbing trees and rooftops. Olga and Michael had been tomboys together. The Emperor's four daughters took the utmost care of their little brother.

Anastasia (standing) and Maria, two of the ill-fated daughters of Tsar Nicholas II.

Anastasia, even when quite small, was a desperate tease, and everybody in her world came in for their share of it, her aunt included. On one occasion the little god-daughter teased her so ruthlessly that the Grand Duchess slapped her. The child did not cry, but her face went very crimson and she ran out of the room. In a few moments she returned, her large, gray eyes smiling, and clasped her godmother's hand.

"She well knew that she deserved that slap. She never sulked," added the Grand Duchess.

Suddenly, as on many earlier occasions, I found it difficult to realize that I was in Canada, thousands of miles away from the palace and park of Tsarskoe Selo. I imagined the nurseries, the vast reaches of the park; I followed those four running after their youthful aunt (Olga was barely twenty-four at the time), all their dogs leaping and bounding 'round about them, the little girls' hair all disheveled, the Grand Duchess's hat certainly askew.

Back in Cooksville, in her shabby little living room, Olga got up from the sofa, opened a drawer of a chest, and turned to me, a large square box in her hands.

"We've been talking about Anastasia," she said softly. "She was such a generous child. I have something to show you—a few of the little gifts I had from her." And she settled down on the old sofa and opened the box, lined with faded and frayed velvet.

There were no great valuables inside, only a tiny silver pencil on a thin silver chain, a small scent bottle, a hatpin surmounted by a big amethyst, and other insignificant trinkets, all kept together, all cherished down the years, taken across one continent and an ocean, so many precious tokens of deep affection. She fingered them one by one, closed the lid, and replaced the box. Somehow the little room was filled with fragrance.

"But she was a *Shvipsik* indeed," the Grand Duchess went on. "As she grew older, she developed a gift for mimicry. Ladies who came to see my sister-in-law never knew that somewhere unseen in the background, their Empress's youngest daughter was watching every movement of theirs, every peculiarity, and later it would all come out when we were by ourselves. That art of Anastasia's was not really encouraged, but oh the fun we had when we heard duplicated the fat Countess Kutuzova, one of my mother's ladies-in-waiting, complaining of a heart attack brought on by the appearance of a mouse. Very naughty of Anastasia, but she was certainly brilliant at it!"

And here Olga's face clouded.

"It is really odd—the child was brimming with vitality, but I always had a presentiment that she would not live long. You see, at least twice the child brushed with death. . . ."

The first time it happened when the Empress took her for a drive in the park at Tsarskoe Selo. For some unaccountable reason, the horses bolted. By a mere chance, Count Ilya Voronzov was riding toward them. He leapt out of the saddle and stopped the Empress's horses as they approached the lake.

Had it not been for his courageous action, the carriage would have been in the water.

The second accident, witnessed by the Grand Duchess, happened at Livadia in the summer of 1906. The Emperor and his four daughters were swimming at no great distance from the beach when an enormous tidal wave rolled over them. When the Tsar, Olga, Tatiana, and Marie swam up to the surface, they saw that Anastasia had vanished.

"Little Alexis and I saw it happen from the beach. The child, of course, didn't realize the danger, and kept clapping his hands at the tidal wave. Then Nicky dived again, grabbed Anastasia by her long hair, and swam back with her to the beach. I had gone cold with terror...."

At the end of 1906, Prince Peter's appointment at Tsarskoe Selo came to an end and the Grand Duchess returned to the mansion in St. Petersburg, but there remained the frequent trips to Tsarskoe Selo and there was the telephone. Olga's interest in and concern for her nieces deepened with every year. On Saturdays she left the capital to spend the entire day with her brother's family. *Tyotya* Olga (Aunt Olga) was an intimate at the Alexander Palace. The children looked upon her as their playmate. The simplicity of her manner won them over. Owing to circumstances beyond their control, the imperial family led a very secluded existence. Few excitements colored the lives of the children, but the Grand Duchess was never bored with anything they had to tell her.

"None of them were brilliantly clever. I still think my little Anastasia was the most intelligent of them all. Once Nicky, Alicky, and I were sitting in Nicky's study. He and I started talking about some funny incidents in earlier years, and we all three roared with laughter. Then we saw a door being pushed ajar, Anastasia stood there, made a wry face, and remarked in a superior voice: 'Very funny indeed, but I don't see the joke at all,' and ran away before her mother had time to scold her...."

There were two things the Grand Duchess was mostly concerned about in connection with her nieces, and the first of them was horsemanship.

"And I am afraid I failed—they liked horses, they were not afraid of them, but they hated riding. They sat their mounts well enough, they were not cowards, but I saw soon enough that getting into the saddle was something done because I wanted them to do it. They had no pleasure in it. Only Anastasia had a taste for riding. I don't suppose she remembered that accident at Tsarskoe Selo. Had she lived, she would have become an excellent horsewoman...."

The second matter was much more complicated. It was the children's seclusion at Tsarskoe Selo. Their parents never lived in St. Petersburg after 1904. Children of court officials were invited to the Alexander Palace on certain occasions and, one by one, the Empress's daughters began leaving the schoolroom and appearing at their parents' luncheon table.

"I wanted them to have some lighter fun," confessed the Grand Duchess. "I discussed it with Nicky and Alicky, and they knew they could trust their children to me...."

Beginning with the end of 1906, every Sunday in the winter meant a day with *Tyotya* Olga, who spent the Saturday night at Tsarskoe Selo. In the morning, four excited girls and their equally excited aunt boarded the train for St. Petersburg. There they had first to go to the Anitchkov Palace for an early lunch with their grandmother, the Dowager Empress. For a couple of hours, the Grand Duchesses, even the otherwise irrepressible Anastasia, looked and behaved in the manner becoming to their rank. They were so prim that their aunt could hardly recognize them.

"Those luncheons were most irksomely formal. Fortunately it would all be over in a couple of hours, and weren't we relieved to leave the Anitchkov!"

The glory of the day broke upon the young people once they were under their aunt's roof. Tea was followed by games and dancing, the Grand Duchess having collected quite a number of equally youthful "eligibles" to share her nieces' fun.

"Intoxicating drinks, of course, were never served—even for the grown-ups in the party. In those days gaiety did not depend on vodka or cocktails. I remember the girls enjoyed every minute of it—especially my dear god-daughter. Why, I can still hear her laughter rippling all over the room. Dancing, music, games—she threw herself wholeheartedly into them all...."

At about ten in the evening one of the Empress's ladies-in-waiting came to fetch the girls and take them back to Tsarskoe Selo.

Those red-letter Sundays continued until 1914, the Grand Duchess having come to look on them as one of her most important tasks.

"At thirteen, poor Anastasia began getting rather lumpy—in spite of all the exercise she took. She was also much shorter than her sisters and quite unaccountably lost all interest in her studies. Her teachers called it laziness. But I am not so sure. I think books as books never said much to her. She so wanted to come to grips with life. I know there were many things that troubled her. She hated the Cossack escort always accompanying their outings and so on, but none of it marred her gaiety. That is how I remember her—brimming with life and mischief and laughing so often—sometimes for no reason at all, which is the best kind of laughter. The child was the gayest Romanov of her generation and she had a heart of gold."

She paused. The crowded living room of that small cottage in Canada became very still. She was deep in her memories, and it was quite a time before I ventured to ask:

"And what happened after?"

"1914," the Grand Duchess answered with effort. "At the very beginning of the war I hurried to the front to join my hospital unit. I returned to the North in 1916 and I never saw my dear little god-daughter again." She paused, and added with an emphasis it would have been impossible to ignore, "That is to say, I never saw the real Anastasia again."

Gathering Storms

As is known only too well, the reign of Nicholas II was beset by difficulties which increased more and more as the years went on. In the opinion of the Grand Duchess, it was not so much the politicians or the intellectuals who brought about the downfall of the crown as the Romanovs themselves.

"It is certainly the last generation that helped to bring about the disintegration of the Empire," she said to me. "It is a fact that all through those critical years, the Romanovs, who should have been the staunchest supporters of the throne, did not live up to their standards or to the traditions of the family." And she added trenchantly, "And that includes myself as well."

The family had grown immensely during the latter part of the nineteenth century. Some of the sons of Nicholas I had six children apiece. They had become a clan, and Alexander III, profoundly conscious of the dignity of the old name and the great responsibilities it entailed, ruled over them all much in the fashion of a patriarch. He could not but have been aware of the factions and rivalries among them. He by no means loved them all. There was little in common, for instance, between him and his younger brothers, particularly Grand Duke Vladimir. Nonetheless, Alexander III succeeded in preserving an outward semblance of dignity and unity. He ruled them and they were afraid of him. He had no use for either idleness or profligacy. It does not follow that all the members of the family led lives as irreproachable as his own. But there were no open scandals. Neither in the Empire nor abroad were there any spicy stories about palace alcoves, sinful extravagances, and suchlike. The Emperor might well be regarded as a

The Russian royal children, Grand Duchess Olga's four nieces and a nephew. From left to right: Grand Duchesses Marie, Tatiana, Anastasia, Olga, and Alexis circa 1910.

dynastic lynch pin. However imperfect the cohesion must have been in its inward aspects, its façade answered his purpose.

But he died far too early, and with his death the cohesion fell apart. Where he had commanded, his son would plead. Alexander III did not always trouble to put a velvet glove on his iron hand. Nicholas II would never have had any need for velvet gloves: his hand was far too gentle. From the very beginning it was obvious that he could not hold his own against all that crowd of uncles and cousins who, when the leash slipped, behaved just as they pleased. Factions were formed. In St. Petersburg Grand Duchess Vladimir, highly intelligent, extremely well educated, ambitious, and intriguing, played the lead during the Dowager Empress's retirement to Gatchina and later during her frequent absences in Denmark and England. Various grand-ducal courts, whatever the rivalries dividing them, were united in their determination to assert themselves and in their dislike of the Emperor's wife.

"Not that there were not some among us who had the intelligence and the capacity to serve the Tsar and their country," said the Grand Duchess, "but there were not enough. The majority of us pestered Nicky and sometimes even made scenes in his presence, in the efforts to further our own interests, our own petty schemes, or else to find fault with whatever he did or did not do. It reached such a pitch that in the end Nicky could not be blamed for avoiding certain members of the family. As I look back on it all"—the Grand Duchess spoke sadly—"I can see that too many of us Romanovs had, as it were, gone to live in a world of self-interest where little mattered except the unending gratification of personal desire and ambition. Nothing proved it better than the appalling marital mess in which the last generation of my family involved themselves. That chain of domestic scandals could not but shock the nation—but did any of them care for the impression they created? Never. A few of them actually did not mind being banished abroad."[1]

There were only two cases of divorce among the Romanovs until the reign of Nicholas II. Peter the Great divorced his first wife, Eudoxia Lopukhina, and had her enter a convent, having accused her of interfering with the progress of his reforms. In 1794, Grand Duke Constantine, Paul's second son and grandson of Catherine the Great, was married to Princess Julie of Saxe-Coburg-Gotha. There were no children; the marriage proved a complete failure, and in 1801 Grand Duchess Constantine left her husband and Russia forever. Not until 1820 did Alexander I consent to his brother's divorce to enable him to marry his mistress, a Polish lady, who was given the title of Princess Lowicz. But Constantine's divorce and particularly his remarriage with a commoner, which involved his relinquishing his right to succession, were regarded in the nature of a state secret.

By law no member of the imperial family was free to marry without the sovereign's consent, nor could they marry divorced persons or commoners. But within a few years of his succession, Nicholas II was faced with a spate of matrimonial rebellions and worse. The procession was opened by his cousin, Grand Duke Michael (one of the six sons of Grand Duke Michael, senior, and grandson of Nicholas I), who married a commoner in the very teeth of the Emperor's ban and settled in England, never to return to Russia again. His wife was given the title of Countess Torby.

Then the Emperor's uncle, Grand Duke Alexis, who constantly neglected his duties as the First Lord Admiral of the Russian Navy, fell in love with Princess Zina, wife of Prince Eugene of Leuchtenberg and reputed to be the most beautiful woman in Europe. In spite of continued protests from his nephew, Grand Duke Alexis and the Leuchtenbergs were always together, and much biting laughter was leveled in European resorts at the royal ménage à trois. There was no divorce in this case, but the scandal was all the greater.

Next, Anastasia, Princess of Montenegro and Duchess of Leuchtenberg, divorced her husband and married Grand Duke Nicholas, the Emperor's cousin. Once again there were remonstrations and protests from the Tsar, but by that time the Romanov clan had got the bit between their teeth. Another uncle of the Emperor, Grand Duke Paul, left a widower,[2] decided to marry a divorcée, the beautiful Madame Pistelkors. On that occasion, the Emperor wrote to his mother:

> . . . *I had rather a stern talk with Uncle Paul, which ended by my warning him of all the consequences his proposed marriage would have for him. It*

had no effect. . . . How painful and distressing it all is and how ashamed
one feels for the family before the world. What guarantee is there now that
Cyril won't start the same sort of thing tomorrow, and Boris and Sergie the
day after? And in the end, I fear, a whole colony of members of the Russian
imperial family will be established in Paris with their semi-legitimate and
illegitimate wives. God alone knows what times we are living in when
undisguised selfishness stifles all feelings of conscience, duty, or even
ordinary decency.

Nicholas II wrote that at the end of 1902. He was proved a sad prophet.
Less than three years later, his first cousin, Grand Duke Cyril, Vladimir's
eldest son, married Victoria-Melita, the divorced wife of the Grand Duke
of Hesse. The Emperor retaliated by banishing his cousin. There followed
a terrible scene with his uncle, Grand Duke Vladimir, who threatened to
resign from all his official appointments unless Nicholas repealed the exile
order, but the Emperor stood firm.

At last there fell a much more overwhelming blow. To the inevitable
scandal was added deep personal grief. Grand Duke Michael chose to flout
the law. What his sisters, especially Olga, must have gone through can hardly
be imagined. In August, 1906, Nicholas wrote in despair to his mother:

Three days ago Misha wrote asking my permission to marry. . . . I will never
give my consent. . . . It is infinitely easier to give [it] than to refuse it. . . .
God forbid that this sad affair should cause misunderstandings in our family.
As it is, life's trials are almost impossible to bear.

The lady who had so infatuated the young Grand Duke was one
Nathalie Cheremetevskaya, daughter of a Moscow solicitor. She first married a tradesman, one Mamontov, and divorced him soon enough. Next, she
married Captain Wulfert of the Cuirassier Guards, a regiment commanded
by Grand Duke Michael. Madame Wulfert became his mistress and immediately divorced her husband in the hope of becoming a Grand Duke's
wife. The scandal spread until people began talking of a secret marriage
between them. It was not known that the Grand Duke did not break the

law all at once, but when Madame Wulfert, having obtained her divorce, left for abroad, the Grand Duke followed her in spite of his brother's warning. The couple moved from place to place, unaware that Russian secret agents kept their eye on them. In the end they were secretly married by a Serbian priest in Vienna.

The Grand Duke had virtually cut himself off from the family some time previously, but the news of his marriage could not be kept secret for long, and he was officially forbidden to return to Russia. Not until the outbreak of the First World War did Nicholas allow him to return and his twice-divorced companion received the title of Countess Brassova. Neither the Emperor nor either of the two Empresses ever received Michael's wife.

"Do you realize what it all meant to Nicky?" asked the Grand Duchess. "Michael was his only remaining brother. He could have given Nicky so much help. I tell you again that all of us were to blame. Of the three sons of Uncle Vladimir, one was banished, another, Boris, was living quite openly with a mistress, and the third, Andrew, was never much use to my brother. Yet those three were the sons of the senior Grand Duke and, after Alexis and Michael, stood next in succession. Nicky had not a single member of the family to turn to, except perhaps Sandro, my brother-in-law, but even there things got difficult in time. What example could we give to the nation? Little wonder that poor Nicky, lacking support on all sides, became a fatalist. He would often put his arm 'round me and say, 'I was born on Job's Day—I am ready to accept my fate.'"

The clouds thickened more and more. The Grand Duchess recalled her memories of the disastrous Russo-Japanese War of 1904–5. Keeping aloof from all politics, she often found herself at sea when reading the papers, but she based her conclusions on everything her brother told her as well as on her own shrewd observations at Tsarskoe Selo. At that time Olga was at the palace every day. In the evenings, after the Tsar had given audiences to his ministers and to the senior commanders of his armed forces, he was able to talk to his wife and to his sister without restraint in the seclusion of his private study.

"I am convinced that my brother never wanted the war with Japan and that he was pushed into it by the so-called war party of politicians and generals who were so certain of a quick and sensational victory—to bring glory to themselves and to the crown, in that order. . . ."

Unfortunately, the campaign, badly planned and carried on in chaotic supply conditions, brought nothing but disasters—ending with the virtual annihilation of the Russian Navy at Tsusima in May, 1905. I had read somewhere that when the telegram announcing the disaster was brought to the Emperor at Tsarskoe Selo, he happened to be playing a game of tennis and that, having read the telegram, he crumpled it up, thrust it into a pocket of his tunic, and continued with his game. I asked the Grand Duchess if the story was true.

"It was a calumny—on a par with thousands of others!" she cried. "And I know because I was at the palace when the telegram arrived. Both Alicky and I were with him in the room. He turned ashen pale, he trembled, and clutched at a chair for support. Alicky broke down and sobbed. The whole palace was plunged into mourning that day."

The disastrous war, together with its humiliating conclusion, was but an isolated incident. Throughout the length and breadth of the Empire continuous battles were being fought. Terrorism became commonplace. One by one, senior servants of the crown were murdered in the streets of St. Petersburg and elsewhere. The countryside was ablaze with peasants, looting, killing, burning down manors. It was no longer considered safe for the Emperor and his family to travel about in the interior.

On Epiphany Day, 1905, the traditional ceremony of the Blessing of the Waters was held on the Neva just in front of the palace. As usual, a dais had been built on the ice for the Emperor, his retinue, and the clergy. Members of the imperial family, diplomats, and the court watched the ceremony from the windows of the palace.

A hole having been cut in the ice, it was part of the ritual for the Metropolitan of St. Petersburg to dip his gold cross into the water, and to pronounce the solemn blessing. This done, the guns from the Fortress of Peter and Paul across the river opened with the customary salute fired with blank charges. But in 1905, in spite of all precautions, a group of terrorists had succeeded in winning their way into the fortress and placing a live charge into the guns. A policeman behind the Emperor was badly injured. Another charge hit the Admiralty. A third smashed a window in the palace—a bare few yards away from the Dowager Empress and the Grand Duchess—and glass splinters fell all over their shoes and skirts. Through the broken window they could hear shouts from below. All was utter confusion—with police and military running in all directions. For some minutes neither mother nor daughter could pick out the small, slight figure of the Emperor. Then they saw him standing where he had stood at the beginning of the ceremony, very still and erect.

They had to wait for him to return to the palace. Once inside, he told his sister that he had heard the shell whizz over his head. "I knew that somebody was trying to kill me. I just crossed myself. What else could I do?"

"It was typical of Nicky," added the Grand Duchess. "He did not know what fear meant. On the other hand, it seemed as if he was resigned to losing his life."

Within a bare three weeks, yet another ugly tempest broke over St. Petersburg. One Sunday, a crowd of workmen, led by a priest, George Gapon, crossed the Trinity Bridge and marched along the quays toward the Winter Palace to see the Emperor. They were told he was at Tsarskoe Selo. They did not believe it. They pressed on. In the end, the brutality of the police and the brutality of the crowd met face to face. Then the Cossacks opened fire. Ninety-two workmen were killed and nearly three hundred injured.

That day went down in Russian history as "Bloody Sunday." It seems that the censors let through all the reports telegraphed abroad by foreign correspondents in St. Petersburg. The facts by themselves would have shaken Europe, but the foreign correspondents, with a few exceptions, multiplied the casualty figures, and dyed the incident a far deeper scarlet than it had really been. No mention was made of the stones hurled at the police, or of the number of vehicles wrecked by the crowd on their way to the palace, nor yet of the fact that the majority of the peaceful inhabitants of the capital spent the day behind shuttered windows and barred doors. The published reports insisted that the march was peaceful, that the workmen wanted nothing except to present their grievances to the Emperor, and that, in fact, there was not a breath of anything revolutionary about it at all.

The Grand Duchess was not in St. Petersburg at the time.

"Nicky had the police report a few days before. That Saturday he telephoned my mother at the Anitchkov and said that she and I were to leave for Gatchina at once. He and Alicky went to Tsarskoe Selo. Insofar as I remember, my Uncles Vladimir and Nicholas were the only members of the family left in St. Petersburg but there may have been others. I felt at the time that all those arrangements were hideously wrong. Nicky's ministers and the chief of police had it all their way. My mother and I wanted him to stay in St. Petersburg and to face that crowd. I am positive that, for all the ugly mood of some of the workmen, Nicky's appearance would have calmed them. They would have presented their petition and gone back to their homes. But that wretched Epiphany incident had left all the senior officials in a state of panic. They kept telling Nicky that he had no right to run such a risk, that he owed it to the country to leave the capital, that even with the utmost precautions taken there might always be some loophole left. My mother and I did all we could to persuade him that his ministers' advice was wrong, but Nicky preferred to follow it, and he was the first to repent when he heard of the tragic outcome...."

In less than a month the terrorists struck again. Olga's uncle, Grand Duke Serge, the governor of Moscow, was blown to pieces by a bomb thrown at his sledge while he was crossing the Red Square. He was buried in Moscow, but few members of the imperial family were present at the funeral: the tension in the ancient capital was such that further attempts could not be ruled out.[3]

"There was such gloom at Tsarskoe Selo," the Grand Duchess recalled. "I did not understand anything about politics. I just felt that everything was going wrong with the country and all of us. The October Constitution did not seem to satisfy anyone. I went with my mother to the solemn *Te Deum* which marked the opening of the first *Duma*. I remember the large group of deputies from among peasants and factory people. The peasants looked sullen. But the workmen were worse: they looked as though they hated us. I remember the distress in Alicky's eyes...."

For two years the Grand Duchess could not get down to Olgino. Peasant risings blazed from the White Sea to the Crimea, from the Baltic to the Urals and even beyond. Peasants burned, killed, raped. Local authorities were unable to quell the risings and the military were sent out, but disaffection began seeping into the armed forces. In the late spring of 1906 there was a bloody mutiny on board some ships of the Black Sea Fleet. It was rapidly followed by a mutiny among the ratings of the Baltic Fleet and for a time Kronstadt was a beleaguered fortress.

"I stayed with my brother and Alicky at Alexandria. Its windows rattled from the roar of the cannonade from Kronstadt. Indeed, those were black years," said the Grand Duchess.

A son had been born to the Emperor and Empress two years before. "It happened during the war with Japan. The nation was really in the depths of depression because of all the disasters in Manchuria. All the same I remember how happy the people looked when the news was announced. You know that Alicky had never quite given up hope that she would have a son born to her, and I am sure it was Seraphim who brought it about."

I must have looked bewildered because the Grand Duchess began to explain. In the summer of 1903 the Emperor invited her to join him and the Empress on a pilgrimage they were about to make to Sarov Abbey in the province of Tambov. There was a definite reason for the pilgrimage: the Holy Synod, after years of deliberation, had decided to canonize one Seraphim, a hermit-monk of the eighteenth century, reputed to have been a healer during his lifetime and after his death. Pilgrimages to Sarov had gone on all through the nineteenth century.

The abbey, its white stone buildings enclosing an enormous courtyard, stood on the high promontory on the bank of the Sarovka. The gilt cupolas and spire of the abbey could be seen for miles around. Seraphim was a peasant youth who decided early to lead a hermit's life and built a wooden hut in a forest at some distance from the Sarovka. There he spent years in prayer. He lived on honey, roots, and wild berries. In spite of his seclusion, however, many people heard of him and began flocking to the forest. His manner was gentle and pleasant. He welcomed and comforted all who came to him and often enough knew of a visitor's particular trouble before it was put into words. There were many wealthy merchants among the visitors. According to an ancient custom they would leave their offerings at the door of his hut. But Seraphim used those gifts to help the poorer among the pilgrims. He had no need of gold and silver. Some highwaymen, thinking that he kept great wealth in his hut, waylaid him in the forest, set upon him, and left him for dead. But Seraphim was alive and when the brigands, having ransacked the hut and found no riches hidden there, returned to hang him on the nearest tree, they found Seraphim guarded by an enormous bear. His wounds healed, he returned to the hut, the bear accompanying him.

"After his death," continued the Grand Duchess, "his miracles continued. My great-grandfather, Nicholas I, had a favorite daughter, Marie, and once she became dangerously ill. Someone living in the province of Tambov sent a little woollen scarf worn by Seraphim to St. Petersburg. It was put 'round the child, and next morning when she woke, the fever was gone. The nurses began taking the scarf away, but she wanted to keep it, saying that she had seen a kindly old man come in during the night. 'The scarf belonged to him,' said the child, 'and he has given it to me. I want to keep it.'"

Time and again the Grand Duchess had been asked if she believed in miracles. And I put the same question to her.

"Believe in them? How could I help believing in them? I saw them happen at Sarov."

The journey to Sarov was exhausting—chiefly because of the heat. On leaving the train they had a whole day's journey in front of them, the carriage rolling through the dusty, tortuous lanes leading to the banks of the Sarovka.

"I suppose we were all spent at the end of that day, but nobody dreamt of complaining. I don't think any of us were conscious of the fatigue. We were so full of fervor and expectation. We traveled in troikas, Nicky and Alicky at the head, my mother and I just behind, with Uncle Serge and Aunt Ella following. There were some other cousins and their wives in the rear. And all along the way we passed thousands of pilgrims making for the abbey. . . ."

That day's journey was broken by several halts. At every village the priest awaited them to give his blessing to the Emperor, who immediately ordered the coachman to stop and left the carriage. "And there he was, in a crowd of pilgrims and others milling 'round about him, all struggling to kiss his hands, his sleeve, his shoulders. It was too moving for words. We were traveling with the customary Cossack escort, but there was not a soul for them to watch. Nicky was just *batushka* Tsar—little father—to all those people. . . ."

At Sarov they were taken to the abbot's lodgings, and the next morning the Emperor, his uncle, and his cousins were all bearers when St. Seraphim's remains were taken from the humble grave in the abbey cemetery and carried inside the gold-domed cathedral specially built for the saint's shrine.

"It was from the banks of the little river that I saw the first miracle. The waters of the Sarovka were considered healing because Seraphim had often bathed there. I saw a peasant mother carry her wholly paralyzed little daughter and dip her into the river. A little later the child was walking up the meadow, and there were doctors at Sarov to testify to the reality of the paralysis and the cure. . . ."

The Empress, in her turn, bathed in the Sarovka and prayed by the shrine. Within a year she had her son, and then, while he was still a baby, the parents learned that he had hemophilia. The Grand Duchess was positive that all her four nieces would have carried the dreaded disease to their male offspring if they had ever married, and insisted that they too bled freely. She recalled the panic which broke out at Tsarskoe Selo on the day that Grand Duchess Marie had her tonsils removed. It was expected to be a routine operation by Dr. Selerioff. The operation had barely begun when the young Grand Duchess began to hemorrhage. Taken by complete surprise, the doctor ran from the operating table in utter fright. And it was then, in a moment of extreme crisis, that the strength of Empress Alexandra was revealed. "Alicky calmly grabbed the trembling doctor by the arm and said quietly but sternly: 'Will you please finish the operation, doctor?' He managed to do so successfully despite the persistent bleeding.

"You might well say that the birth of a son, which should have been the

Tsar Nicholas II, accompanied by his son Alexis, inspecting the Cossack Guard at Livadia, 1910.

happiest event in the lives of Nicky and Alicky, became their heaviest cross," the Grand Duchess concluded sadly.

Meanwhile the shadows continued to thicken. A cloak of frustration seemed to fall on the country. According to the Grand Duchess, terrorism reached such a pitch by the middle of 1906 that the monarchy would have fallen then and there if it had not been for the appointment of Peter Stolypin as Prime Minister in July.

"He held the office for five years, and he would have stayed on, I am sure. His long tenure of office should be a challenge to all those who said that my brother had no use for anyone except reactionaries. Stolypin was a liberal, and it is not known to this day that Nicky chose him for the office. Goremykin's dismissal that summer of 1906 surprised everybody, including Stolypin himself who was then Minister of the Interior. My brother did not lack insight altogether—he knew that Stolypin was the man for the hour and he was proved right...."

Stolypin, a statesman of great vision and courage, came from the ranks of landed nobility. His mother was born Princess Gorchakov and his father had won distinction in the Russo-Turkish War of 1877. Stolypin's outlook was that of a convinced liberal, but he knew his country too well not to realize that a naked and untidy realization of liberal ideas would lead to chaotic results. He longed to see reforms come gradually so as to allow the national mind to get accustomed to their color. A great landowner himself, knowing all the peasant problems at first hand, Stolypin's ultimate aim was an immense agrarian reform which would turn the peasants into small landowners and then create a healthy social stratum, a mainstay of the crown and a strong bulwark against all revolutionary onslaught in the future.

"He could be ruthless," admitted the Grand Duchess. "He taxed the upper classes without mercy; he insisted on the breaking-up of a large estate on the death of the head of a family. Important landowners up and down the Empire hated him, and even some of the family including my cousin Nicholas[4] were very bitter against him, but most of us were wholly on Stolypin's side. We felt he was both strong and genuine. He had not a shred of self-interest. Russia alone mattered. Some books I have read said that my brother was jealous of his Prime Minister and did all he could to undermine Stolypin's work. That is a shoddy lie—on a par with so much else. I remember perfectly well Nicky saying to me, 'Sometimes Stolypin is so high-handed that I get annoyed, but it does not last, and he is the best Prime Minister I have had.'"

Yet good statesmanship in Russia seemed to be doomed. Stolypin's reforms were still in their infancy when an assassin's bullet put an end to all agrarian progress. A member of a revolutionary group shot at Stolypin at a Kiev theater during a gala performance of Rimsky-Korsakov's opera *Tsar Saltan*. The Emperor and two of his daughters were in the opposite box.

They saw the Prime Minister slump down in his seat, then turn his head towards the imperial box and make the sign of the cross. The murderer was caught. The Prime Minister was rushed to the hospital where he died a few days later.

"I shall never forget Nicky's horror and sorrow. When Stolypin died, Nicky was at Chernigov. He hurried back to Kiev, to the hospital, and there knelt by Stolypin's body. People who said Nicky was relieved to hear of Stolypin's death are too wicked for words. My brother was very reserved, but he never shammed. His grief for Stolypin was utterly genuine, I know...."

While Stolypin was at the helm, however, conditions in Russia grew calmer. The imperial family felt that, with the tension relaxed, they could, as it were, take a holiday. In the spring of 1907, Grand Duchess Olga went to Biarritz to stay all by herself at the Hotel du Palais. Later, much to her pleasure, her sister Xenia, with her husband and their six children, came to join her.

"But, oh," Olga laughed, "such a crowd arrived with them—members of their household, tutors and governesses, and servants. The Hotel du Palais had not enough room for them all. They had to rent an enormous villa in the neighborhood. Thank goodness," added the Grand Duchess, "that I used to travel very simply in those days."

I took the remark at its face value. It was not till after the Grand Duchess's death that I learned the exact meaning of the adverb "simply" as applied to her travels. Nancy, Viscountess Astor, told me that she was at Biarritz at the time and heard a lot about the "simple" habits of Grand Duchess Olga. She discovered that Olga's retinue consisted of thirty people. Yet, on the whole, this was rather a conservative number for a Romanov traveling abroad. The Dowager Empress's retinue was two hundred. In those days, the visits made by the Romanovs to the Riviera practically kept the whole hotel business going. They required much for their own needs, they entertained lavishly, and they settled their bills with pleasing promptitude. All their traveling expenses were met by funds deposited in England, France, and elsewhere.

From Biarritz the Grand Duchess went back to Russia. It was nearly five

Tsar Nicholas II inspecting the Preobragensky Regiment, outside Peterhof Palace, with his son Alexis. The officer on the right is Grand Duke Michael.

years since she told her husband of her wish to part from him, but apparently, Prince Peter of Oldenburg, having stipulated a seven-year interval, considered that the extraordinary modus vivendi would continue indefinitely. He still gambled, still went to dine at his parents' on the Palace Quay, and still behaved like a perfect husband in public. But society could not be deceived; nobody knew about the Grand Duchess's jealously hidden romance, but Prince Peter's reputation was an open secret. As usual, those who knew nothing pretended to be very familiar with the conditions in the Oldenburg household.

Meanwhile Olga waited. It would have been a lonely spell indeed if she had not had her loyal old Nana. She seems to have had hardly any intimates among her own family. Her favorite brother was banished. Her sister grew increasingly busy with a family of seven. There remained Tsarskoe Selo, where her brother and his wife now lived permanently. In St. Petersburg, the Winter Palace would be opened only for official functions.

During Stolypin's term of office the Empire was certainly quieter, but hostility towards the imperial couple did not lessen. That ill-feeling, as the Grand Duchess never tired of telling me, did not come from the masses but from society, grieved at the lack of court functions and, alas, from other members of the Romanov clan.

It is true that life at Tsarskoe was run on virtually cloistral lines. Ministers and other senior officials arrived with their reports and ambassadors were received in audience, and they would be invited to luncheon, but there was practically no other entertainment, and the Emperor worked harder than ever.

"Nicky and Alicky had few private moments during the day," said the Grand Duchess. "There were always people for lunch—often served in a big hall away from their apartments. But in their own wing they had no dining room. Breakfast, tea, and dinner were served anywhere on a small portable table. Children would sometimes appear at tea—Nicky often worked after dinner. His study was across a short passage which led from their bedroom. Not only did they share a room, but they slept in one bed. Once Nicky jokingly complained that Alicky kept him awake by crunching her favorite English biscuits in bed...."

Nicholas, who was extremely athletic, had a small exercise room attached to his study and gymnastics were his sole relaxation. "I remember finding him swirling around the exercise bar one day when I expected him to be deeply engrossed in his study. 'I need the blood in my head to be able to think.'" said Nicholas with a smile when he saw the puzzled expression on his sister's face.

In the summer of 1908 they all went by sea to Reval to meet King Edward VII and Queen Alexandra.

"That was a great historic event. It sealed the new Anglo-Russian entente which had been so desired by Nicky. Relations with England had almost reached breaking point during the war with Japan. The British government and people did not conceal where their sympathies lay, so Uncle Bertie's arrival brought all the more pleasure to us all. We felt that at last the affection between the two reigning houses would work for a better understanding between the two countries...."

King Edward arrived on board the *Victoria and Albert*, the Emperor on the *Standard*, and his mother on the *Polar Star*. The visit lasted for three days.

"I had lots of leisure, my mother being fully occupied with Aunt Alix. There were endless comings and goings. I particularly enjoyed meeting Admiral Fisher again. I had made friends with him some time before at Carlsbad. But I am afraid I disgraced myself shockingly. Admiral Fisher could tell the funniest stories and my laughter was known to carry far. At a dinner on board the *Victoria and Albert* I laughed so loudly that Uncle Bertie raised his head and asked Admiral Fisher to remember that we were not in the gunroom. I felt dreadful but there was nothing to be said at the moment. I had to wait until dinner was over and I could tell Uncle Bertie that it had all been my fault."

The illuminations and fireworks over the Bay of Reval brightened the northern skies and certainly lightened a few moments for the Grand Duchess. But soon afterwards the Emperor and his wife made state visits to Sweden, France, and England, and Grand Duchess Olga, who stayed in Russia, accompanied her mother on the usual round of deadening social functions. But at least none of them took place in the morning, and she still had a few precious hours for her walk, her painting, and, all surreptitiously, her work at a hospital. Her Aunt Ella's dedication to a life of relieving people's suffering had greatly moved her.

In 1912 the Dowager Empress paid her last visit to England before the First World War, and Olga had to accompany her. The Grand Duchess never liked leaving Russia. This time she felt more spirited than ever. The seven years had come and gone, but Prince Peter never made the least allusion to the promise he had given in 1903. He felt apparently satisfied with conditions as they were, and Olga, deeply conscious of what all the earlier scandals had meant to her brother, hesitated to add her own share to that record.

The long stay at Sandringham did nothing to hearten her. "It was all so sad. Aunt Alix had aged so much and was more deaf than ever. She and my mother did nothing but sit in the house and talk about the past. Victoria and I went driving and riding. When we four sat down to a meal, I had a feeling that we were all shelved, as it were. I was just thirty—but I felt desperately old. And things were not much better when we left Norfolk to stay with Georgie and May at Buckingham Palace. All the time I had an odd foreboding that something would happen. One evening I went to the theater with my dear friend Lady Astor. There I was taken ill."

The Grand Duchess returned to Russia, her health still giving cause for anxiety. She had had a breakdown in England and for about another year she was on the verge of another collapse. But the Dowager Empress evidently did not understand illness except in terms of high temperature or spots. She meant to meet her sister again—this time in Denmark—in the autumn of 1912, and she considered that her younger daughter was well enough to accompany her. So the *Polar Star* sailed once again—making for Danish waters.

"It lasted a fortnight, I think," Olga told me, "but I was too thankful when it was over. We stayed on board—so I could not escape anywhere. It meant endless hours on deck listening to Aunt Alix recalling all the happy times of their youth. . . ."

How thankful she was to get back to Russia, to Tsarskoe Selo, to listen to her nieces' artless chronicles, to try and relieve the Empress's deepening anxiety about little Alexis. "By that time," said the Grand Duchess, "Alicky was indeed a sick woman. Her breath often came in quick, obviously painful gasps. I often saw her lips turn blue. Constant worry over Alexis had completely undermined her health."

There was not much privacy for any of the Romanovs during the tercentenary celebrations of the dynasty in 1913. Among other things, a great ball was given by the St. Petersburg nobility in honor of the sovereigns.

"Such splendor, such dazzling pageantry," the Grand Duchess said sadly, "but to me it all seemed unreal and forced. Alicky was exhausted and nearly fainted at the ball. As I watched all those illuminations in honor of the dynasty and went from one ball to another, I had an odd feeling that though we were carrying on as we had done for centuries, some new and terrifying conditions of life were being formed by forces utterly beyond our control."

The Empress was too ill to travel, and it fell to the Grand Duchess to accompany her brother into the heart of the country, particularly to Kostroma, the cradle of the Romanov family.

"That was certainly better than St. Petersburg ballrooms," she said with deep feeling. "Wherever we went, we met with manifestations of loyalty bordering on wildness. When our steamer went down the Volga, we saw crowds of peasants wading waist-high in the water to catch a glimpse of Nicky. In some of the towns I would see artisans and workmen falling down to kiss his shadow as we passed. Cheers were deafening. Nobody, seeing those enthusiastic crowds, could have imagined that in less than four years Nicky's very name would be spattered with mud and hatred."

The Grand Duchess certainly needed heartening at that time. In the late spring of 1913 her faithful old Nana died in her sleep at the house in Sergievskaya Street. Olga had her buried in the park at Gatchina, at the spot where Mrs. Franklin often used to watch her little charge play games with her favorite brother. "Nana's death was a great blow. And she was not so terribly old either. Little did I guess in 1913 how relieved I was to be in the near future that she had been spared the horrors of 1917 and all that followed...."

Tsar Nicholas II is taken by surprise in this picture, as he inspects the Russian army in 1914. He was certain war would never occur. The picture was taken by Grand Duchess Olga.

And so to 1914. People began talking about the tension in Europe and the Kaiser's intentions. "I spoke to Nicky and he replied that Willy was a bore and an exhibitionist, but he would never start a war. And somehow I thought of my father and Uncle Bertie. Both hated war, and so did Nicky. Both were strong, and I wondered if Nicky was. Both were feared by Willy—but did Willy fear Nicky or Georgie?[5] I did not think so."

Tension reached its peak after Sarajevo, and in July, 1914, President Poincaré of France came to St. Petersburg on a state visit.

"Alicky being ill, I had to accompany Nicky everywhere—banquets and dances, a reception at the French Embassy, a command performance at the Mariinsky Theatre, and a luncheon on board La France. Poincaré did not

impress me in the least. He was a short, podgy man—with an artificial smile. I found him evasive in conversation. He showered compliments and presents on us all and he kept making grandiose speeches about mutual friendship and respect. But he meant none of the flowery things he said. Barely three years later he behaved despicably toward my family."

She stopped for a moment.

"It is all such ancient history now, I suppose, but all the evils of the century spring from 1914. And do you know who is to be blamed for that outbreak? Great Britain. If only Georgie's government had made it clear from the outset that England would join Russia and France if Germany made trouble, Willy would never have dared to make a single move. But I can tell you that Count Pourtalès, Willy's ambassador, told us in my own drawing room that he was convinced Britain would never enter the war."

On August first, 1914, the day war was declared, the Grand Duchess and the Tsar attended a parade of troops at Krasnoe Selo. Upset by persistent rumors of war, the Grand Duchess asked her brother if he thought she should stay at Krasnoe so that she could see her regiment off in case war should be declared.

"Don't worry, dear," replied the Tsar. "There won't be a war. You can go home and sleep in peace."

"Reassured, I left Krasnoe Selo for St. Petersburg that same evening. I was just having a bath when a special messenger from Nicky arrived to tell me that war had suddenly been declared and that I should return immediately to Krasnoe Selo."

Olga rushed back to Krasnoe Selo to see the officers and men of her regiment, the Akhtyrsky Hussars, leave for the front. Other regiments were leaving too. She caught a glimpse of Nikolai Koulikovsky. They touched hands for a second, they exchanged a whisper or two, and he was gone. "I watched him. I gave him up to God. And with him gone there was nothing to keep me in St. Petersburg. The city had become a prison. So I went to my husband to tell him that I was going as a nurse to the front and that I would never return to him. He made no reply. I don't think he believed me."

The very next day she was at the Warsaw station, boarding a train bound for the West.

The Last Tsar, Nicolas II, and his ill-fated family. At the Tsar's right is Empress Alexandra Feodorovna and their children. From left to right: Grand Duchesses Marie, Tatiana, Olga, and Anastasia (Grand Duchess Olga's favorite niece). Five-year-old Alexis, who suffered from hemophilia, is at his father's feet. The Tsar's family was executed the night of July 16, 1918, in Ekaterinburg, Russia.

The Rasputin Legend

Possibly no other country in the world could have produced such an embodiment of ambiguities and contradictions as Rasputin.[1] No labels really fit him, and to call him a schizophrenic does not explain him. For all that violent extremes met in his nature, he was neither saint nor devil. When blind adulation on one side and frenzied strictures on the other have had their say, the man emerges like a chameleon, whose words and actions changed their color according to the varied needs of the people he met, the environment, and, finally, his own moods. Religious fervor and fatalism, generosity and selfishness, sagacity and an almost wooden obtuseness, kindness and cruelty, humility and arrogance—the list of opposing qualities could well be carried further. Now a mere plaything of chance, now an architect of events, this man without a surname came out of obscurity at the very moment when the country was sick almost to death, when the Manchurian disasters, coupled with savage lawlessness within her own borders, reduced the nation's hopes to a faint flicker, and when the Emperor and Empress, secluded at Tsarskoe Selo, were in the grip of sharp anxiety about their little son.

As has already been said, Grand Duchess Olga was a great intimate at the Alexander Palace. "I think," she admitted, "they did appreciate my not prying into their purely personal affairs. I made it a principle never to ask questions, or to give uncalled-for advice, still less to interfere in their private life. . . ."

I had certainly hoped that the Grand Duchess would talk about Rasputin. Rather to my surprise, she was at first very reluctant to discuss him.

"Rasputin has become the central figure of a story the world has long

Rasputin, the "Siberiak" (literally, "the man from Siberia").

since accepted as true. Anything I might have to say about him would either fall on deaf ears, or else be dismissed as a fable. Anything written about the man is so colored and twisted that it is virtually impossible for the public to sift fact from fiction."

But I continued my arguments and in the end succeeded in convincing the Grand Duchess that she owed it to her family not to exclude Rasputin from her memoirs. I pointed out to her that, of all the Romanov survivors, she had the strongest case, and that, on her own showing, she was the only member of the imperial family permitted to share the privacy of her brother and his wife. The Grand Duchess listened very patiently. I could see that the whole subject was deeply distasteful to her. On the other hand, I had no alternative: her memoirs had to include Rasputin.

At last she said: "I suppose you are right. Yes, not only did I know Nicky and Alicky far too well to believe any of the ugly rumors, but I also knew the *Siberiak* [literally 'man from Siberia'] and knew too the limits of his influence at the palace. Volume upon volume had been written about it all—but who among all those authors had access to first-hand information? I can only think of two." She did not mention either name, but said that all the others relied on popular hearsay, gossip from various grand-ducal courts, and endless chatter in the drawing rooms of St. Petersburg and Moscow. "Take the memoirs of Paléologue, the French ambassador, as an example. His Embassy was just a great social center in St. Petersburg. He boasted of his friendship with Aunt Michen.[2] His supposed exclusive information concerning my brother, his wife, and Rasputin was no more than a digest of all the tittle-tattle heard in the drawing rooms of St. Petersburg, particularly Aunt Michen's salon. He did meet the man once or twice, but he had never been to Tsarskoe Selo informally, and audiences are not the occasion for private confidences. But Paléologue chose to set himself up as an authority and the reading world accepted his claim."

I hesitated before putting my next question to the Grand Duchess. "Didn't you think the man was an evil genius?"

My use of the last word was rather unfortunate. Grand Duchess Olga looked almost angry. "Yes, of the stature of a Mephistopheles, I suppose." She spoke mockingly. "That is the picture in the public mind today, created by unbridled imagination, and they started creating the legend in Rasputin's lifetime. I know that what I am going to say will probably disappoint a great many people always avid for spicy revelations, but I think it is high time the man was reduced to his proper size and standing. He was neither saint nor devil. To Nicky and Alicky he remained what he was—a peasant with a profound faith in God and a gift of healing. There was no mystery whatever about his meetings with the Empress. All those elements were born in the imagination of people who had never met Rasputin at the palace. Someone turned him into a member of the staff. Many others made him monk or priest. He had no position either at court or in the church. And apart from his undoubted gift of healing, Rasputin was neither as impressive nor as exciting as people think. He was just a *strannik*."

A *strannik* is literally a lay pilgrim. There were great numbers of them in old Russia. They wandered from monastery to monastery, from village to village, giving counsel and comfort, sometimes curing the sick, and begging their bread on the way. The Orthodox hierarchy did not always look upon *stranniky* with a benevolent eye, often suspecting them of heresy. They were liable to be imprisoned if they were caught preaching to the common folk. Yet Rasputin could not rightly be described as a *strannik*. None among them possessed families or homes. Rasputin had a wife and three children and a hut of his own at Pokrovskoye, and the Grand Duchess told me that in his wandering from place to place he never forgot his family. He was deeply attached to them all.

Nothing is known of Rasputin's grandfather. His father, Efim, settled down in a Siberian village on the way to Tobolsk. There, at Pokrovskoye, the family were called simply *novye*, "newcomers." Rasputin, the name under which Efim's son went down in history, was a derisive nickname given to Gregory after one or two unsavory episodes in connection with some young girls in the neighborhood of Pokrovskoye. He chose to retain it after his conversion as a token of humility. (The word has two meanings: a vagabond and a debauchee.)

He was first heard of in St. Petersburg in 1904. The saintly John of Kronstadt met him and was deeply moved by his repentance. Rasputin made no attempt to screen his unsavory past. John, having seen him at prayer, was convinced of his sincerity. Two sisters, Anastasia, then Duchess of Leuchtenberg (later Grand Duchess Nicholas), and Militza, Grand Duchess Peter, who were both deeply attached to John of Kronstadt, received the *Siberiak* in their palace. Whoever met him was convinced that he was "a man of God." But Rasputin, in spite of all that happened in St. Petersburg, did not linger there: he soon left it on one of his pilgrimages.

It was in July, 1906, that the Emperor recorded their first meeting at a monastery in the neighborhood of Peterhof. In the original, the sentence in Nicholas's diary ends with an exclamation mark. It was October, 1906, that Rasputin was summoned to the palace for the first time. "He came at 6.30 P.M., he saw the children and talked to us till 7.15 P.M." So Nicholas wrote in his diary.

By that time, as the Grand Duchess was to learn later, there were vague rumors floating about concerning Rasputin.

"It is important to remember that Nicky and Alicky were fully aware of Rasputin's past. It is completely false to suggest that they regarded him as a saint incapable of evil. I say it again—and I have the right to say so—neither of them had been duped by Rasputin, or had the least illusion about him. The unfortunate thing was that the public did not know the truth, and neither Nicky nor Alicky, because of their position, could fight the lies which were being spread. Now let us get it right. First, there were thousands upon thousands of common folk who firmly believed in the man's gift of prayer and healing. Then came the bishops and archbishops. Society, always hungry for the unusual, followed the lead. Finally, Nicky's own cousin accepted the *Siberiak* and introduced him to my brother and his wife. And when did it happen? In 1906 when the cruel truth about my little nephew's health gave them endless anxiety. I read somewhere that Rasputin was, as it were, smuggled into the palace by Anna Vyrubova[3] who hoped to increase her own influence by doing so. That is pure rubbish. Anna Vyrubova never had any influence. Many a time did Alicky say to me how sorry she was for 'that poor Annie.' She was utterly irresponsible, childish to silliness, and much addicted to hysterical outbursts. She did cling to Rasputin as to an anchor, but she never brought him to Alicky's notice.

"It is perfectly true that after he had been to the palace a few times, wildly exaggerated reports about his influence at court made many people try to turn him into a tool to further their own ambitions. Rasputin was besieged with petitions, and presents were showered on him, but he never kept anything for his own use. I know he helped the poor of St. Petersburg and elsewhere. And not once did I hear him beg for any favors from Nicky and Alicky. I often heard him make requests for others. I am sure that his attachment to my brother and his wife was utterly devoid of self-interest. He might so easily have amassed a fortune, but he died owning a Bible, some clothes, and a few things given him by the Empress for his personal use. Even the furniture in his flat in Gorokhovaya Street in St. Petersburg did not belong to him. It is true that he received large sums of money, but all of it was given away. Rasputin kept just enough to provide food and clothing for his family in Siberia. And if, at the very end, he became conscious of the political power he could exert, it was only because some ruthless and unscrupulous people forced him into it."

Here the Grand Duchess stopped and looked at me rather quizzically.

"I do know that all I have said so far may well seem to turn me into a devotee of Rasputin's. But let me say it straight out: I never liked the man. All the same, the interests of history cannot be served by a false perspective."

She vividly remembered the day in the autumn of 1907 when she first met Rasputin at the Alexander Palace at Tsarskoe Selo. She was then living in St. Petersburg, but she went to Tsarskoe two or three times a week, sometimes oftener. On that particular day she was asked to dinner. There was no other guest present. When the meal was finished, her brother said: "Will you come and meet a Russian peasant?"

She followed the Emperor and his wife up the flight of stairs into the children's nurseries. The four girls and their little brother, all in white pajamas, were being put to bed by their nurses, and in the middle of the room stood Rasputin.

"When I saw him I felt that gentleness and warmth radiated from him. All the children seemed to like him. They were completely at their ease with him. I still remember their laughter as little Alexis, deciding he was a rabbit, jumped up and down the room. And then, quite suddenly, Rasputin caught the child's hand and led him to his bedroom, and we three followed.

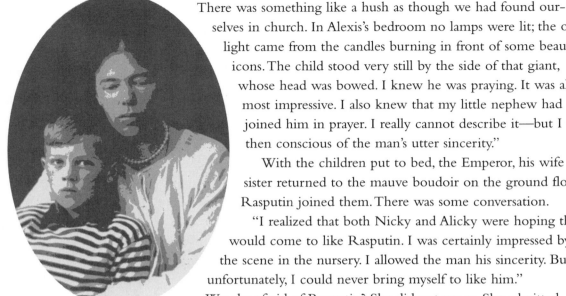

Grand Duchess Olga with her son Tikhon.

There was something like a hush as though we had found ourselves in church. In Alexis's bedroom no lamps were lit; the only light came from the candles burning in front of some beautiful icons. The child stood very still by the side of that giant, whose head was bowed. I knew he was praying. It was all most impressive. I also knew that my little nephew had joined him in prayer. I really cannot describe it—but I was then conscious of the man's utter sincerity."

With the children put to bed, the Emperor, his wife and sister returned to the mauve boudoir on the ground floor. Rasputin joined them. There was some conversation.

"I realized that both Nicky and Alicky were hoping that I would come to like Rasputin. I was certainly impressed by the scene in the nursery. I allowed the man his sincerity. But, unfortunately, I could never bring myself to like him."

Was she afraid of Rasputin? She did not say so. She admitted being impressed by his eyes, which looked blue and brown in turn, and rolled about in a frightening manner, but she did not see any magnetism in them.

"I never felt I was hypnotized by Rasputin. I did not think that his personality had anything irresistible in it. If anything, I found him rather primitive. His voice was very rough and uncouth, and it was almost impossible to keep up a conversation with him. That very first evening I noticed that he leapt from one subject to another, and he did use so many biblical quotations. They did not impress me in the least. . . . I knew enough about the peasants to realize that a great many among them knew whole chapters of the Bible by heart."

"What was the main reason for your disliking the man at that first meeting?" I asked. "You were impressed by him in your nephew's bedroom. You liked what you saw of him in the nurseries."

The Grand Duchess replied promptly: "It was his curiosity—unbridled and embarrassing. In Alicky's boudoir, having talked to her and Nicky for a few minutes, Rasputin waited for the servants to get the table for evening tea and then began plying me with most impertinent questions. Was I happy? Did I love my husband? Why didn't I have any children? He had no right to ask such questions, nor did I answer them. I am afraid Nicky and Alicky looked rather uncomfortable. I do remember I was relieved at leaving the palace that evening and saying 'Thank God he hasn't followed me to the station' as I boarded my private coach in the train for St. Petersburg."

A little later the Grand Duchess met Rasputin again, this time not at the palace but at Anna Vyrubova's cottage at the park gates. The Grand Duchess had spent a day at Tsarskoe and she accompanied her brother and sister-in-law to Mme. Vyrubova's after dinner.

"Rasputin was there, and he seemed very pleased to meet me again, and when the hostess with Nicky and Alicky left the drawing room for a few moments, Rasputin got up, put his arm about my shoulders, and began stroking my arm. I moved away at once, saying nothing. I just got up and joined the others. I'd had more than enough of the man. I disliked him more than ever. Believe it or not, on my return to St. Petersburg I did a strange thing—I sought my husband out in the study, and told him all that had happened at Anna Vyrubova's cottage. He heard me out and with a grave face he suggested that I should avoid meeting Rasputin in the future. For the first and only time I knew my husband was right."

A few weeks later, when the Grand Duchess was alone in her drawing room, Anna Vyrubova was announced. She came in, disheveled, flushed and obviously excited, and flung herself down on the floor by the Grand Duchess's chair. She had come to ask Olga to receive Rasputin in her own house.

"I remember her repeating, 'Oh please, he wants to see you again so much,' and I refused very curtly and I kept to my refusal. From then on, I only saw Rasputin at Anna Vyrubova's cottage when I accompanied Alicky. Nicky would not have him at the palace again—because of all the spreading slanders. To the best of my knowledge Nicky put up with the man solely on account of the help he gave to Alexis and that, as I happen to know very well, was genuine enough."

Here I asked if there were any truth in the widely spread assertions of Rasputin's insolence to the Emperor and his wife. Examples of it were supposed to happen at the palace and elsewhere.

"Such stories were invented by people who had not the slightest personal knowledge either of my brother or of Alicky and who were equally ignorant of the peasant make-up," the Grand Duchess said heatedly. "In the first place, such behavior would never have been tolerated for an instant. And secondly and even more importantly, Rasputin was and always remained a peasant in whose eyes the Tsar's person was sacred. He was always respectful, though I don't suppose he ever learned anything about etiquette. He called them *batushka* and *matushka*, 'little father' and 'little mother.' They always spoke to him and of him as Gregory Efimovich. On his rare visits to the palace he came either to pray for Alexis, or to speak on religious themes with Alicky. To judge by some of the absurdities written about him, you would imagine he practically lived at the palace."

And the Grand Duchess referred to a book published fairly recently where the author gave a description of the dining room at the Alexander Palace, with the Emperor and the Empress and all their five children seated at table and anxiously waiting for Rasputin's arrival. The Empress was supposed to say in despair that she felt sure of a mishap. Rasputin had never before been late for a meal.

"The whole incident is a complete and most grotesque fabrication," the Grand Duchess said angrily. "To begin with, the children never dined with their parents. Nicky and Alicky—except when they had guests—had their dinner served either in the mauve boudoir or in the little drawing room. In point of fact, there was no proper dining room in their wing at Tsarskoe Selo. And I was too much of a habituée there not to know that Rasputin never had a meal at the palace. People who write that kind of nonsense have not the slightest idea of the way Nicky and Alicky lived. And what has been written about my nieces and Rasputin is even worse. I had known those girls since their babyhood. I stood so close to them that they would sometimes confide their little secrets to me which they felt they couldn't bring to their mother. I know what their upbringing was down to the tiniest detail. The least sign of what is known as "freshness" on Rasputin's part would have bowled them over! None of it ever happened. The girls were always glad to see him because they knew how greatly he helped their little brother."

And, still angry, the Grand Duchess went on to tell me that vicious rumor ended by laying every moral lapse among the palace staff at Rasputin's door. One of those stories, concerning the rape of a nursery maid, reached the Emperor who immediately ordered a thorough investigation. It proved that the girl had indeed been caught in bed—with a Cossack of the imperial guard.

"And I do remember hearing in St. Petersburg that my sister-in-law poured money like water on Rasputin. Once again, there was not any foundation to it. Alicky was very careful, as you might say. It would have been utterly out of character for her to throw money about. She gave him shirts and a silk belt she had embroidered, and also a gold cross which he wore."

Nor, according to Olga, was there any truth in the story that the Empress was put into trances at spiritualist séances arranged by Rasputin at Anna Vyrubova's cottage.

"That would be laughable if it were not wicked. Alicky's piety may well have been exaggerated, but she was staunchly Orthodox and our church bans all such activities. And again you may remember that in a book written by Katherine Kolb, who had several noms-de-plume, Princess Katherine Radzywil among them, you read that Vyrubova had a key to my sister-in-law's diary, and knew all her secrets. Now, Alicky's diary had no lock to it and she was never a very good diarist. During the last years she was far too busy and ill and stopped making entries altogether."

Although the Grand Duchess disliked Rasputin so much and found it rather difficult to follow his thickly slurred Siberian accent, she never criticized him openly either to her brother or his wife.

"I felt that their friendship with the man was their private concern and that not even I would have been justified in interfering. I had plenty of opportunities to do so since, for years, I used to see Nicky and Alicky practically every day. But I never did—partly because I could well gauge that Rasputin's reputed influence was non-existent where Nicky was concerned, but mainly because of Alexis."

The Grand Duchess found it difficult to understand why hardly anyone in Russia would believe that her nephew's terrible illness was the only reason for the Empress's trust and friendship with Rasputin.

Faith in the power of prayer, in the gift of healing, and in miracles was common enough among the people. And Rasputin certainly possessed that gift of healing.

"There is no doubt about that. I saw those miraculous effects with my own eyes and that more than once. I also know that the most prominent doctors of the day had to admit it. Professor Fedorov, who stood at the very peak of the profession and whose patient Alexis was, told me so on more than one occasion; and all the doctors disliked Rasputin intensely."

As is well known, the least accident in Alexis's case could lead, and often did, to an agonizing struggle between life and death, and the first crisis happened when he was barely three years old. He had a tumble in the gardens at Tsarskoe Selo. He did not cry and his little leg was hardly bruised, but the fall had started internal bleeding, and within a few hours the child was racked by excruciating pain. The Empress rang up the Grand Duchess who at once rushed to Tsarskoe Selo.

"I wonder what Alicky must have thought—and that proved the first crisis out of many. The poor child lay in such pain, dark patches under his eyes and his little body all distorted, and the leg terribly swollen. The doctors were just useless. They looked more frightened than any of us and they kept whispering among themselves. There seemed just nothing they could do, and hours went by until they had given up all hope. It was getting late and I was persuaded to go to my rooms. Alicky then sent a message to Rasputin in St. Petersburg. He reached the palace about midnight or even later. By that time I had gone to my rooms and early in the morning Alicky called me to go to Alexis's room. I just could not believe my eyes. The little boy was not just alive—but well. He was sitting up in bed, the fever gone, the eyes clear and bright, not a sign of any swelling on his leg. The horror of the evening before became an incredibly distant nightmare. Later I learned from Alicky that Rasputin had not even touched the child but merely stood at the foot of the bed and prayed, and, of course, some people would at once have it that Rasputin's prayers were simply coincidental with my nephew's recovery. In the first place, any doctor would tell you that an attack of such severity cannot be cured within a bare few hours. Secondly, the coincidence might have answered if it happened, say, once or twice, but I could not even count how many times it happened."

Once Rasputin's prayers had the same effect when he was in Siberia and Alexis in Poland. In the autumn of 1913, at Spala, his father's hunting lodge near Warsaw, the boy, scrambling out of a boat, knocked his right knee against the gunwale. At once, urgent wires were sent to Professor Fedorov and others. The Grand Duchess was then in Denmark with the Dowager Empress. She heard from Professor Fedorov that it proved the very worst attack in the boy's life. Then his mother wired to Pokrovskoye for help. Rasputin replied: "God has seen your tears and heard your prayers. Be anxious no longer. Your son will recover."

"Within an hour my nephew was out of danger," said the Grand Duchess. "Later that year I met Professor Fedorov who told me that the recovery was wholly inexplicable from a medical point of view. Now I have heard it said that the public might have understood Rasputin's position better had they known about my nephew's illness. That is pure calumny. It is true that his illness was not, as it were, broadcast as soon as Nicky and Alicky knew it, but it could not be kept a secret for long. They all blamed my poor sister-in-law for having transmitted the disease to her son and then they blamed her for trying all she could to find a remedy. Was that just? Never did either my brother or Alicky believe that the man was endowed with any supernatural powers. They saw him as a peasant whose deep faith turned him into an instrument for God to use—but only in the case of Alexis. Alicky suffered terribly from neuralgia and sciatica, but I never heard that the Siberiak helped her."

And the Grand Duchess, her eyes sad, remembered her nephew's sunny nature, his fortitude, his patience, the quiet way in which he accepted the fact that a boy's ordinary healthy pastimes were not for him.

We were now reaching a point where I felt somewhat at a loss because I did not know how best to approach it without causing distress to the Grand Duchess. There were the Empress's own letters to her husband in 1915 and 1916, with their innumerable references to "Our Friend," the advice given by him on matters which had nothing to do with Alexis's illness, such as ministerial nominations, all of it presenting a curious enough picture as though the Empress were convinced that the fate of the Empire stood or fell by Rasputin. The material, as I saw clearly, had been greatly misused, one writer going to the length of suggesting that the Emperor never arrived at an important decision without first consulting Rasputin.

"I was away—nursing at the front during that time," the Grand Duchess said calmly, "but I couldn't help hearing a lot. In the first place, knowing Nicky as I did, I must insist that Rasputin had not a particle of influence over him. It was Nicky who eventually put a stop to Rasputin's visits to the palace. It was again Nicky who sent the man back to Siberia and that more than once. And some of Nicky's letters to Alicky are proof enough of what he really thought of Rasputin's advice. Things were going from bad to worse at the time Nicky was at Moguilev and Alicky all by herself at Tsarskoe Selo. I admit that her letters do indicate that she was paying more and more attention to Rasputin's advice. But don't forget that she saw him as her son's savior. Harassed almost beyond all endurance, unable to find support anywhere else, she ended by imagining the man to be the country's savior. But Nicky never shared that idea of Alicky's. For all his devotion, he dismissed and appointed men against her wishes. Sukhomlinov was replaced by Polivanov at the War Ministry after the Empress had implored him not to do it, and Nicky dismissed Sturmer from the Foreign Office and sent Samarin to the Holy Synod, again acting on his own initiative. Then again some people were only too ready to remember that Rasputin had been dead against us fighting Germany in 1914. So in 1916 it was found convenient to start a campaign of the grossest calumnies against Alicky—that she was all for a separate peace with Germany, urged by Rasputin, who now, so they said, was just a tool in the hands of the Germans. This rubbish has now been disproved—but what untold harm it did at the time!"

She paused a little, and then continued:

"I, having been so close to them both, never interfered, either with advice or criticism. I knew little or nothing of purely political matters, and the rest was their own affair. But look at the family! My mother and Aunt Ella alone had Nicky's interests really at heart—but neither my mother nor my aunt knew all the details as they were. They, too, had based their judgments on rumors. Yet at least they were quite sincerely anxious. All the

others began coming to Tsarskoe Selo to give uncalled-
for advice, to utter violently worded warnings, even to
make scenes. Some even thought that Alicky should be
sent to a convent. Nicky's young cousin Dimitri, with
some friends of his, gave full support to a vile conspir-
acy. There was just nothing heroic about Rasputin's
murder. Remember what Trotsky said about it—that it
"was carried out in the manner of a scenario designed
for people of bad taste." You could hardly call Trotsky a
champion of the monarchy. I think that for once the
Communists were not severe enough in their judgment.
It was a murder premeditated most vilely. Just think of
the two names most closely associated with it even to
this day—a Grand Duke, one of the grandsons of the
Tsar Liberator, and then a scion of one of our great
houses, whose wife was a Grand Duke's daughter.[4] That
proved how low we had fallen!"

Olga added, with deep revulsion in her voice and
eyes: "What did they hope to achieve? Did they really
believe that the killing of Rasputin would mend our fortunes at the front,
and bring to an end the appalling transport chaos and all the resultant
shortages? I've never for a moment believed it. The murder was so staged as
to present Rasputin in the guise of a devil incarnate and his killers as some
fairy-tale heroes. That foul murder was the greatest disservice to the one
man they had sworn to serve—I mean Nicky. The involvement of two
members of the family did nothing but reveal the appalling decadence in
the upper social strata. It did more. It created a panic among the peasants.
Rasputin was flesh of their flesh and bone of their bone. They felt proud
when they heard of him being the Tsarina's friend. When they heard of his
murder they said, 'There, let one of us get near the Tsar and the Tsarina,
and princes and counts must needs kill him out of jealousy. It is always they
who will stand between the Tsar and ourselves.'"

*Grand Duchess Olga in her
nurse's uniform.*

In and Out of Chaos

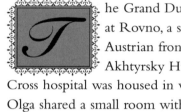he Grand Duchess spent the first months of the war at Rovno, a small town not far from the Polish-Austrian frontier where her own Hussar regiment, the Akhtyrsky Hussars, was fighting at the time. The Red Cross hospital was housed in what had been the artillery barracks, and Olga shared a small room with another nurse. The hospital was terribly understaffed. They worked fifteen hours a day and sometimes even longer. There was no time to think of one's own problems or discomforts. Fresh casualties kept arriving every day, and soon enough the Grand Duchess came face to face with the utter inefficiency of the Russian war machinery. There were constant shortages of medical supplies, clothing, bed linen, and ammunition.

"Soldiers in our ward told us that they had to meet German machine guns with sticks in their hands. The head surgeon, Nikolai, kept begging me to write to Nicky. Even General Ivanov, who then commanded the south-eastern front, once came to Rovno to ask if I could ask the general staff for reinforcements."

To her, such revelations were horrible. She felt as if she were personally responsible for the chaotic conditions. She felt shamed and her humiliation deepened when she realized there was nothing she could do. The hospital at Rovno was but one unit among hundreds. The soldiers could hardly believe it when they were told that the smiling, petite nurse tenderly caring for them was the sister of their Tsar. Many crossed themselves, thinking they were seeing a vision. Contrary to the imperial tradition of each Grand Duchess being in charge of her own hospital, the Grand Duchess Olga

Grand Duchess Olga on her way to the Red Cross Unit in Rovno at the Russian-Austrian frontier after the outbreak of hostilities in August, 1914.

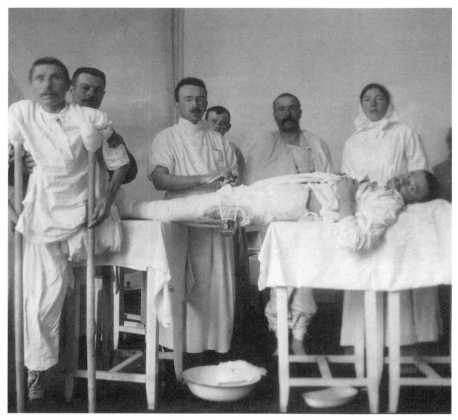

Grand Duchess Olga in the operating room of a temporary hospital on the Austrian frontier in 1915.

chose to serve as a simple nurse instead. It was only later, in recognition of her tireless work, that the hospital was named after her.

Yet, mismanagement and all, the war started brilliantly for her country. In East Prussia, her brother's armies were steadily advancing. In Galicia, the Austrian retreat was rapidly becoming a rout. Lemberg fell to the Russians in the middle of March, 1915, and a few days later the fortress of Przemysl, considered impregnable, surrendered too, and the garrison of 126,000 officers and men, vast quantities of ammunition, food, and medical supplies fell to the Russians. All the bells were ringing in triumph up and down the Empire, and many people thought that the end of the war was in sight.

The Grand Duchess left Rovno to join the Emperor in Galicia, and she rode by his side as they entered Lemberg.

"The people gave us a tumultuous welcome, and flowers were thrown from every window. Nicky had been warned of the danger, as some snipers were still hiding behind chimneys. I, too, had heard of this risk, but at that hour, neither peril nor death meant much. It was for the very last time that I sensed that mysterious bond between my family and the people. I could never forget that triumphant entry into Lemberg."

There were few joys ahead for the Grand Duchess. On August twenty-sixth of the same year, Hindenburg routed two Russian army corps at Tannenberg. Nearly all the guards regiments perished in the Mazurian marshes. The Russians began retreating virtually on every front. Grand Duke Nicholas was relieved of the supreme command—now assumed by the Emperor against everybody's advice.

"It was a noble thing to do," insisted the Grand Duchess. "We hoped it would raise the sagging morale of the troops and the people. Alas, it did not—but Nicky had no alternative but to shoulder the responsibility. As usual, Nicky chose the course of total honor and, as usual, it turned out to be a catastrophe."

Her own hospital was moved as far back as Kiev. Reverses continued. Morale was worsening everywhere.

"I soon noticed that many among the doctors and nurses avoided looking at me. Discipline slackened among the men and everybody took to discussing politics in a heated manner. Then things moved to a climax. I narrowly escaped having my skull smashed by a nurse one evening when she and I were working in the dispensary. I have no idea what made me turn my head at that moment—I saw her, eyes blazing, mouth twisted, an enormous jar of vaseline held high in her hands. She was just about to drop it on my head when I screamed and she dropped it on the floor instead and ran out into the street. She was taken into a convent."

A few days later when Grand Duchess Olga was on the ward, she heard that someone had come to see her. She went to the door and all the patients saw the Tsar's sister throw herself into the open arms of a very dirty and unshaven officer. It was Colonel Koulikovsky, her "*Kukushkin*," come to spend a week's leave near her hospital. When his leave was over the Grand Duchess went to Petrograd.

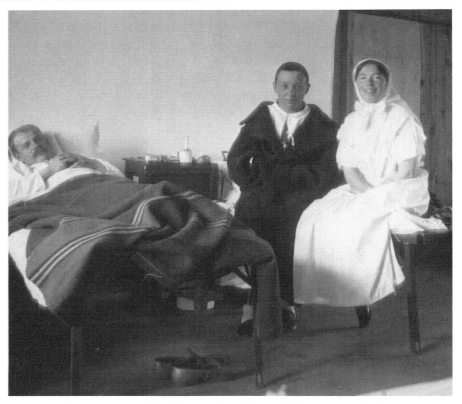

Grand Duchess Olga in the hospital named after her in Kiev.

It was the autumn of 1915 and, though she did not know it, it proved her last visit to the city she loved so much. She gave a year's pay to all her servants at the house in Sergievskaya Street. She also went to Tsarskoe Selo.

"Poor Alicky was all agony and dejection. Of course, I never told her about all the fantastic rumors. She told me how she missed Nicky. We both cried at parting. Yet the visit I had most dreaded was to my mother. I had to tell her of my decision to marry the man I loved. I had been prepared for a terrible scene, but my mother remained quite calm and said that she understood. And that was something of a shock in its own way."

The Grand Duchess found the capital full of the most fantastic calumnies directed against her family. Some people even forgot that she was the Emperor's sister and spoke of those things in her presence. There were also whispers of a family plot against the Tsar. Now one grand-ducal name would be mentioned, now another.

"I longed to get back to the front and my nursing. There was just nothing to keep me in Petrograd. The city was gripped in the clutches of hysterical defeatism. To listen to some people, you would have thought the war was lost."

On returning to her hospital, Olga at once sensed a sharp decline in the atmosphere. Some nurses from Petrograd had come during her absence and they were quite openly "Red." There were incidents daily in every ward, and the least detail of the routine became charged with political flavor. To Olga's relief, her mother decided to close the Anitchkov Palace in Petrograd and came to Kiev. The Grand Duchess dined with the Dowager Empress every day and was grateful for that brief escape from the ever-mounting tension at the hospital. War work brought Grand Duke Alexander into the Ukraine. He lived on board his own train just outside Kiev station. There was a bathroom in his coach, and Olga was glad of a chance to have a bath now and again. The fuel shortage in Kiev had led to a scarcity of hot water, even in the hospitals.

The last months of 1916 were rather exciting for the Grand Duchess. First of all, her brother Michael arrived from the North for a few days. She had not much leisure, but she gave him every moment of it. They did not discuss the shadowy present. They went back to their shared childhood and laughed about those remote days just as though they were children again—enjoying stolen sweets. But when the Grand Duke's stay came to an end and his sister went to see him off at the station, she wept unashamedly.

They were never to see each other again.

Early in November, the Emperor came from Moguilev for an inspection of Kiev hospitals.

"I was shocked to see the change in Nicky, so pale, thin, and tired he looked. My mother was worried by his excessive quiet. I knew he would have liked a long talk with me, but there was not a moment—there was so much to do and so many people for him to see." For her, the most memorable moments of the Emperor's visit came in the ward of her hospital.

"We had a young wounded deserter, court-martialed and condemned to death. Two soldiers were guarding him. All of us felt very troubled about him—he looked such a decent boy. The doctor spoke of him to Nicky who

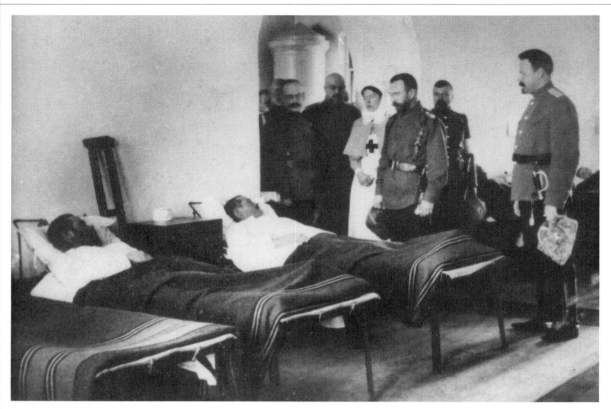

Tsar Nicholas II inspecting his sister's ward at the hospital in Kiev a few months before his abdication. This was the last time Grand Duchess Olga was ever to see her brother.

at once made for that corner of the ward. I followed him, and I could see the young man was petrified with fear. Nicky put his hand on the boy's shoulder and asked very quietly why he had deserted. The young man stammered that, having run out of ammunition, he had got frightened, turned, and run. We all waited, our breath held, and Nicky told him that he was free. The next moment the lad scrambled out of bed, fell on the floor, his arms 'round Nicky's knees, and sobbed like a child. I believe all of us were in tears—even those very difficult nurses from Petrograd. And then there fell such a hush in the ward—all the men had their eyes on Nicky and what devotion there was in their look! Just for that moment, all the hard and disturbing elements had gone. Once again the Tsar and his people were at one." The Grand Duchess dropped her voice. "I have cherished the memory all down the years. I never saw Nicky again."

Hardly had Nicholas II left Kiev than general discontent began to deepen: wilder and still wilder rumors seeped into the city, shortages increased, and food queues grew longer and longer. Whenever Olga met Grand Duke Alexander, he would warn her about the future.

The gloom in Kiev was at its deepest the day Olga heard that her brother had ratified the annulment of her marriage to Prince Peter of Oldenburg. Now she could marry the man she had loved for thirteen years. The wedding took place immediately in a very small chapel. It is unlikely that any other Romanovs had ever gone to the altar in such a way.

"My mother and Sandro came. There were two or three officers of the Akhtyrsky Regiment and the very few friends I had at the hospital. It was such a small dark chapel. My wedding dress was my Red Cross uniform. Later the hospital staff gave us a dinner. The same evening I was back on the ward. But I did feel happy. Something like new strength came to me, and then and there, in that chapel, standing beside my beloved Kukushkin, I resolved to face the future whatever it brought. I was so deeply grateful to God for granting me such happiness."

Christmas came and went. Rumors thickened as the last days of the monarchy drew to their close. There were hardly any letters from Petrograd. The Dowager Empress, Olga, and Sandro did not know what to believe.

"The news of Nicky's abdication came like a thunderbolt. We were stunned. My mother was in a terrible state and I stayed the night at her house. The next morning she left for Moguilev and Sandro went with her, and I returned to my work at the hospital."

The Grand Duchess did not know what she could expect there, and the immediate warmth and understanding she met at the hospital moved her very deeply. The soldiers clasped her hand as she passed by. No words were spoken, but many of them cried like children. When a Communist nurse ran up to the Grand Duchess and began congratulating her on the abdication, some of the orderlies present caught hold of the girl and pushed her out of the ward.

The Emperor came under a heavy fire of criticism, some of it made by his close relatives. "Nicky must have lost his head," wrote Grand Duke

Alexander in his book, *Once a Grand Duke.* "Since when does a sovereign abdicate because of shortage of bread and ... disorders in his capital? ... He had an army of fifteen million men at his disposal...."

But the Grand Duchess was staunch in her defense of her brother's difficult decision.

"Not only did he want to prevent further disorders when he gave up his crown but he had no other choice. He found himself deserted by all his army commanders, who, with the exception of General Gourko, favored the provisional government. Nicky could not even rely on the men in the ranks. He saw nothing but cowardice, treachery, and deceit all 'round him, and Michael, with that wife of his, could not possibly succeed him. And yet even my mother could not understand the reasons behind the abdication. On her return, she kept telling me that it was the greatest humiliation of her life. I shall never forget the day when she returned to Kiev."

In spite of the abdication, the Dowager Empress had left for Moguilev, and all the customary honors had been paid to her. She had driven to the imperial platform at the station, the Cossack escort following, and the governor of Kiev, Count Ignatiev, had seen her off. But nobody met her on her return; the imperial platform was barred off, and there were no Cossacks to accompany her carriage. In fact, there was not even a carriage. The Dowager Empress drove to her house in a hired cab. Within a few minutes, Grand Duke Alexander rushed to the hospital, where Olga, who was now expecting her first baby, was still working. She must come and calm her mother, he said.

"I was on duty, but I had to go. I had never seen her in such a state. She could not sit still for a moment. She kept pacing the floor, and I saw that she was more angry than miserable. She understood nothing of what had happened. She blamed poor Alicky for just everything.

"It was an afternoon to turn your hair gray," went on the Grand Duchess. "In my hurry to get to her I had missed my footing and fallen rather badly just as I was getting out of the car. All the time I tried to pacify my mother, I kept wondering if the fall had injured my baby."

The Dowager Empress continued in her refusal to accept the reality. She persisted in visiting the Kiev hospitals—to the distress of everybody near her, the Grand Duchess included. The public mood grew worse and worse. Prisons having been opened by the mob, streets teemed with released murderers and burglars who, still wearing their prison uniforms, were wildly cheered by the crowds.

"I could see them from a hospital window. The police were all gone. Streets were patrolled by awful-looking thugs who, though they were armed to the teeth, could not keep order. Filthy slogans against Nicky and Alicky were chalked on walls, and the double eagle torn off all the official buildings. It was not pleasant to brave those streets on the way to my mother's house."

Grand Duke Alexander wanted them to leave for the Crimea immediately. Olga was ready to go, but the Dowager Empress rejected the mere idea of flight. She must stay in Kiev because of her sons and Grand Duchess Xenia who were all in the North.

At last, a shock brought the Empress Marie to her senses. One morning she drove to the main hospital in Kiev. She arrived to see the gates being closed in her face, and the head surgeon rudely said that her presence was no longer wanted. He was supported by the entire staff of doctors and nurses. The Dowager Empress came back to her house. Next morning she told her daughter that she would go to the Crimea.

The Romanovs were in great peril in Kiev—but to leave it proved a task so difficult that it might never have been accomplished except for the initiative and the herculean efforts of Grand Duke Alexander. The Communists would never have allowed them to leave from the station. Within a few days Sandro succeeded in having a train assembled on a deserted siding behind a wood outside the city. He was successful in enlisting the cooperation of a small unit of sappers, still loyal to the crown, who were building a bridge across the Dnieper. They volunteered to man the train all along that most uncertain and perilous journey to the Crimea.

The party left the city by night, all going separately. The Dowager Empress, Grand Duke Alexander, Olga and her husband boarded the train in silence. They were followed by a few members of the Empress Marie's household. Olga's own maid, her loyal Mimka, had volunteered to travel alone to Petrograd, to rescue some at least of her mistress's valuables from the house in Sergievskaya Street.

"It was a bitter night. I wore nothing but my nurse's uniform. To avoid all suspicion I had not put on a coat when I left the hospital. My husband covered me with his greatcoat. I had a very small dressing case in my hands. I remember the moment when, looking upon that small case and my crumpled skirt, I realized that I owned nothing else in the world."

Early in January, 1917, the Grand Duchess had written to her house steward in Petrograd to ask that her jewelry should be sent to Kiev. He replied that he considered the transit risks were too great and that he had everything put in a bank vault. The Dowager Empress was far more fortunate. Kiki, her faithful maid, had some of her mistress's jewels packed and brought to Kiev.

The Grand Duchess never knew how they succeeded in reaching the Crimea at all. At every station there were scenes of wild confusion, with crowds of refugees trying to board the train. But the sappers kept their word. Their bayonets drawn, they guarded the door of every coach. It took them four days to reach Sebastopol. The sappers did not stop at the station but drove the train to a siding on the outskirts. There, a few cars were waiting. They had come from the Military Aviation School at Sebastopol, its personnel still loyal to the monarchy.

"When we left the train, I saw a group of unkempt and untidy sailors staring at us. It was sheer anguish to be aware of their hatred. There were few of them and they could not harm us because of the loyal sappers. Nonetheless, Nicky's sailors had been my friends since my childhood. It was a shock to realize that they were now enemies."

They did not go to Livadia. They drove to Ai-Todor, Grand Duke Alexander's estate, about twelve miles from Yalta, and a few days later Grand Duchess Xenia and her children arrived from the North.

"Those few weeks at Ai-Todor were almost too good to be true. It was spring, and the park rioted in blossom. Somehow there was hope. We were left in peace, nobody interfering with us. But of course, we were anxious for Nicky and all the others. There were so many rumors. With the exception of one smuggled letter, we had no news from the North. We only knew that he, Alicky, and the children were still at Tsarskoe Selo."

Soon enough, other refugees reached the Crimea. Prince and Princess Yusupoff came to Koreiz, an estate neighboring Ai-Todor. Grand Duke Nicholas and his family were at Dulbert nearby, and the summer of 1917 went by, with nothing to mar their peace except anxiety for those left in the North. On August twelfth, the Grand Duchess had her first born, a son, who, according to her promise, was christened Tikhon.

And then, suddenly, conditions changed for the worse. The provisional government sent a commissioner to the Crimea, "to keep an eye on the Romanovs." The local Communists began raising their voices. At Ai-Todor they heard of Lenin's bid for power in July. They had no news from or about Tsarskoe Selo. The Grand Duchess's joy in her first born sustained her through those weary days when the Dowager Empress complained to everybody that she should never have let herself be persuaded to come to the Crimea, that she should have gone to Petrograd to support her son abandoned by the entire family. And the atmosphere at Ai-Todor was not lightened by the arrival of Olga's faithful maid Mimka, who had indeed succeeded in finding her way to the Crimea—but she came almost empty-handed. The Grand Duchess's jewels had nearly all been requisitioned.

"So dear Mimka brought just everything that caught her eye—a huge hat trimmed with ostrich feathers, a few dresses, and a silk kimono some-body had brought me from Japan years ago. She also brought my little Maltese poodle!"

The Crimea was peaceful no longer. At no great distance from Ai-Todor stood the house of the Goujons, prominent Petrograd industrialists of French origin. Grand Duchess Olga and Colonel Koulikovsky were very friendly with them and often spent evenings at their villa. Late one night the Goujons' doctor came running to Ai-Todor to tell them that a band of Communist brigands had raided the Goujons' villa, murdered the husband, and knocked the wife down unconscious.

This proved a bloody preface to a long chapter. Soon the Black Sea Fleet went over to the Bolsheviks, into whose hands fell the two largest cities in the Crimea, Sebastopol and Yalta. News of one ghastly massacre after another reached Ai-Todor, and in the end the Sevastopol Soviet forced the provisional government to issue a search warrant which enabled them to enter Ai-Todor and make an investigation of its "anti-revolutionary activities."

At about four one morning, the Grand Duchess and her husband were awakened by two sailors marching into their room. They were told to keep still. The room was searched. Then one sailor left, and the other sat down on the sofa. Presently he got bored with having to watch two harmless people and confided to them that Ai-Todor was supposed to shelter German spies. "And we are looking for firearms and the secret telegraph," he added. After several hours, the two young sons of Grand Duke Alexander crept into the room to report that the Dowager Empress's room was full of sailors with whom she was furiously arguing.

"Knowing my mother, I began to fear the worst," said the Grand Duchess, "and, defying our guard, I ran to her room."

She found the room in chaos and her mother in bed, her eyes blazing with anger. All the drawers were emptied. Clothes lay all over the floor. Pieces of wood from wardrobe, table, and desk were ripped off. So were the curtains. From under the wild scatter on the floor, bare boards showed here and there, the sailors having torn up the carpet. The mattress and bedclothes were half pulled off the bed where the tiny Dowager Empress lay, her dark eyes still ablaze. The invective she poured on the marauders did not affect them in the least. They went on with their work until a particularly biting phrase from the bed made one of them say that they might just as well take the old hag along with them. Only the intervention of Grand Duke Alexander saved the Dowager Empress from being dragged out of her room. But, in going, the Communists took with them all the family photographs, letters, and the family Bible greatly treasured by Empress Marie.

That frantic search, accompanied by so much wanton destruction, revealed nothing except about two dozen old sporting guns. The Communists went and nobody at Ai-Todor could tell when the sailors would return. At the end of that day, the Dowager Empress's chauffeur decided to join the Communists and drove away in the only car there was. The only vehicle left at Ai-Tudor was an ancient pony cart. Nearby, at Dulbert, Grand Dukes Nicholas and Peter and their wives also had the whole place searched for ammunition.

Freedom left Ai-Todor the day sentries were posted at the gates. No one was allowed to come in or go out. The only exception was made for Colonel Koulikovsky and his wife who, having married a commoner, was no longer considered a Romanov.

"That ramshackle pony cart came into its use. My husband and I were kept very busy all day long buying food, calling on friends, gathering what news there was about the latest developments in the Crimea and beyond. But little by little the guards realized that we were human beings and not wild animals. Some of them even saluted my mother when they met her in the park...."

It was finally decided that the Grand Duchess and her husband should leave the great house and move into the so-called "cellar" on the edge of the park, a barnlike building with a large wine cellar and a room for storing grapes. There were two small rooms above. To the cellar went the Empress Marie's large jewel box. Having ransacked her bedroom from floor to ceiling, the raiders had never even looked at the box which had been left in full view on the bedroom table.

"We transferred everything in small cocoa-tins. At the least sign of danger, we hid those tins in a deep hole at the bottom of a rock by the seashore. Because of the many holes in the face of the rock, we marked the one in which we had hidden the jewels by placing at the front of it the white skull of a dog. One day we arrived to find the skull lying on the beach. We didn't know what to think. Had somebody discovered our hiding place? Or had the wind just blown it to the ground? I still remember the cold drops of perspiration forming on my forehead as I watched my husband sticking his hand deep in every possible hole in the precipice. What a relief when he finally pulled a cocoa-tin rattling with jewels out of one hole!"

No visitors might call at Ai-Todor and few ventured to go to the cellar except Dr. Malama, Grand Duke Nicholas's physician, who, being allowed to offer his services in the neighborhood, was as good as a weekly paper to Olga and her husband. There was also a gentleman appointed by the provincial government to look after Koreiz, the area to which Ai-Todor belonged. But the Soviets being established to the right and the left of him, the poor man had no authority left him. So he often called at the cellar to drink acorn coffee, and sometimes to weep.

"He was the gentlest creature in the world. His only wish was for peace and order. He shuddered at the very mention of violence. Officially he was called Commissar—but there was nothing of a commissar about him. We could almost imagine him at the head of a kindergarten. We knew that he was fighting a losing battle with Yalta and Sevastopol. . . ."

As she walked about the small villages, the Grand Duchess was often recognized in spite of her peasant smock and apron and her clumsy boots. The people, however, were friendly.

"Those Tartars were still loyal to Nicky and many of them had met him in happier days—but unfortunately they were no fighters. Had those Tartar village folk been like the Cossacks, Communism would have been crushed in the Crimea. As it was, we knew it was gaining ground every day. . . ."

Gradually, the atmosphere at Ai-Todor changed for the worse. The small community cooped up in the house, seeing nobody but one another, perplexed by conflicting rumors, and, be it admitted, idling their time away, began reacting to their imprisonment in anything but a happy way. The Empress Marie never accepted Olga's husband as an equal and pointedly excluded him from all family gatherings. Grand Duke Alexander became a shadow of his former self and lost interest in everybody and everything, and Grand Duchess Xenia was in the depths of despair. Her children, with nobody thinking of any routine to fill their days, were hard to discipline. Members of the household spent their time in idle tittle-tattle and futile regrets for the past. And the servants, catching the general mood of frustration, became lazy and insolent by turn. About the only common link between them all was their anxiety about the Emperor and his family.

"We heard so many wild rumors. We did not know what to believe. Some of us hoped that they had escaped to England. Then we heard that they were all taken to Tobolsk and this, alas, was no rumor. A dentist in Yalta was suddenly sent by the Soviet to Siberia. The good man succeeded in smuggling a few letters and some small gifts from Nicky and Alicky...."

That proved the last communication they would receive from Siberia. With the fall of the provincial government, the end had really begun.

Three or four weeks before Christmas, 1917, a giant of a sailor, one Zadorozhny, was installed at Ai-Todor to represent the Sebastopol Soviet.

"He was a murderer but a charming man," remembered the Grand Duchess. "He never met our eyes. Later he confided that he could not bear to look at those he would have to kill some day. As time went on, however, his manner became much kindlier. Yet, for all his good intentions, it was not Zadorozhny who saved our lives in the end—but the fact that the Soviets in Sebastopol and Yalta could not agree as to which of them had the prior right to chop our heads off...."

Apparently the Yalta Soviet wanted to execute all the Romanovs at Ai-Todor and Dulbert without any delay. But Sebastopol, from where Zadorozhny received his orders, insisted on waiting for definite instructions from Petrograd. And Zadorozhny exploited the rivalry to the very best of his abilities.

Tension between the two Soviets sharpened in February, 1918. Then Zadorozhny had all his prisoners at Ai-Todor removed to Dulbert, a gray, fortresslike house, encircled by a stout high wall, a place which could be defended far more easily than the exquisite white palace at Ai-Todor.

"Once again my husband and I were left at liberty. Never before had I imagined how worthwhile it could prove to be a commoner."

Yet soon enough both husband and wife came to regret their freedom. They were left alone at Ai-Todor, completely at the mercy of chance raiders. Nor could they get in touch with anyone at Dulbert. Zadorozhny was taking no risks and the place was heavily guarded day and night. Sometimes the Grand Duchess walked as far as the hill overlooking Dulbert in hopes that she might catch sight of someone. Once or twice she caught a glimpse of her mother.

The sharper realization of peril produced a beneficial change in the Ai-Todor party. At Dulbert they found themselves cheek by jowl with Grand

Dukes Nicholas and Peter, whose wives were disliked by the Empress Marie and her daughters. But there were no quarrels and later Olga would hear from her mother that everybody could not have been nicer.

On March third, 1918, the Brest-Litovsk Treaty was signed. One of its clauses surrendered to Germany many vast reaches of land in Western Russia. Another gave them the right to occupy the Crimea. The Yalta Soviet decided to "liquidate" the Romanovs before the arrival of the Germans.

Zadorozhny's scouts warned him of an artillery attack planned by Yalta. The man, aware that he, with a comparatively small number of men under him, could never hold Dulbert against a major attack, risked his life in hurrying to Sebastopol to seek reinforcements. But Yalta was nearer to Dulbert than Sebastopol. Dr. Malama warned the Grand Duchess and Colonel Koulikovsky that the danger was imminent.

"That afternoon I felt nearly faint with anxiety. My husband had gone out to meet our gentle Commissar who was almost beside himself. Then Dr. Malama called again. He had hardly sat down when we heard appalling shouts along the road. We ran to the door to see some Tartar women running past our cottage. One screamed at me, "They'll kill us all!"—and at that moment my husband came back. I wrapped the baby up in blankets and we picked our way down to the shore. . . ."

There they hid in the rocks for some hours. Eventually they made their way towards Dulbert. Everything seemed quiet enough.

"And there stood I, a Romanov, begging to be taken prisoner by the Communists! It was nearly dusk by then. . . ."

The sentries would not let them in. They heard that, earlier in the day, a strong contingent from Yalta had tried to get in and drag the prisoners out, but Zadorozhny's men had repulsed them.

"Then the Yalta men promised to return the next day. They ran into our poor gentle Commissar on their way back and bayoneted him. . . ."

Cold, hungry, exhausted, anxious for the baby, Olga and her husband trudged on up yet another hill to seek shelter at a friend's house where they were given a welcome, food, and beds.

"Excited voices woke us in the morning. My heart almost missed a beat when someone's smiling face appeared in the room to tell us that the enemy had been routed during the night. Our people at Dulbert were free...."

By the Kaiser's order, an advance German column had been rushed to rescue the imperial prisoners from the clutches of the Yalta Soviet and the firing-squad. The Germans arrived at dawn when the Yalta contingent had already battered down the gateway. The Empress Marie and all the others were within a hair's breadth of death.

"I did not know whether to feel happy or sad. Here we were, the Romanovs, being saved from our own people by our arch-enemy, the Kaiser! It seemed the ultimate degradation...."

At Dulbert, the German officer in charge wanted to have all the Communists shot immediately, including Zadorozhny's men and Zadorozhny, who had only just returned from Sevastopol, too. The German was amazed when all the Grand Dukes pleaded with him to spare the men's lives.

"That German," said the Grand Duchess, "must have thought that the long imprisonment had affected our minds! And the last grotesque touch was added by my mother. She, still holding that Germany was at war with Russia, refused to receive the German officer who had saved her from the Russian firing-squad...."

A few days later, Zadorozhny and his men left Ai-Todor. They addressed their one-time prisoners by their titles and kissed their hands.

"I watched them go, a deep gratitude in my heart. They had been decent. Not only did they save our lives but they restored our faith in the innate kindness of the Russian people. To me, at least, this was almost more important than my life."

With the Germans in possession, a semblance of peace settled over the Crimea. The Romanovs seemed safe enough, but the Grand Duchess, for all her personal happiness, had premonitions of further disasters. Soon enough these were realized. News from the North began trickling into the South. There were wholesale arrests and massacres. Petrograd, Moscow, and other cities were clutched in the grip of the Tcheka. In the Crimea they heard of

Grand Duke Michael's exile to Perm in Siberia; of Grand Duchess Serge and others also taken across the Urals; and, finally, of the Emperor and his whole family being removed to Ekaterinburg.

Yet, in spite of all her premonitions, the Grand Duchess, now staying with her mother and all the others at Harax on the coast much nearer to Yalta, refused to believe in the rumors and was still hoping for the best. With the bitter tension of Ai-Todor and Dulbert behind them, all of them relaxed. They walked, gardened, fished, and the younger ones began printing a weekly newspaper. The Grand Duchess even mentioned picnics, "but all of us had to bring our own food—because of the shortages." And all of them, surrounded by the civility of the Germans and the friendliness of the Tartars, thought that it was just an interlude, that something would happen, and they would return to their palaces and live down the nightmare.

"It was really tragic that none of us, in spite of all the violence we had seen in 1917, foresaw the terror of 1918. I believe that lay at the root of our downfall: we still imagined that the armed forces and the peasants would come to our support. It was blindness and worse; and how many of us paid with our lives for the blunder!"[1]

But the semblance of peace along the Crimean coast was shattered before 1918 reached its end. In November, the Germans having surrendered, their troops began evacuating the peninsula. The road into the Crimea soon lay open. True, the Allied ships were at anchor in Sebastopol harbor, but the sporadic efforts to organize resistance against the Communists could delay, but never stem, their advance to the South. The White Armies in the Don and Kuban areas lacked cohesion and all unity of purpose. Some favored a republic. Others were for the return of the monarchy. Still others remained neutral. They were all short of ammunition. By February, 1919, the Red Army had overrun the whole of the Ukraine and was threatening Odessa, occupied by the French.

From time to time the Dowager Empress received senior British officers, all of them urging her to leave on board their ships.

"But my mother was adamant. She kept telling them it was her duty to remain in Russia. She disliked the very idea of a flight. Moreover, she rejected what she called the rumors about the Ekaterinburg murders. As a matter of fact, we all did at the time...."[2]

The Grand Duchess was pregnant again. She by no means discounted the dangers menacing the Crimea. She felt torn in two. Her duty to her mother seemed to demand of her that she should stay at Harax. But Olga had other duties now, and to follow them she needed to move into a safer area.

"It was a terrible decision to make. To make matters more difficult, Sandro, who alone might have helped me, had already left on board a British destroyer. He meant to go to Paris, there to urge the necessity of crushing the Communist danger. I was my mother's daughter. But I was also a wife and mother...."

In the end, she and her husband decided to leave for the Caucasus, where the Red Army had been beaten far back by General Wrangell. But the Dowager Empress refused to move from Harax, insisted that Olga's duty was to remain with her, and blamed Colonel Koulikovsky for all he had done and not done.

"It was a sad and bitter way to say good-by. I wept as I left her. She was so angry. She said she would never forgive my husband. And I, knowing what the dangers were, wondered if I would ever see her again."

The little party left the Crimea by steamer for Novorossiysk on their way to the Caucasus. They were hardly overburdened with luggage. They were five in number: the Grand Duchess, her husband, their little son, Mimka the maid, and Timofey Yachik, a loyal member of the palace bodyguard. A man of Caucasian origin, he offered himself as a guide and his services were invaluable. The long and wearisome trek was begun just in time.[3]

They reached Novorossiysk and made their way to the station in the hope of finding places in a train for Rostov. They found quite a few trains—all crowded to bursting with soldiers on their way to join the White Army units. All hope gone, Colonel Koulikovsky and his wife were turning toward a shed off the platform to spend the night when, by a mere chance, they ran into General Koutepov, who, recognizing the Grand Duchess in spite of her sadly disheveled hair and battered clothes, at once offered them

Grand Duchess Olga in her nurse's uniform during World War I.

his own coach and had it coupled to a small train leaving for Rostov almost immediately.

"We felt we were traveling in the lap of luxury, even though the coach teemed with bugs and other vermin...."

General Denikin's advance had indeed cleared the Don area of the Red Army. Yet traveling in that territory was by no means safe. Excesses committed by the White Army during their advance had not endeared them to the local population, and Communist agents lost no chance to exploit the discontent. Somehow or other, the entire countryside heard that the Tsar's sister was on board that particular train. At every halt, and there were many of them, crowds of peasants would bunch together, craning their necks to stare at a tiny woman in rough, torn clothes, with a crumpled kerchief on her head, who sat by the window, a baby in her arms. They stared silently, unsmilingly. At one station, someone tinkered with the couplings of the coach. It would have been wrecked if it had not been for the bravery of Colonel Koulikovsky, who crawled across the roofs of the coaches ahead and succeeded in reaching the driver who stopped the train and put right the loose coupling.

Rostov was a disappointment. Denikin refused to see the Grand Duchess.

"He was supposed to feel sympathetic toward us, but he could not afford to show any sympathy. He sent a messenger to tell us that we were not wanted at Rostov."

Then Yachik persuaded them to make for his own village, Novo-Minskaya in the Ekaterinodar area of the Caucasus, where, as he knew, his family would look after them. They left Rostov by train; they changed to a cart; they ended the journey on foot. But Novo-Minskaya was a paradise after Rostov and other places. They could rent a hut there, and a peasant woman offered to come and help about the place. Some six weeks after their arrival, the Grand Duchess gave birth to her second son. There were no doctors. A village woman came to help.

It was a pleasant summer for Olga and her husband. She learned the ways of a kitchen garden, hoed and weeded, ground the corn bought from a neighboring farmer, baked bread, washed what little underwear they

possessed, nursed her baby son, and looked after Tikhon. She often walked barefoot. Her husband worked at a farm nearby and his wages came in kind. They were neither hungry nor thirsty, they had their sons, and day by day they heard news of General Denikin's further triumphs. By the end of June he had driven the Red Armies out of East Ukrainia. The Crimea was once again free. In August Denikin captured Odessa and Kiev. By September his men were at Kursk, pressing on to Voronezh and Orel. Denikin was within two hundred and fifty miles of Moscow.

But the entry into Orel proved the last triumph. Denikin's supply-lines were broken. His men's excesses turned the population against them. When in October, 1919, the Red Army started its counter-offensive, Denikin's victories melted away. By November Kiev was reoccupied by the Reds. Denikin's army, the last shreds of discipline gone, ceased to count.

One bitter November night, four Cossacks from a garrison nearby ran into the Koulikovskys' hut. The Red advance units were within the neighborhood of Novo-Minskaya. No time must be lost. They wrapped up their sons, grabbed whatever they could carry, and, followed by Mimka, fled from the village.

The next two months proved to be a time of indescribable hardship, danger, and well-nigh Spartan endurance. The four Cossacks, their own lives in jeopardy, followed them in that nightmare flight to the Black Sea coast. But it was winter, they often had to spend their nights in derelict barns, and, looking at the wan face of her baby, Olga wondered if he would survive.

Fighting raged all over the country. There were no battles but an endless sequence of skirmishes between Red and White bands, both equally given to arson, looting, and murder. On one occasion the refugees were fortunate to find a train, but the loyal Cossacks, on hearing that the next station was held by the Reds, lifted the Grand Duchess and her little sons out of the moving train. They crawled across some frozen fields to get into a temporarily safe area, to get nearer Rostov.

Rostov was still nominally in the hands of the Whites, but Communists were already converging on it and the station master threatened to have the train blown up. One of the four Cossacks pulled out a revolver and shouted: "If this train does not leave in five minutes, I mean to blow your brains out!"

There were a few British ships at Novorossiysk, but the town teemed with thousands and thousands of tattered, haggard, starving refugees, all fleeing from the Terror, all hoping to be evacuated. The Grand Duchess and her companions arrived destitute and hungry. Between them they had not enough to pay for a jug of milk. Her little sons looked like skeletons, and typhus was already raging in the city.

They found shelter at the Danish Consulate, already crowded with refugees, among them a circus troupe from Moscow, but typhus had already got into the house.

"We, who were all right, gave up our beds to the sick and slept on the floor. I was terribly worried about my husband and babies. I didn't care about my own life. I had seen such horrors that something seemed dead within me. But I had to get through somehow."

One morning when, half-dazed after a night of misery, she sat down to rest, she heard a voice she knew break into an English song:

"For she's the cutest little thing, for she's the cutest little thing—Itchiku, Itchiku, Itchiku..."

Olga sprang from her chair. She thought she was losing her mind. But it was Jimmy all right, with the silly little song he used to sing during his stay at Olgino in the days gone forever. Jimmy—now Flag-Captain James aboard Rear-Admiral Sir George Hope's flagship H.M.S. *Cardiff*, just berthed at Novorossiysk. He was engaged on his first task ashore, which was to check the rumor that the Tsar's sister was in the town and, if true, to find her.

Tattered as they were, Olga and her husband accepted the invitation to have tea on board the *Cardiff*. There, Olga was given a whole piece of navy-blue cloth—"the most wonderful present. I at once started making clothes for us all and we looked respectable at last."[4]

Just before leaving Novorossiysk, Olga heard that her Aunt Michen, the formidable Grand Duchess Vladimir, had arrived after a harrowing escape from the Caucasus.

"I went to see her. I was amazed to learn that she had reached the town in her own train, manned by her own staff, and still had her ladies with her. For all the dangers and privations, she still appeared every inch a Grand Duchess. There had never been much love between Aunt Michen and my own family, but I felt rather proud of her. Disregarding peril and hardship, she stubbornly kept to all the trimmings of by-gone splendor and glory. And somehow she carried it off. When even generals found themselves lucky to find a horse cart and an old nag to bring them into safety, Aunt Michen made a long journey in her own train. It was battered all right— but it was hers. For the first time in my life I found it was a pleasure to kiss her. . . ."[5]

One February morning Olga and her party at last boarded the merchant ship that was to take them to safety. Overcrowded as it was, they had a tiny cabin to share with the other passengers.

"I could not believe that I was leaving my country forever. I was certain I would return. I felt that my escape was cowardly, though I had reached the decision for the sake of my small sons. Still, a feeling of shame nagged at me all the time. . . ."

Two days later the steamer reached Turkish waters, but the Grand Duchess was not permitted to go ashore. Together with thousands of refugees she found herself interned at an improvised camp on the island of Prinkipo in the Sea of Marmora. The first thing ordered by Turkish authorities was the fumigation of the refugees' clothes.

"They needed it," she laughed a little ruefully, "but that rough and ready process did not improve their appearance, and our footwear shrank most horribly."

Life at Prinkipo proved a mercifully short interlude, but it was crammed with miseries—inadequate food, occasional lack of water, ghastly sanitary arrangements. But nothing daunted the Grand Duchess. She organized some kind of a committee and, poor as they were, they collected their pennies together and sent a telegram to King George V expressing their gratitude for sending his ships to help them escape from Russia.

Here I could not help interrupting the Grand Duchess:

"But why didn't you send a personal wire to him? He was your first cousin. For you to be interned in a common refugee camp—"

She shook her head almost angrily. "They were not common. They were all human beings. For all I knew, most of them had gone through far worse hardships than had fallen to my lot. And anyway, I was a commoner's wife, and my husband and our sons were there."

But though Olga did not think of appealing to the King of England, an old friend of hers had been busy on her behalf. Jimmy had written to Captain W. W. Fisher, Chief of Staff to the British High Commission in Constantinople, and within two or three weeks Olga and her small party were permitted to leave Prinkipo for Constantinople. From there they left for Belgrade, where King Alexander met them with a warm welcome.

"History is full of ironies. Here was I, granddaughter of a Tsar who had freed Serbia and Montenegro from the Turkish yoke, arriving in the Serbian capital—a tired, destitute refugee. But how kind they all were to us."

King Alexander hoped the Grand Duchess would choose his country as her home in exile. She would have liked to do so, but the Empress Marie, now settled in Denmark, wanted her. So, after a fortnight's rest, Olga and her husband left for Copenhagen.

"We got there on Good Friday, 1920. I was happy to see my mother again, but we all felt sad. Deep within ourselves we knew what we never dared put into words—that the remainder of our lives would be spent in exile."

The Bread of Exile

The Grand Duchess had loved Denmark since her childhood. Her earliest associations with Fredensborg and Copenhagen went back to the years when nearly all the royal families in Europe would gather under the roof of her hospitable grandfather, King Christian IX.

But all of that lay in the past. It was 1920, and Olga found the Empress Marie installed in one of the wings of the castle of Amalienborg in close proximity to her nephew, King Christian X, who made no effort to hide the dislike he felt for his dispossessed relatives.

"Fortunately, other members of the family and the Danish people did not share his opinion of us," said the Grand Duchess, "otherwise I really don't know how we could have borne it. I remember his Queen Alexandrina, whom we called Adine, bursting into tears, so ashamed was she of her husband's behavior." Olga recalled how one evening she and her mother were sitting quietly knitting in the living room of their palace when the door opened and a footman of the King's household walked in. The man was obviously awkward and hesitant. "His Majesty has sent me over," he said in a whisper, "to ask you to switch off all these lights. His Majesty said to mention to you that the electricity bill he had to pay recently was excessive." The Dowager Empress grew deathly pale but said nothing to the man. With imperial dignity she rang for one of her own servants and in front of the King's messenger ordered him to light up the entire palace, from cellar to attic. "The King would even come himself and stroll about the rooms where, naturally, every stick of furniture and most of the ornaments belonged to him. I remember him staring about. If he thought that

One of the living rooms at Villa Hvidøre.

Grand Duchess Olga (right) with her mother, Empress Marie Feodorovna, at Villa Hvidøre until her death in 1928

some bibelot or a miniature were missing, he would not scruple to ask my mother if she had pawned it! It was all too bitter for words...."

The refugees' finances were in a chaotic condition, made all the worse by the Empress Marie's reckless generosity. Thousands of Russian émigrés all over the world wrote to her and asked for help, and she considered that it was her duty to satisfy them all.

"It never occurred to my mother that there was hardly enough to support our own establishment," continued Olga, "but I really cannot blame her too much. She looked upon all the émigrés, whatever class they belonged to, as one family. Moreover, none among us, my father excepted, ever had any business sense."

Yet constant financial aid posted to the four corners of the globe was by no means the end of the Empress's extravagances. Several exiles from among the nobility converged upon Denmark. Little by little, they somehow attached themselves to the little court at Amalienborg. The Empress would not turn anyone away. For a time many wealthy friends in Denmark gave what support they could afford, but the situation grew from bad to worse, and finally a Danish-born American bluntly told the Empress that it could not continue much longer.

When it came to King Christian X's knowledge that his aunt was in financial difficulties, he said that she could always sell her jewelry. For the Empress Marie had succeeded in bringing the famous box to Denmark. At Amalienborg she kept it under her bed. Occasionally, when a nostalgic mood fell on her, she would open the case and touch all those pearls, diamonds, rubies, sapphires, and emeralds. Except for a diamond brooch given her by her husband on their wedding day, the old Empress never wore any jewelry now. That incredible glittering hoard, however, stood for the last link with the vanished splendor; she would not think of parting with even the least important of the trinkets.

In the end, her nephew in England came to the rescue and settled an annual pension of £10,000 on his "dear Aunt Minnie." King George V also asked Sir Frederick Ponsonby whether some arrangements might not be

Villa Hvidøre, just north of Copenhagen. The house was purchased by the Empress Marie Feodorovna and her sister Queen Alexandra of England so they would have a place of their own when they visited Denmark.

made to keep his aunt's establishment solvent, and Ponsonby asked a retired Danish admiral, Andrup, an old friend of the Empress, to try and get the old lady accustomed to plan her expenditure according to her means. It was a well nigh herculean task but the Admiral acquitted himself nobly.

One of the first measures suggested by him was a move. They left Amalienborg—to the undisguised relief of the King and their own slightly less obvious pleasure—and moved to Hvidøre, a spacious-enough place to enable the Empress to keep her entourage, but certainly not a palace to warrant an expenditure on the scale demanded at Amalienborg. Hvidøre, built by the three daughters of King Christian IX, was in their joint ownership, but now Queen Alexandra and the Duchess of Cumberland made it over to their less fortunate sister.

There, all the pictures, furniture, and ornaments spoke of a precious past. Once at Hvidøre, the Empress Marie stepped further and further back into a world where harsh realities had no meaning for her. In her mind, Nicky was still the head of his Empire. She kept studiedly aloof from all the rival factions among the exiled Romanovs. The names of Grand Duke Nicholas, Grand Duke Cyril, and even Grand Duke Dimitri were all in turn mentioned to her as possible successors to her son, and supporters of each kept writing to Denmark to beg the Empress to acknowledge one or other of them. She ignored all these letters. Her stony refusal to face the truth was not shaken even by the arrival of the sad relics salvaged from among the ashes in the wood at Four Brothers near Ekaterinburg—half-burnt pieces of clothing, a few buttons, bits of broken jewelry, and suchlike. The Empress's two daughters wept over the little box before it went to France, there to find its last resting place together with a few other relics in the Russian cemetery outside Paris.

The Empress Marie continued to think and to talk as though her son and his family were still alive. "Yet I am sure that deep in her heart my mother had steeled herself to accept the truth some years before her death," said the Grand Duchess.

From one point of view at least, the Empress's dignity answered its purpose. She was not ignored by her relations, and all—with the exception of King Christian X—treated her with affectionate respect. The Grand Duchess recalled the visit of Queen Olga of Greece, who left her own exile in Italy to see her god-daughter Olga and the Dowager Empress at Hvidøre. The Greek Queen brought Prince Philip, her six-year-old grandson, along. "I remember young Philip as a wide-eyed youngster with blue eyes sparkling with humor and mischief. Even then, when a mere child, he possessed a mind of his own, though he seemed rather subdued in the presence of mother. I served him tea and cookies, which vanished in a split second. I could never have imagined then that this lovely child would one day be the consort of the Queen of England."

The King continued to humiliate his aunt. On some occasions, however, his rudeness was defeated by her calm dignity. One such incident happened during the state visit of the King and Queen of Italy. King Christian X had no intention of inviting his poor relatives to the banquet at the palace or to any other festivities. He merely sent a telephone message to say that he and his guests would call at Hvidøre one afternoon. On arrival, the royal party were met not by one of the Empress's gentlemen-in-waiting, not even by the steward or the butler, but by a footman saying:

"Her Imperial Majesty deeply regrets that, being indisposed, she does not receive today."

King Christian was furious. His aunt's decision was partly a reply to his rudeness, but largely based on the fact that Italy had recently recognized the Soviet government.

"We were not very happy about it," the Grand Duchess said sadly. "We did so want to meet Queen Elena again. She was a Montenegrine, brought up and educated in Russia, and we all loved her, but my mother remained intransigent. As a matter of fact, she kept being so outspoken that we lived in constant fear of her being kidnapped by the Reds. About 1925, I think, they said that the Russian church in Copenhagen, having been attached to the imperial Embassy, was their property. The Danish government allowed the claim, and the Reds took possession and turned the church into an annex to their Consulate. All the émigrés were broken-hearted, but my mother would not admit defeat. She engaged one of the finest Danish lawyers, had the case taken to the High Court, and won it. She was badly crippled by lumbago and arthritis at the time, but nothing prevented her from attending the first service after the reopening of the church."

The hallway at Villa Hvidøre.

The Grand Duchess greatly admired her mother's undaunted spirit. Nonetheless, those first years of exile proved very hard for Olga. Her sister Xenia, whose husband Grand Duke Alexander now lived in France, did not wish to stay on in Denmark. She and the Grand Duke were not divorced, but they had separated for good, and the British government would not allow the Grand Duke to come to England. In the end, Grand Duchess Xenia and her children left Denmark for England. Olga was constantly at the beck and call of her mother, carrying out the varied duties of companion, nurse, lady's maid, and secretary. There were many servants at Hvidøre—to say nothing of the ladies in attendance on the Empress—but the latter insisted on having her younger daughter always at hand. The younger daughter had a husband and two lively sons. It was impossible to

Grand Duchess Xenia (at right) was a frequent visitor at Villa Hvidøre. Here she sits with her mother, Marie Feodorovna (middle) and the Grand Duchess Olga.

keep the boys always out of the Empress's earshot. They were lively, they were noisy, and often enough they made a nuisance of themselves.

"Can't you keep those boys under control?" the grandmother would ask angrily if the boys happened to be playing a noisy game not far from her windows. In her exasperation, Olga would answer that she could do so only when they were asleep.

Her life was not made much easier by the Empress's studiedly formal manner toward her husband. To the very end, Marie treated Colonel Koulikovsky as an intruder and a commoner. When guests arrived and Olga would be invited to have either luncheon or tea in her mother's rooms, her husband was excluded from the invitation. When on very rare occasions the Empress had to attend some formal function at Amalienborg or elsewhere, she made it obvious that she expected Olga and Olga alone to accompany her.

"My husband was wonderful. He never complained either to me or any-one else. However, things might have been much worse, and we did go on with our efforts to bring up our sons and to get more or less accustomed to that strange life in exile."

In 1925 the Grand Duchess left Denmark to spend four rather momentous days in Berlin. Neither the Empress Marie nor Colonel Koulikovsky wished her to make the journey. They thought that its purpose was both imprudent and unnecessary, and later the Grand Duchess would have to admit she should never have gone, but her aunt, the Duchess of Cumberland, urged very strongly that she should meet the woman sup-posed to be the only survivor of the Ekaterinburg massacre. "Just to clear up the case once and for all," pleaded the Duchess, and there was no doubt that Olga was the one person best qualified to recognize her dearly loved niece and god-daughter, Anastasia, the youngest daughter of Nicholas II. And apart from the insistence of her aunt, and her uncle Prince Valdemar of Denmark, Olga felt an irresistible impulse to draw closer to the mystery and to solve it if it were at all possible.

The whole world knows the beginning of the story—how a young girl, now known as Mrs. Anderson, of no provable identity, was rescued from a canal in Berlin in 1920. It was a case of attempted suicide, and the entire Anastasia legend sprang from that incident.

Anna Anderson, the woman who claimed to be Grand Duchess Anastasia, in Berlin, 1926.

"It was on that night that the saga had its beginning," the Grand Duchess said wryly. "That attempt to drown herself is probably the only indisputable fact in the whole story." Rescued, she was taken to a hospital. Presently a neighbor of hers in the ward, a German who had once been a dressmaker in St. Petersburg, thought that she recognized the Romanov features. "The woman was not a court dressmaker," commented Olga. "I very much doubt if she had ever seen any of my nieces."

Little by little, the extraordinary escape story became known in Berlin. Some people believed it, the Danish ambassador being among them. The young woman then called herself Mrs. Tchaikovsky. She alleged that she had been rescued by two brothers, one of whom she had married and who subsequently was supposed to have been killed. The other was said to have vanished without leaving a single trace. The whole story teemed with improbabilities and impossibilities. Nonetheless, some among the Russian émigrés in Berlin claimed to have recognized their Emperor's daughter, and the number of her supporters grew and grew.

The Empress Alexandra's elder sister, Princess Henry of Prussia, went to Berlin in 1922.

"It was an unsatisfactory meeting, but the woman's supporters said that Princess Henry had not known her niece very well and all the rest of it."

M. Gilliard, who had been tutor to the Emperor's children for thirteen years, and was married to Shura Tegleva, Grand Duchess Anastasia's nurse, also visited the hospital in Berlin. The patient recognized neither of them. A lady-in-waiting to the Empress Alexandra, Baroness Buxhoeveden, traveled all the way from England and returned with the same negative results. But the Anastasia supporters claimed that they were right. In their view, "the Grand Duchess" could not always recognize her visitors owing to the lapses in her memory.

"Unfortunately," said Olga, "the same excuse came to be accepted by some of our relatives. My Uncle Valdemar began sending money to

Berlin—since the woman appeared to be quite destitute. And there was the Duke of Leuchtenberg who had her to stay at his castle in Bavaria,[1] and Princess Xenia invited her to America, but that happened some time after my visit."

Colonel Koulikovsky and his wife went to stay at the Danish Embassy in Berlin. The ambassador, M. Zahle, was a fervent supporter of the lady.

"He had never met my niece, but he was a scholar, and the whole story seemed to him the greatest historical puzzle of the century, and he was determined to solve it."

The Grand Duchess was met in Berlin by the Gilliards, husband and wife, who accompanied her to the Mommsen Nursing Home. When Olga entered the room, the woman lying on a bed asked a nurse: "*Ist das die Tante?*"

"That," confessed Olga, "at once took me aback. A moment later I remembered that the young woman, having spent five years in Germany, would naturally have learnt the language, but then I heard that when she was rescued from that canal in 1920, she spoke nothing but German—when she spoke at all—which was not often. I readily admit that a ghastly horror experienced in one's youth can work havoc with one's memory, but I have never heard of any ghastly experience endowing anyone with a knowledge they had not had before it happened. My nieces knew no German at all. Mrs. Anderson did not seem to understand a word of Russian or English, the two languages all the four sisters had spoken since babyhood. French came a little later, but German was never spoken in the family."

The Grand Duchess spent nearly four days by Mrs. Anderson's bed. Hour by hour, Olga went on searching for the least clue to establish the woman's identity.

"My beloved Anastasia was fifteen when I saw her for the last time in the summer of 1916. She would have been twenty-four in 1925. I thought that Mrs. Anderson looked much older than that. Of course, one had to make allowances for a very long illness and the general poor condition of her health. All the same, my niece's features could not possibly have altered out of all recognition. The nose, the mouth, the eyes were all different."

The Grand Duchess remarked that the interviews were made all the more difficult by Mrs. Anderson's attitude. She would not answer some of the questions, and looked angry when those questions were repeated. Some Romanov photographs were shown to her, and there was not a flicker of recognition in her eyes. The Grand Duchess had brought a small icon of St. Nicholas, the patron saint of the imperial family. Mrs. Anderson looked at it so indifferently that it was obvious the icon said nothing to her.

"Naturally, all of that may have been due to the badly shattered memory," acknowledged the Grand Duchess. "All the same, memory lapses could not account for everything. There were so many other discrepancies. I knew the story of the supposed journey from Ekaterinburg to Bucharest. To begin with, Mrs. Anderson maintained that she had kept away from her cousin Marie[2] because she was pregnant at the time and was afraid of going near the Queen. Now please remember that it all happened in 1918 or 1919. If Mrs. Anderson had indeed been Anastasia, Queen Marie would have recognized her on the spot. All my nieces had known their cousin since their childhood. Our two families were most closely united. Marie would never have been shocked at anything, and a niece of mine would have known it. But the whole story is palpably false. I was convinced then, and I am now, that it is so from beginning to end. Just think of the supposed rescuers—vanishing into thin air, as it were. Had Nicky's daughter been really saved, her rescuers would have known just what it meant to them. Every royal house in Europe would have rewarded them. Why, I am sure that my mother would not have hesitated to empty her jewel box in gratitude. There is not one tittle of genuine evidence in the story. The woman keeps away from the one relative who would have been the first to recognize her, understand her desperate plight, and sympathize with her. Instead the woman makes her way to Berlin in order to ask help from an aunt who was one of the most straitlaced women in her generation. My niece would have known that her condition would indeed have shocked Princess Henry of Prussia. No and no again," said Olga decisively, "none of it makes sense to me, and after all I stood nearest to Anastasia."

She paused for one moment and glanced at the chest where she kept her niece's souvenirs.

"That child," she went on softly, "was as dear to me as if she were my own daughter. As soon as I had sat down by that bed in the Mommsen Nursing Home, I knew I was looking at a stranger. The spiritual bond between my dear Anastasia and myself was so strong that neither time nor any ghastly experience could have interfered with it. I don't really know what name to give to that feeling—but I do know that it was wholly absent. I had left Denmark with something of a hope in my heart. I left Berlin with all hope extinguished."

But although the Grand Duchess put no credence in Mrs. Anderson's story, she was deeply sorry for the woman.

"Somehow or other she did not strike me as an out-and-out impostor. Her brusqueness warred against it. A cunning impostor would have done all she could to ingratiate herself with people like Princess Henry of Prussia and myself. But Mrs. Anderson's manner would have put anyone off. My own conviction is that all of it started with some unscrupulous people who hoped they might lay their hands on at least a share of the fabulous and utterly non-existent Romanov fortune. The woman looked ill enough in 1925. She must have been far worse in 1920. I had a feeling that she was "briefed," as it were, but far from perfectly. The mistakes she made could not all be attributed to lapses of memory. For instance, she had a scar on one of her fingers and she kept telling everybody that it had been crushed because of a footman shutting the door of a landau too quickly. And at once I remembered the real incident. It was Marie, her eldest sister, who got her hand hurt rather badly, and it did not happen in a carriage but on board the imperial train. Obviously someone, having heard something of the incident, had passed a garbled version of it to Mrs. Anderson. Then again I heard that at a party in Berlin, when she was offered some vodka, Mrs. Anderson said: "How nice! It does remind me of the days at Tsarskoe Selo!" Vodka certainly would not have brought any such reminder to my niece." The Grand Duchess's voice rang very dry. "My nieces never touched either wine or spirits—and indeed how could they at their age? Alicky, having drunk nothing but water in her early life, had an occasional glass of port with her meal. Only when there were guests for dinner would vodka and hors d'oeuvres be served before the soup, but the children did not dine with their parents. As to Nicky, I should say that he was the most abstemious Romanov in history."

The interviews at the nursing home had begun on a very strained note, but on the third day of the Grand Duchess's visit, Mrs. Anderson became much more friendly and began talking more easily.

"I had the impression that she was getting tired of playing a part someone had assigned to her. She nearly admitted to me that some people always told her what she was to say on certain occasions. She did in fact admit that a scar, allegedly resulting from the blows on her head at Ekaterinburg, had been caused by her tubercular condition. I felt really sorry for the woman by the time I left her. And how really imprudent I was in going at all! My mother was right. I can't tell you what stories some unscrupulous people made out of my visit. My refusal to recognize my niece in Mrs. Anderson was attributed to a telegram I was supposed to have received from my sister Xenia in England instructing me not to acknowledge the relationship on any account. I never received any such telegram. And then people switched 'round and said that I had recognized my niece because of the few letters and a scarf I sent to her from Denmark. I know I should never have done so, but I did it out of pity. You have no idea how wretched that woman looked!"

Having read Mrs. Anderson's autobiography, I asked the Grand Duchess if the account of her visit which appears in the book tallied with what really happened. In the book, Olga, wearing a red coat, her face expressing excitement and pleasure, came into the room and at once embraced and kissed Mrs. Anderson.

"It's a complete fabrication," insisted the Grand Duchess. "For one thing, I did not possess a red coat. For another, I neither hugged nor kissed the woman. Indeed, I spoke very formally, using the German *Sie* all through. I would not have dreamt of saying *Du* to a stranger."

When I asked what in her opinion was the reason for it all, Olga had no hesitation in saying that she believed that some of those who had first "sponsored" Mrs. Anderson had their eye on a great Romanov fortune abroad, more specifically in England. There was no truth in any of those stories. Olga said that all the Romanovs had withdrawn their deposits in foreign banks to help with the war effort in 1914. In particular, the Emperor's foreign investments had helped to pay for the entire Red Cross equipment. The only sum which could not be withdrawn was in a bank in Berlin. The amount ran into millions, but after the defeat of Germany and the dizzing fall of the mark, those millions were not enough to buy a pack of cigarettes.

"That is the reason why none of us who managed to escape had funds to enable us to live comfortably in exile. Most malicious rumors about that 'fortune' began floating about soon after Mrs. Anderson's appearance in Berlin in 1920. I heard that it ran into astronomical figures. It was all fantastic and terribly vulgar. Would my mother have accepted a pension from King George V if we had any money in England? It does not make sense."

At the end of 1925, Queen Alexandra died at Sandringham. The two sisters were like twins in everything except their age. The Queen's death dealt an irreparable blow to the old Empress. At first, it left her stunned. When she recovered from the first shock, she had the air of someone who had lost her way in a wilderness. Almost overnight, Marie gave in to the demands of her years. She became feeble. She lost all zest for life. She ceased going out, and Hvidøre held her a virtual prisoner for the remaining three years of her life.

Those three years were very hard for Olga. Her mother, all her varied ailments notwithstanding, kept refusing medical help. She became suspicious of her ladies-in-waiting and of all the servants, and insisted on her daughter being continually in her bedroom. The poor Grand Duchess hardly ever had a moment to spare for her husband and children. And week by week, month by month, the aged Empress stepped further and further back into the past.

"My mother never spoke of Nicky or the children, though she would look for hours at their photographs which were all over her bedroom. Then she began worrying about her jewel box. She was convinced that burglars were after it and she had it moved from under her bed so that she might look at it whenever she wished. Xenia sometimes came over from England on a short visit, and she and I would ask my mother for a keepsake or two, and she always refused. I believe she knew perfectly well that neither of her two daughters had any business sense. She would merely say, "You will have all of it when I am gone." There was certainly no Romanov gold in any bank in England, but there was a sizable fortune in my mother's bedroom at Hvidøre. I often saw her looking at that box with such anxiety in her eyes—just as though she foresaw all the trouble to come."

The Empress Marie was right. The Romanovs were certainly anything but practical. Olga would not have had a single trinket if it had not been for her faithful maid's cunning and courage. Grand Duchess Xenia had succeeded in bringing most of her jewels out of Russia. The collection included her famous black pearls, but, according to what Olga told me, Xenia lost almost everything by entrusting the sale of these priceless gems to others who mismanaged the whole affair.

Grand Duchess Olga with her second husband Nicholas Koulikovsky and sons Goury (in Olga's arms) and Tikhon. Denmark, 1921.

The Empress's last years were not made any easier by her relations' pressure that she should part with her famous collection. In truth, it was a great treasure trove, its value considerably increased by several beautiful pieces bequeathed to her by Queen Alexandra. Presently King Christian X began dropping broad hints that he expected a share from the sale. Again, Grand Duke Alexander, writing from his comfortable retreat in France, repeatedly urged the Empress Marie if not to sell, then at least to pawn the jewelry in order to enable the family to open a paper factory, which, according to the Grand Duke, would bring untold benefits to all the Romanovs. In England, Grand Duchess Xenia found herself in difficulties she did not see a way to solve except by the sale of her share. In brief, the Empress Marie's box interested everybody.

Colonel Koulikovsky, keeping strictly aloof from all these family plans, conjectures, and wrangles, could not but notice how seldom, if at all, his wife's opinion was asked. In the end, he advised Olga to try and look after her own interests, but from all I learned from her, the Grand Duchess does not seem to have done anything about it.

"All of it was so distasteful," was her comment.

From England, King George V wrote to his "dear Aunt Minnie" to suggest that her jewelry should be deposited in some bank vault in London. He also promised that he would himself see to the arrangements for the sale. "Dear Aunt Minnie," however, stonily refused to be parted from her box—in spite of the arguments of her nephew in England and all the Romanov relations. The famous box remained in her bedroom until the day of her death.

In October, 1928, Marie fell into a coma. Xenia, who had arrived from England a week earlier, and Olga kept a vigil in her room for three days and nights. The Empress never recovered consciousness and died on the thirteenth of October.

Her body was taken to Amalienborg Castle. The final decision about the funeral rested with the King who at first declared that there was no need for his aunt, an ex-Empress, to have a state funeral. That on its own would not have greatly mattered to her daughters, but they felt it was a deep injury to their mother's rank and dignity. "In the end," Olga told me, "my cousin had to change his mind owing to the pressure of public opinion."

But having given a reluctant consent, the King hedged it 'round with unpleasant conditions, one of them being that Father Leonid Koltcheff, the Empress's private confessor, was not permitted to enter the cathedral in the vestments of a Russian Orthodox priest for fear the Roman Catholics might demand the right to hold services in the cathedral of the predominantly Protestant Danes. This, however, did not faze faithful Father Koltcheff. He managed to sneak in, wearing a long coat over his flowing robes, and whispered a Russian prayer over the imperial coffin.

The Dowager Empress leaving her car on her way to the Russian Church in Copenhagen, 1928. Her faithful Cossack Yashchek is assisting her on this rare venture out from Villa Hvidøre.

The coffin, draped in imperial purple, was taken to Roskilde Cathedral, the traditional burial place of the Danish royal family. For the last time, all the pageantry of imperial Russia came to life, however briefly, as a tribute to the last Empress. Every royal house in Europe was represented, and Russian émigrés in their hundreds flocked to Denmark, many members of the Romanov House among them.

"It was really ironic—so many of them hardly gave a thought to my mother during her years of exile, but all hurried to the funeral—even my cousin, Grand Duke Cyril, who should have had the grace to stay away," Olga said grimly.[3]

Barely two or three days after the funeral, King Christian X called on Olga for the sole purpose of ascertaining if her mother's jewelry was still at Hvidøre. The Grand Duchess, appalled, answered that she did not know for certain. She believed the box was on its way to London.

In his memoirs, the late Sir Frederick Ponsonby admitted that he had been instructed by King George V to have the jewels brought over to England for safety. Ponsonby asked Sir Peter Bark[4] to go to Denmark. He told the story of Bark going to Copenhagen and meeting the two Grand Duchesses. Bark explained that the King had sent him and that it was thought advisable to have the jewels taken to London, there to be kept in a bank-safe until the sisters had decided what they wished done with them. According to Ponsonby's account, both Grand Duchesses accepted the suggestion. The jewel box was sealed in their presence, taken to the British Legation in Copenhagen, and then shipped to England immediately.

But Grand Duchess Olga told me that the story in Ponsonby's memoirs was inaccurate. She did not see Bark, nor was the box sealed and removed in her presence. Her sister Xenia alone knew of the arrangement.

"I knew nothing at all until the next day when Xenia told me that the box was already out of Denmark. I approved of the general plan and I felt very grateful to Georgie for his concern on our behalf. What happened in Copenhagen was no fault of his. Xenia took it upon herself to arrange things. I was given to understand that the matter could not concern me very closely because I had a commoner for a husband." The matter of the jewel box had obviously made a gulf between the sisters.

To make the situation even more humiliating for Olga, she stayed in Denmark but Xenia hurried back to England almost at once. She was present at the opening of the box at Buckingham Palace when Ponsonby had his first and last chance to appraise the fabulous jewels before their dispersal. They proved to be even more magnificent than he had thought. "Ropes of the most wonderful pearls were taken out, all graduated, the largest being the size of a big cherry. . . ." he wrote in his memoirs. "Cabuchon emeralds and large rubies and sapphires were laid out. . . ."

The jewelry was valued by Messrs. Hennel & Sons, who were prepared to make an immediate advance of £100,000 on the contents of the box. Ponsonby says that "eventually those jewels fetched £350,000."

King George V asked Sir Edward Peacock, a Canadian-born director of the Bank of England, to look after the financial affairs of his two Romanov cousins. After Grand Duchess Olga's death, I was told by Sir Edward that the sum entrusted to him in 1929 was exactly £100,000, of which £60,000 went to Xenia and the remainder to Olga. Yet, according to Ponsonby's account, there was the balance of £250,000. I mentioned the discrepancy to Sir Edward Peacock, but he could not throw any light on the subject, though he said that Ponsonby's memory may have failed him in this instance.

That, however, can hardly be the case. Ponsonby might well have been mistaken about some minor point, but hardly about the aggregate value of the Romanov jewel hoard. Moreover, it is common knowledge that the collection was worth infinitely more than £100,000. Some people, including Sir Peter Bark, estimated its value at half a million pounds. There are no grounds for doubting Sir Edward Peacock's statement about the sum eventually given to the two Grand Duchesses. Therefore, the mystery of the missing £250,000 still remains unsolved.

Soon after the sale, some of the more important pieces in the collection appeared in Queen Mary's possession, as the Grand Duchess told me, adding that Lady Bark had also acquired a Romanov jewel.

The bedchamber at Villa Hvidøre, where the Dowager Empress died in 1928.

What could be the answer to the puzzle? Did the authorities feel that they were justified in retaining the balance of £250,000 to recoup themselves for the upkeep of the Empress Marie, her family, and her little court in Denmark? If such was the case, would not Queen Mary have made it clear to her cousins who believed themselves to have been dependent on the generosity of their English kin? It would have made a vast difference to the morale of the refugees if they had known that their debt to England had been settled in full.

The Grand Duchess always avoided the subject. On one occasion only did she shed her reserve a little.

"Yes, indeed," she said, "there are certain aspects in this affair which I could never understand, and I have tried not to think about it too much, and certainly I've never talked to anyone, except my husband. I know that May was passionately fond of fine jewelry. I remember how in 1925 the Soviet government, being badly in need of foreign currency, sent a lot of Romanov jewels to be sold in England, and I heard that May had bought quite a few—including a collection of Fabergé's Easter eggs. I also know that at least one item of my own property, looted from the palace in Petrograd, was among the lot shipped to England, but its price proved too high even for May, and I suppose it is still in the Kremlin. It was one of my wedding presents—an exquisite fan made of mother-of-pearl and studded all over with diamonds and pearls."

I could see that the Grand Duchess did not really care about the ultimate fate of her mother's treasure trove or even about the apportioning of the money. What had bitten hard into her was the way in which all the transactions were carried out. She, Olga, might not have existed for all the notice taken of her during those difficult weeks after her mother's death.

Hvidøre, as Olga realized only too clearly, could never be her home in the future. It was far too big and its upkeep beyond anything she dared to contemplate.

After Xenia's departure for England, Olga and her family stayed at Amalienborg. But they were not allowed to stay there for long. King Christian sent a cousin of his, Prince Axel, with a peremptory message that they were to leave the palace as soon as possible.

A Danish millionaire, Mr. Rasmussen, came to the rescue. He owned a large estate in the neighborhood of Hvidøre, and he engaged Colonel

Koulikovsky, an expert horseman, to manage his stables. The Grand
Duchess and her husband were only too happy to escape from the gloomy
Amalienborg, where the King, enraged by the disappearance of his aunt's
jewelry, never lost an opportunity to bring humiliation to his cousin's door.

Presently, Olga's lien on Hvidøre was confirmed. She was able to sell
it and she bought a property with the proceeds. But all of it took nearly
four years. Not until 1932 did she and her family take possession of
Knudsminde, a large farm in Ballerup about fifteen miles northwest of
Copenhagen.

"We felt we had reached a haven, there to spend the rest of our lives in
peace. We never envisaged another move. Amalienborg receded into a distance. Knudsminde was wholly ours, and the King's bad temper and malice
could not touch us there. It was a humble farmhouse—a far cry from
palace and castle, but it was a home. It meant hard work, and I welcomed
all of it. I realized that it was a thousand times preferable to be a poor exile
among poor peasantry than among rich royalty and aristocracy. I came to
love those sturdy, hard-working folk. I believe they accepted us in their turn
not for what we were but because we worked hard."

There was plenty of hired labor to be had, but the Grand Duchess and
the Colonel took their share in everything. They kept horses, Jersey cattle,
pigs, and poultry. The housework was divided between the indefatigable
Mimka, Olga's personal maid, and Tatiana Gromova, who had been nurse
to Grand Duchess Anastasia and who, escaping through Finland, joined
Grand Duchess Olga in 1934. Also women from the neighboring village
came and lent a hand.

For the first time since 1914, Olga felt that she belonged to herself. Now
a certain amount of leisure fell to her share, and she turned to her painting,
neglected for so many years. Little by little, her delicate studies of flowers
and trees began to be sold in Copenhagen and elsewhere.

"Those were peaceful years," she admitted to me. "I had my husband and
my sons. Nobody interfered with us. We were not wealthy, but we managed
to pay our way. We all worked hard, and it was gorgeous—living a family
life under our own roof."

She persisted in calling herself a farmer's wife, but she was daughter and sister of Tsars, and her royal relations came to Knudsminde. Occasionally Olga went to Germany and France. All the émigrés loved and respected her, but she kept herself aloof from all factions. Once a year she went to Sweden, to Sophiro by the sea, to stay with the Crown Prince and Princess.

"I used to go to Sophiro in the old days when Oscar II was King. I did not much like it then. But Gustav and Louise transformed the place. That red-stone castle was just like a home—so welcoming they were. I loved my annual holiday with them. Gustav is a keen archeologist, and a botanist too. He always gave me plants to take back to Denmark. And Louise was just incomparable. Do you know that they had a household rule—no tips to be given to the servants? It was such a relief for a poor relation like myself. And always I found such gaiety at Sophiro. I would feel younger and more buoyant on my return home."

Yet the Grand Duchess, for all her affection for the Swedish cousins, was never sorry to return to Ballerup. The gray walls of Knudsminde stood for home. Her mother's blood began stirring in Olga, and she learned at last that Denmark spoke in accents not altogether alien to her. Her two sons, their education ended, entered the Royal Danish Guards. Presently both of them married Danish girls. The Grand Duchess, painting, walking, or gardening, felt that she had earned a right to a peaceful sunset in her mother's country.

But no permanent peace seemed ordained for the sister of the last Romanov sovereign. The thunders of 1939 rolled across Europe and by the end of 1940 the Nazis had overrun the whole of Denmark. At first things were relatively quiet, but later King Christian X was interned for his implacable refusal to cooperate with the invaders. The Danish army was dissolved, and Olga's sons were in prison for several months.

"And then the Luftwaffe opened a camp in Ballerup. The German officers, on hearing that I was the Tsar's sister, came to pay their respects, and I had no alternative but to receive them."

Hitler's invasion of Russia brought a terrible complication into Olga's life. Untold thousands of Russian émigrés, trusting Hitler's promise to free Russia from the Communists, enlisted under the German colors, and great numbers of them came to Denmark for no other purpose than that of seeing the sister of their martyred Emperor. A temporary camp was set up in the neighborhood of the farm, and the Grand Duchess did not close her door to those compatriots of hers. But to the Danes, humiliated by the German occupation, the mere sight of those Russians in the hated German uniform was more than a passing provocation, and Olga found herself torn in two.

The Danish resistance began gathering momentum. Many Danes risked their lives and often lost them in trying to get free of the hated alien yoke. And here was a Russian Grand Duchess, daughter of a Danish princess, who had lived among them for so many years, and now she joined issue with them and dispensed her hospitality to the enemy and the enemy's friends. It would have been impossible for the Danish farmers and peasants to see the situation from Olga's point of view, nor did she expect them to do so.

She, having kept aloof from politics all her life, now found herself involved in a whirlpool of dangerous intrigues. As a Romanov, she could not but take her stand with the Allies against Hitler. She had by no means forgotten the Kaiser's war, her sons were in the Danish army, and she owed much to Denmark. But she was a Russian, and she felt that she must extend help and sympathy to those countrymen of hers who wore German uniforms in the hope that Hitler's victory would bring about the downfall of Communism in Russia. Those unfortunate Russian émigrés were wholly misled. Some of them came to Europe from the four corners of the world, and all alike were blindly ignorant about the conditions within Russia and lulled themselves with the idea that the Communist forces would never withstand the panzer onslaught. They did not think of Hitler's victory except in those terms. It never occurred to any among them that the Nazi triumph would have put the whole of Europe under a yoke as bitter and vicious as that of the Kremlin.

In the end, all the émigré hopes were crushed into dust. To add to the peril, Stalin's troops were almost at Denmark's door. The Communists began making one attempt after another to have the Grand Duchess extradited on the charge of having helped some among her countrymen to escape to the West, and Denmark was hardly in a position to resist the Kremlin demands at the time. The charge was not wholly unfounded, though it would not have constituted a crime in anyone else's eyes. After the German collapse, many Russians who had fought in Hitler's army came to Knudsminde seeking asylum. The Grand Duchess could offer no real help to them all, though she admitted to me that a man was hidden in her attic for several weeks. Yet those émigrés were in truth between the devil and the blue sea, and those who had come from the Allied countries realized that few doors in Europe would now be open to them.

But the Grand Duchess and her family stood in peril of their own lives. Russian pressure was increasing. The atmosphere in Ballerup grew more and more tense, and it became obvious that their days in Denmark were numbered.

It was by no means easy for Olga, now aged sixty-six, to be uprooted once again. After many heart-searchings and family councils, they decided to emigrate to Canada. The Danish government realized that the Koulikovsky family must leave as quickly and unobtrusively as possible. The danger of the Grand Duchess being kidnapped by the Russians was not at all imaginary.

Civilian traveling was not easy in 1948 and many difficulties had to be overcome. Sir Edward Peacock helped greatly with the numerous preliminary negotiations. In the end, the Koulikovsky family were permitted to go to Canada as "agricultural immigrants," which meant that they would have to work on a farm once they got there. It proved easy enough to sell Knudsminde, but to get the purchase money and what other funds Olga possessed out of Denmark meant almost insurmountable difficulties. Nothing but the help offered by the American wife of Prince Vigo would have solved the problem. She it was who opened a dollar account in New York in the Grand Duchess's name and agreed to accept payment in Danish currency.

All the plans were made in great secrecy. Nonetheless, there must have been some leakage somewhere. They were first going to England, and a few days before a clerk from a shipping firm appeared with the tickets for their cabins on board S.S. *Batory*. One of the directors of that firm was

Prince Axel. The boat's name s
aid nothing at all to the Grand
Duchess, but when she mentioned
it to some friends in Copenhagen,
they were aghast.

"You can't possibly leave by
that Polish boat," they told her. "It
is a trap."

"I shivered," the Grand Duchess
told me, "when I realized that once
aboard a Communist ship, all of us
could be taken off by Communist
agents and sent to Moscow—for a
so-called trial on a charge of high treason. I pretended to be ill and the
Batory left without us."

*The farmhouse at
Knudsminde.*

Not until May, 1948, did the Koulikovsky family leave Denmark on
board a Danish troopship bound for London, but the Grand Duchess by no
means left all danger behind when she said good-by to Denmark. Just how
real and immediate that danger was can be gathered from the following
account given me by Mr. J. S. P. Armstrong, Agent General of the province
of Ontario in England. It was obvious that both the British and Canadian
governments considered themselves responsible for the Grand Duchess's
safety and took the strictest security measures for her protection.

After the war [Mr. Armstrong wrote], Scotland Yard was in frequent
touch with me, as a security check, about many foreigners wishing to
migrate to Canada. I think it was mid–April 1948 when they first con-
tacted me about the Grand Duchess. In her case it was to ascertain
whether or not she would be welcome, given sanctuary and normal
protection or whether her presence would create difficulties and
embarrassment for our authorities. I stated that I was confident she
would be welcome and that both Canadian and Ontario authorities
would give her every reasonable protection.

From the conversations it appeared there was some urgency about

Princess Marina of Greece (on left) and the Grand Duchess Olga at Knudsminde, Denmark.

the matter, that it had received consideration on the highest level, and that for her safety it was important that the Grand Duchess and her family leave Britain as soon as possible. I subsequently learned they had been seriously threatened in Denmark and this had necessitated their quick departure. The same people were making efforts to locate their whereabouts in England. I was sworn to secrecy and asked if I would do what I could to assist in their going to Canada, if this course was finally adopted. I agreed to help in every way.

About a week later Sir Edward Peacock asked to speak to me on a confidential matter, seeking my advice on whether I thought Ontario would be a suitable home for the Grand Duchess and if she would be well received. He told me the history of the family and their serious plight, and I expressed my opinion that they would be welcome and offered assistance.

Sir Edward asked me to see the Grand Duchess at her home and advise her and her family, giving details about the Canadian way of life, cost of living, housing, agriculture, etc. He arranged my first interview, stressing the need for security as regards their address and future plans.

I well recall the circumstances surrounding my first call at one of the grace-and-favour apartments of Hampton Court Palace where Queen Mary had given them temporary quarters. It was in a section of a low row of houses on a public street, and I had difficulty in finding it. On approaching the number I noticed a man who for no apparent reason was standing in the rain on the opposite side of the street. I suddenly thought that as I drove a big Canadian car with "Canada" plates on it, it would be stupid to park outside the house so I drove on for two blocks to a side street and walked back. The man was still there in the heavy rain—and I presumed he was a plain-clothes policeman.

I was ushered into what appeared to be a small dining-room, sparsely furnished, on the ground floor, with no fire in the grate and the curtains drawn. It was so cold and damp that I did not take off my coat. Within a few minutes the Grand Duchess came and introduced herself, asking me to take off my coat and be seated, and she thanked me for coming. She was warmly dressed in a long outfit of heavy dark material from her neck almost to her ankles, and had a heavy woollen shawl over her shoulders. She was very nervous. The Grand Duchess was a most charming, intelligent and fascinating personality. She possessed a regal bearing, like her great friend, Queen Mary. When I saw her, she appeared tired, sad and harassed with strain and worry, but in spite of this there was evidence of determination and courage in every bone of her body. She was searching for a haven where they could live in peace and security—a simple rural life—with the minimum of publicity and social life. She did not fear death for herself, and her main concern was to save her children and grandchildren from extinction.

During the talk she brought in her husband, Colonel Koulikovsky, and her sons, and they asked me questions. The Colonel was not very well, and although he did not ask many questions, he listened intently. I was offered some refreshment and the Grand Duchess, who apparently made all major family decisions, instructed me to proceed with the arrangements.

She spoke very quickly and clearly, explaining their problem and how vital it was that she and her whole family leave Britain as soon as possible. She thought they would be safer in Canada than the U.S.A. She stated she was grateful for my offer of help, and for over an hour fired questions at me on matters concerning immigration, transportation, finance, cost of living, cost of a farm, suitable location, agriculture, and Canadians in general. Although the sons seemed pleased with her quick decision, the husband did not show the same enthusiasm and thought the matter should receive more consideration. There was no argument. The Grand Duchess said they were going, and showed me to the door.

A time was set for our next talk to report on progress made. Only

Grand Duchess Olga with her grandchildren, Xenia and Leonid, in the garden at Knudsminde in Denmark, the day before her departure to Canada, 1948.

Grand Duchess Olga and Colonel Kouilikovsky with their son Goury at their Knudsminde farmhouse in Denmark, near Copenhagen.

personal contact was possible and for security reasons neither telephone nor mail could be used. I made two further calls on the Grand Duchess in May and she, her husband and two sons came to see me at Ontario House just before departure to thank me for my help.

Mr. Armstrong's narrative is here inserted in full because of its twofold value. In the first place, it presents Olga in a light she herself would have been only too pleased to hide under the bushel. Having reached an important crossroads, she, a daydreaming, impractical artist, seemed to have put on a different personality—active and vigorous in spite of her weariness, quick at grasping issues that mattered and at arriving at the decision more or less independently of her family's reaction. The second point carries a much wider implication.

The year was 1948, precisely thirty-one years after the October Revolution of 1917. One would have thought that the Romanov family would have ceased to trouble the Kremlin, but all the facts point to the contrary. In Denmark, with the Soviet troops massed so near the frontier, the peril was immediate. That it should have been so in England speaks for itself. The magic of the Romanov name was by no means dead, and the peril menacing the Grand Duchess was not born in anyone's idle imagination.

In their hurry to leave Denmark, nobody had remembered to get a passport for Olga's faithful and indispensable Mimka, now aged eighty-three. Departure had to be delayed for a fortnight before Emilia Tenso's papers were ready, and the Grand Duchess left Hampton Court fairly frequently, her activities adding fresh burdens to Scotland Yard.

"I rather welcomed the delay," she told me. "There were so many

people to see. I even managed
to find some relatives of my dear
old Nana, and there was also
Jimmy, gone to Buckinghamshire to
spend his retirement. I had tea with
him. He had one of my paintings
on a wall. When I saw it I cried, "I
never knew I could paint so well!"
It was such fun to see him and to
talk over the old days. There was
also May's eighty-first birthday party
and quite a few private calls at
Marlborough House."

"Did you mention the matter of
the jewelry to Queen Mary?" I
ventured to ask.

Olga shook her head vigorously.
"Why create unnecessary bitterness?" she asked.

On June second, 1948, Grand
Duchess Olga and her family

boarded the *Empress of Canada* at Liverpool and one more day of sad
farewells was added to her life. Besides the sixty-six-year-old Grand
Duchess and her sixty-seven-year-old husband, the party consisted of their
two sons, Tikhon, aged thirty, and Goury, a year younger, their Danish-born
wives Agnete and Ruth, and two grandchildren, Xenia, aged six, and
Leonid, five.

The Grand Duchess Olga with her family outside the farmhouse at Knudsminde, Denmark, the day before their departure to Canada, 1948. From left to right: Agnete, Tikhon, Olga, Nicholas, Ruth, Goury, and in front, Xenia and Leonid.

"As the gray shores of England receded in the mist, something like a
curtain seemed to fall over a lifetime spent in Russia and Denmark. Of
course, I knew perfectly well that I would never see Europe again. I also
knew that I would keep many dear and tender memories to the end of
my days."

A New World in the Evening

Her past chequered and darkened with so many griefs, perils, and hardships, it could easily have been imagined that the Grand Duchess, stepping forth into an absolutely new world, would have been dismayed at the prospect of yet again having to adapt herself to utterly unfamiliar conditions on a continent where, for all she knew, old ways and customs would hamper rather than help. The years had not broken her, but inevitably, they had left scars.

But conscious of the finality of her farewell to Europe, she did not permit herself to indulge in prolonged nostalgia. Canada began looking like an adventure, and adventures must be started whole-heartedly or not at all. Her high spirits were put to severe test during the voyage. It proved to be the worst crossing ever made by the *Empress of Canada*, so the captain told the Grand Duchess. Nearly all the passengers, including her own family, were stricken and kept below. She and her Mimka were not ill, and Mimka watched over her mistress and kept an eye on an old jacket Olga had bought for her in the Crimea all those years ago. Mimka kept the jacket under her pillow during the night and wore it all day long. The jacket would have seemed surprisingly heavy to anyone picking it up in a casual way, but Mimka saw to it that nobody had a chance of picking it up. In between the cloth and the lining, the faithful old servant had sewn in several little chamois leather bags, containing all that was left of her mistress's jewelry. Neither the number of the trinkets nor their quality could be compared with the late Empress Marie's treasure trove, but in Mimka's eyes even a slim gold pin of no particular value could evoke the pithy and comforting Russian equivalent of "it may come in useful"—*prigoditza*.

Grand Duchess Olga's youngest son, Goury, and his first wife, Ruth Schwartz, in Grand Duchess Olga's living room at the farm in Campbellville. In the background are Grand Duchess Olga's many icons and photographs, many of which appear in this book.

"The old liner kept tossing and rolling all the time. I don't think we had many quiet hours on board. I could not understand why I was not seasick like the rest of my family. Never in my life have I been a really good sailor. I would often succumb on board the *Standard*—to my nieces' distress."

Some among the crew spoke about the boat as "the drunken Duchess." The joke was overheard by a Danish journalist on board, he took it to be a reference to Olga, and brought his indignant complaint to the captain. "It is most disrespectful and grossly unfair—Her Imperial Highness is well known for her abstemious habits," said the Dane, and the captain assured him that the joke had no reference whatever to the Grand Duchess. Somehow or other, she came to hear of the incident, and was immensely amused. She said she would not have minded in the least if the joke really referred to her.

The *Empress of Canada* docked at Halifax. The Grand Duchess and her party, met by the Danish Consul General and many officials of the C.P.R., at once boarded a train for Montreal. The bad crossing left its aftereffects on her family. Colonel Koulikovsky's spine, injured during the First World War, began troubling him again. Olga's grandchildren were restless, and the rest of the party wondered rather uneasily about the prospects awaiting them at the end of the journey.

But the Grand Duchess chose to plunge herself into the moment. Having settled her husband on the train as comfortably as she could, she turned to the window.

"The immense spaces I saw deeply impressed me. I felt at home. Everything spoke to me of the vastness I had known in Russia."

At Montreal they were welcomed by a group of enthusiastic Russian émigrés, many among whom had traveled for hundreds of miles to welcome the Tsar's sister. A couple of them even claimed to be distantly related to the Grand Duchess. "I did not know at the time that these 'relatives' stood at the head of an endless procession of imaginary cousins, nephews and nieces, and other imposters who seemed to spring from every corner of the globe. The American continent was particularly suited to producing them. They thrived there better than anywhere else."

The arrival of the Koulikovsky party in Toronto was quieter. To her dismay, she discovered that "the agricultural immigrants" had a splendid suite reserved for them at the Royal York Hotel, supposed to be the largest of its kind in the Commonwealth.

"All thick carpets, exquisite curtains, masses of exotic flowers, and what-not! I just couldn't endure it, and my family disliked that grandeur just as much as I did—except for poor, dear Mimka who kept arguing that the place being more or less the size of a palace, it was fitting that her mistress should stay there. But we had to disappoint her. In two days we moved to a very humble guesthouse run by a friendly émigré couple. There were no rich carpets or comfortable armchairs, but what a pleasure it was to see icons hanging in every room and to have cabbage soup served with those tiny patties which we call *pirozhky*. Everybody in Toronto was most kind and helpful to us," added Olga warmly.

At that time the American consul was Mr. Malcolm Doherty, who proved of great assistance to the family. He and his wife had once stayed with the Koulikovskys at Knudsminde in Denmark.

However, the Koulikovskys had not come to Canada to be fêted or to enjoy little meat patties made in the old Russian way. They had to begin looking for a farmhouse to purchase. That took a little time. The lack of business experience notwithstanding, the Koulikovskys were spared all possible pitfalls because of the generously offered help of Mr. A. H. Creighton, an official of the C.P.R. All the necessary negotiations were conducted by him, and he did not disclose the identity of the prospective buyer. The glamor of a fabled fortune stiff clung to the Romanov name, and most real-estate agents would certainly have made capital of it. Day by day, the Grand Duchess, her husband, and Mr. Creighton toured the countryside.

"Oh, and I mustn't forget to mention Mimka. She insisted on coming with us every time. She made things rather difficult—so many farms were judged by her to be utterly unsuitable. Knudsminde hadn't mattered so very much since we did keep in close touch with my royal cousins. But here, in Canada, with no kings, dukes or princes to establish us, as it were, poor Mimka hugged the delusion that the bigger the farmhouse the better it answered my rank. However, her ways were so endearing that we always forgave her."

Not until the autumn of 1948 did they find a suitable steading, a two-hundred-acre farm in Halton County near Campbellville, some fifty miles west of Toronto. Even Mimka, however grudgingly, admitted that they might have done much worse. The large red-brick house stood among generously planned lawns. A private lane, edged by tall maples, led to it from the road. The whole produced an impression of a small country estate. Owing to Mr. Creighton's astuteness, the place was bought for fourteen thousand dollars, considerably less than it would have been if Olga's identity had been known from the start.

"It was a joy to move from Toronto, and I worked like a slave to turn the house into a real home. All our belongings turned up eventually, and there were dear mementos of the past in every one of the ten rooms. The place was a paradise for flowers...."

It seems good to realize that those first months in Canada proved some of the happiest in Olga's life. Day by day, week by week, she breathed more amply. The countryside 'round about the farm spoke to her in a voice she could recognize. All her hours of leisure were given to rambles. Echoes of a home she would never see again came from tree, shrub, and flower. Memories dearer than life itself grew clearer and clearer as Olga learned the landscape of Canadian spaces. She was more than satisfied; she felt happy. Her excitement like a brightly burning candle, she wrote to a friend:

"I found my favorite spring plants in the bush about here—the blue anemones—it was a happy moment because I adore them and thought I should never set eyes on them again. Now I have so much to look forward to—when they will begin to bloom I shall feel still more at home in Canada.... The woods were blue in spring at home with these same flowers...."

But that was a leisure pastime. They were farmers, and the Grand Duchess never forgot it. She gave all the help she could—particularly in the poultry yard. Gradually Colonel Koulikovsky got together a sizable herd of cattle. They decided to keep a few pigs as well. As farms went, their steading seemed small enough and manageable.

Yet difficulties greatly troubled them from the start. All the machinery, shipped over from Denmark at a considerable cost, proved virtually useless in Canada. Replacements were hard to get and cost dear. Farm labor proved difficult to find in Halton County. After a brief spell, Olga's two sons decided to look for some business opening in Toronto. They left Campbellville, together with their wives.

The Grand Duchess was grieved, but nothing seemed to daunt her for long. She had been a farmer's wife in Denmark, and she settled down to a similar existence in Canada. No longer conscious of being "an animal put on show in a gilded cage," Olga took keen pleasure in ordinary household tasks—cooking always excepted. She liked good food when it was placed

The Koulikovskys' mailbox enduring, as Grand Duchess Olga did, the harsh Canadian winter. Despite the excitement the community felt over the Grand Duchess, the Koulikovskys were, as this photo shows, just like everyone else.

before her, but she never missed it when it was not there, and she considered all elaborate culinary preparations a sheer waste of time which, as she thought, might have been employed in walking, painting, or even daydreaming. Mimka, her rheumatism gaining on her, did what she could, but it did not amount to much. Olga had a certain cunning with vegetables and she loved making bread. Otherwise, the household had to depend on the tins bought in Campbellville.

Inevitably, the Grand Duchess's arrival created a sensation in the neighborhood. All the farmers in Halton County proved kind, helpful, and deferential from the start. Bewildered by the complexities of Russian titles, they sometimes spoke of the Colonel and Olga as "the Tsar and his Queen." They were greatly intrigued by the rumor that Colonel Koulikovsky had been the owner of one thousand Palomino horses in Russia, the story probably originating from the fact that his regiment, the Akhtyrsky Hussars, had indeed possessed a big stud of those horses. The neighborhood never forgot that Olga was a Romanov, daughter and sister of Emperors, but her clothes, her simple manner, her undisguised pleasure in so many common things in life, all these soon put everybody at their ease. In no time she became "Olga" to the neighbors, and she gloried in being addressed in such a way.

To everybody's astonishment, the Grand Duchess not only endured but delighted in the long, cold Canadian winter. The snowy landscape warmed her heart. The generous log fires, the ice embroidery on window panes, the crunching of the snow under her feet, the peculiar wintry stillness of wood and field were all pages of a book she had read and loved since childhood.

Unfortunately, Olga's retirement in the heart of the Canadian countryside in no way discouraged reporters and press photographers. She had abhorred all publicity when living in a palace. Now she hated it more than ever and she was powerless to put a stop to it. A journalist from Copenhagen crossed the Atlantic for no other purpose than that of getting "the story" of a granddaughter of King Christian IX living in the Canadian wilderness. Presently, publishers in New York became interested. The Grand Duchess would be offered high sums for the rights to her autobiography. The offers must have been a temptation, since the grand-ducal finances continued limping from bad to worse, but Olga rejected all those offers even when the money might have extricated her from all immediate difficulties. But she could not write letters of refusal to reporters who descended upon her without any warning. Try as she would to avoid them, the Grand Duchess did not always succeed. They streamed to Halton County in dozens, they waylaid her in the garden, the poultry yard, and in the fields. They took snapshots of the slight old woman among cows, hen houses, and flower beds. They caught her seated at her ease, or trying to darn a sheet. They even peered through the windows and caught her at her heroic and decidedly inadequate efforts with broom and duster.

Reporters came and went away, and had to build their stories on what they had seen rather than on what they had heard, the mistress of that farmhouse having been very polite and taciturn.

In spite of all the difficulties, Canada proved good for her soul. Olga was no longer a poor relation in exile, her former splendor and its disappearance continually mourned by many among her more fortunate kin. In Canada, she was on her own.

The German Anastasia was by no means a solitary claimant to the Romanov name. When Olga went to Berlin in 1925, she could hardly have foreseen how many more encounters of that nature lay in the future. In fact, imposters haunted her to the very end of her life. She said to me:

"It was a good thing that I ended by getting, as it were, immune to their attacks. Otherwise they might have driven me mad. I had rather hoped that indifference would prove the best method of dealing with those people, but such a strategy did not always work. You have no idea how impertinent, callous, and obstinate some of them can be."

The Grand Duchess was harassed from the very beginning of her life in Halton County when a stranger in Toronto began writing frequent and lengthy letters to her. The woman did not say who she was but merely repeated that, being "a very close relative," she had the right to ask for an interview and to tell her story to the Grand Duchess. At first Olga merely ignored the letters. At last, however, she got exasperated and sent a short note refusing to see the woman.

That did not silence the "very close relative," but it made her change the way of approach.

"She started sending such really piteous letters that in the end I relented and said that I would see her just once. A date was arranged and my husband drove to Moffat to meet the train from Toronto, but he never brought the woman to the farmhouse. As soon as he saw her, he knew he could not possibly let me meet the woman. He told me she was just impossible. I have no idea how he managed it, but somehow or other he kept her talking on the platform and then succeeded in getting her on board the very next train for Toronto. He must have said something to silence her for good and all. I never heard from her again and I have no idea who she pretended to be."

Another imposter was a new and extremely vociferous Anastasia who lived in a small town in Illinois. She, too, began pestering her "beloved Aunt Olga" with interminable letters and it did not trouble her in the least that her beloved Aunt Olga never answered them. The woman ran an Anastasia Beauty Salon and her business apparently flourished. After a while, the lady in Illinois got tired of writing letters to Canada. She traveled all the way to Toronto, determined to make the "beloved aunt" see her. The Illinois Anastasia meant to get down to Campbellville but, on reaching Toronto, she heard a rumor which made her hurry to the German Consulate.

It so happened that just about that time Mrs. Anderson had brought her case before the German courts in an attempt to have her claim recognized in law. To Olga's anger and disgust, two German lawyers flew to Toronto to establish some details about the Grand Duchess's visit to Berlin in 1925. The German consul begged Olga to give them a brief interview. Her first impulse was to refuse: she wished to have nothing more to do with the case. But the consul continued pleading with her, and in the end she agreed, however reluctantly. "The brief interview" dragged on and on until the Grand Duchess began wondering if she were being trapped into answering questions which she did not properly understand. Angry and tired, she got up, said she had no more information to give, and walked out of the room, the embarrassed consul following her and murmuring his apologies. In the corridor outside, they almost ran into the Illinois Anastasia, who, having heard about the lawyers' arrival in Toronto, was waiting for the consul to see her so that she might state her own case and accuse the German Anastasia of fraud. The Illinois Anastasia overheard the consul's apologies addressed to an "Imperial Highness." It took her less than an instant to guess at Olga's identity and she rushed forward, crying:

"Aunt Olga! Dear Aunt Olga! At last!"

The Grand Duchess, too angry for speech, walked past her without a glance. Later it came to Olga's knowledge that the Illinois Anastasia had tried to win supporters in Toronto by insisting that she had recognized her dear aunt by her upper lip.

"For the first and only time in my life," said Olga wryly, "I learned that I can be recognized by some mysterious peculiarity of my upper lip. I suppose the woman went back to her beauty parlor in Illinois. At least, she stopped wasting stamps on letters to me."

Those were but two cases out of many. A woman, living in a luxurious villa on the shores of Lake Como, made herself out to be Grand Duchess Olga, Nicholas II's eldest daughter. In her turn, she insisted that the German Anastasia was an imposter since there were cast-iron proofs that all her three sisters had been murdered in 1918. The Lake Como pretender seemed to be in possession of considerable means. The appointments at the villa spoke of opulence. She was supposed to be secretly engaged to a royal gentleman, whose name and nationality were never disclosed. There even appeared an Anastasia in Japan! The Russian bishop in Tokyo, an old friend of the Grand Duchess, wrote that the woman was creating a stir even in Asia. "You must do something to stop it," he pleaded with Olga.

"What was there that I could do?" the Grand Duchess asked me. "All my relations and myself received conclusive proofs of the massacre. It was pure cruelty on the part of those adventurers to assume those identities—always with the hope of material gains. But there was nothing for me to do. I could not stoop to expose those shameful tricks. I could only ignore them. But all of it tortured me."

Once, when she and her husband were already in Cooksville, there was a knock at the door one evening. The Colonel went to open it and saw an undersized, unpleasantly featured man, who grinned and said in French:

"I don't suppose you will recognize me after all these years. I am Alexis. Please could I see Aunt Olga? I have brought her the story of my life."

The Grand Duchess heard. She felt nearly faint. The Colonel tried to prevent the stranger from entering the cottage, but the little man squeezed past him into the living room, put a bulky, greasy manuscript on the table, and stood there babbling away about some soldiers at Ekaterinburg who had taken pity on him all those years ago.

"I was very badly wounded but I was still alive, and they smuggled me out of the cellar. Later they handed me over to the French. An officer adopted me and brought me to France. I have always known whose son I was, but I did not wish to make it public. But I think it is time I did so, and I have written my life. I am sorry—I have forgotten all my Russian."

The Grand Duchess had long since schooled herself to accept the horrors of the Ekaterinburg massacre. She fervently believed that her brother and his entire family were at rest with their God. She held them both in prayer and in thought. Even when she decided to communicate her memories to me, she never said much about Ekaterinburg, nor would I ask her questions. I knew that it had never ceased to haunt her.

And here, under her own roof, was an unkempt little Frenchman talking on and on about the ghastliness of that July night in 1918. The Colonel may well have wanted to kick him outside. But the Grand Duchess listened and agreed to read his manuscript, though, of course, she knew he was no more her nephew than the dog lying by the fireplace.

In the end, the little man burst into tears and confessed his fraud. He was a Frenchman, had been to sea, and was now a dishwasher in New York. As I sat listening to Olga, I could well imagine what agony that evening must have brought to her door. And all she said was: "We were very sorry for him...."

The most recent Anastasia appeared in Montreal at the beginning of 1960. That woman, her real identity unknown, proved so persistent that the chief of Montreal police finally decided to send one of his men to Cooksville.

"I was asked if I would agree to have a color film of myself shown to that woman in Montreal," Olga said. "I agreed. I wanted to settle the silly business once and for all."

But some weeks later when the Grand Duchess lay very ill in a Toronto hospital, a Montreal police officer, accompanied by the latest imposter, walked into her room, in spite of the "No Visitors" sign on the door. The harassed Olga closed her eyes and pretended to be asleep in the hope that they would leave her in peace, and she heard the woman say:

"I still remember that she always pretended to faint whenever she wanted to get something out of my father."

"Now," said Olga to me when I came to visit her and was aghast by what she had told me, "never once did I either faint, or pretend to faint, in Nicky's presence. There was never any need of pretense with him. I know I often badgered him and I hope he has forgiven me, but there was never any falsehood between him and me."

All the insolent persistence notwithstanding, the Montreal Anastasia vanished into the shadowy background where she really belonged.

Unbelievably, the Grand Duchess was once accused of impersonating herself. Some articles of mine about her were published in a Canadian magazine. Suddenly I received a long letter in Spanish from a woman in Montevideo. She claimed that she was the genuine Grand Duchess Olga and that the woman in Canada was an imposter. The writer warned me that she was coming to Canada to start legal proceedings and "to protect

the honor and dignity of the Romanov family." I showed that letter to
Olga and she laughed.

"Incredible what crackpots there are in the world, isn't it?" she said.

The woman in Montevideo was never heard of again.

How proud and reserved was the Grand Duchess, and how bitterly all
those imposters must have hurt her! I can still hear her voice:

"I know I am very near death and now at the end of a long life I
think I have told you everything I remember about Anastasia. There is
nothing to add to it. I think I have done my duty to the memory of
my poor *Malenkaya*."[1]

I knew that she had done so, and I also knew her ardent hope that the
Anastasia legend might soon come to be buried. Olga's reverence for the
memory of her brother and his family plumbed a depth far greater than the
ordinary level. The wound left by the Ekaterinburg crime had never turned
into a scar. All the pretenders who took their assumed identity to the international market did far more than merely harass the Grand Duchess. They
crashed through the door of a very private sanctuary where none but the
Grand Duchess and her sister Xenia had the right to be. A truly dedicated
daughter of her Church, her strong anchor its teaching and symbols, Olga
had regarded her brother as God's anointed, his power bestowed on him
not by men but by God. I once ventured to ask if she prayed for him. She
took a little time to reply:

"Not for him—but to him. He is a martyr."

Having once settled down at Campbellville, Olga rather hoped for a more
or less complete retirement, but there came invitations to luncheons, dinners, and cocktail parties, and at first she accepted them if only for the sake
of her daughters-in-law. The Grand Duchess went everywhere, wholly
unconscious of her shabbiness. She had had to pay some attention to her
wardrobe during her mother's lifetime. With the death of the Empress
Marie, Olga felt she was free to neglect her wardrobe as much as she
pleased, but clothes could never interfere with her dignity and poise.

In the old days, the Grand Duchess's indifference to clothes would send
her dressmakers into despair, and the elaborate court dress she had to wear

on certain occasions made her feel as though she were in a cage and could not get out of it. This indifference grew with the years. She regarded clothes as purely functional. They covered her body and protected her from cold, and nothing else mattered.

Olga's favorite garment was a very shabby leather jacket which she would slip over an equally ancient dress of indeterminate shape, color, and material. She seldom wore stockings, and thrust her feet into a pair of shoes which looked almost past cobbling. Her only hat was a beret of great antiquity. One morning, on leaving the house, she was seen wearing a blouse torn at the back, and her son tried to remonstrate with her.

"But what does it matter?" asked the Grand Duchess, genuinely astonished that he should have noticed such a trivial detail. "It's at the back. Nobody need see it."

Yet if matters of haute couture and fashion said nothing to her, Olga still felt a deeply sentimental attachment to one or two things in her possession. How well I remember coming to the cottage one morning to find her wearing an old sweater so pulled out of shape that it hung, all bunched up in folds, from her shoulders.

"Look," she said triumphantly, "I've just come across it in a drawer! I'd no idea I still had it. I remember knitting it twenty-five years ago. I am so glad I've found it again. I am very fond of it." And she stroked a sleeve proudly and lovingly. I would see that sweater often enough in the weeks and months that followed.

She had lent me some of her most precious icons for the Byzantine Art Exhibition in Toronto, and I was naturally anxious that she should come to its opening. She promised she would. It proved a brilliant occasion, the female society of Toronto, richly gowned and bejeweled, turning up in strength. Into that hall, crowded with men in uniforms and women in the latest creations, came the Grand Duchess wearing an old gray cotton dress and worn brown brogues. Anyone else would have cut a grotesque figure at such a gathering. Not so Olga. Her poise was the true Romanov poise. The simplicity of her manner enchanted everybody. She looked what she was born.

"I agree," she told me once, "that I do look like something left by a cat

As a rule, any royalty visiting Canada came to visit Grand Duchess Olga at her home outside Toronto. Here the Duchess of Kent, a cousin of Olga's, is seen with Olga and her sons Tikhon (right) and Goury (left, and behind Marina). When Queen Elizabeth was in Canada, Grand Duchess Olga (Queen Elizabeth's aunt) was one of the first to be invited for lunch aboard the royal yacht Britannia. Grand Duchess Olga is wearing her favorite gray cotton dress, which she also wore at the opening gala of the Byzantine Art Exhibition.

on the doorstep. Well, what does it matter? But it seems to worry some of my friends. The other day a kindly woman, who is a great friend of mine, suggested that I might do something about my wrinkles. I do know they are getting deeper and deeper. Well, I am proud of them and I told her so, for they make me look like a Russian peasant woman. My father would have understood my feeling."

The Grand Duchess never fussed about getting ready for any occasion. In June, 1959, the Queen and Prince Philip came to Toronto, and the Grand Duchess was among the first to be invited to luncheon on board the *Britannia*.

Her friends and indeed the entire neighborhood had a terrible time over it. In the words of the Grand Duchess, "they were at me morning, noon, and night, urging that I should buy a new frock." She complained to me that they did not see that she was far too old to start buying new clothes.

In the end, however, after endless argument and persuasion, Olga agreed to go to a store in Toronto. Once there, she insisted on being given full liberty of choice. A sale was going on, and she got a plain blue and white cotton dress for thirty dollars. A friend who accompanied her suggested a new hat and one or two accessories, and Olga, feeling very happy about the cheapness of the frock, agreed.

Half Cooksville turned out to see her off that memorable morning. Her clothes, however simple, were new, and the little blue straw hat certainly became her. The neighbors knew all about the shopping expedition. "All this fuss, just to go and see Lizzie and Philip!" she said.

In spite of the warm welcome given by Canada, life in Halton County proved a thorny road from the start. To begin with, the Koulikovskys had the aforementioned disappointment of seeing their two sons leave the farm. In Toronto, they carried letters of introduction to heads of business firms, but good jobs were not as easy to find as they had hoped. They had been soldiers, but they had no business experience. The posts they eventually got were anything but lucrative, and Olga had to bear many a financial burden. To Olga's sorrow, both her daughters-in-law decided to get separated from their husbands. One of them, taking her youngest child with her, went back to Denmark.

And early in 1952 both the Grand Duchess and her husband realized that they could not continue running the farm much longer.

"I had grown to love the place. It was so spacious. It breathed of freedom. The house had grace. It felt a home. And the countryside was enchanting. It was heavenly to spend my leisure rambling about those woods and fields. I could paint out of doors there. But my husband found it harder and harder to carry on. Our sons were gone, and hired labor was not easy to come by. The hands we did engage were not always satisfactory."

It was a bitter time for Olga—a time made even more bitter by the fact that a few months earlier some of her most valuable jewelry had been mysteriously stolen. Of greatest distress to her was the loss of a priceless ring which had a sapphire the size of a cherry surrounded by tiny bands of diamonds and sapphires; this had been given to her by her mother when her first child, Tikhon, was born. The ring and a few other jewels were in a small box which was kept in a briefcase along with some important family papers. According to the Grand Duchess, there was no fear that the briefcase would be stolen since it was always kept in open view beside the Colonel's rocking-chair and, in any event, only the family was aware of its contents.

One day, however, the briefcase mysteriously vanished. The police were immediately called and a careful search was conducted in the house and its grounds. In addition, everybody was interrogated, especially two farmhands then working on the farm. After hours of intensive searching, the empty briefcase was found hidden in the barn. In a bush nearby, the family papers lay littered on the snow. None of the jewels, including the ring, was ever recovered. The police were certain it was an inside job.

"The irony of it all was that, had we entrusted the safekeeping of the jewels to good old Mimka, the theft would never have occurred," said the Grand Duchess. For faithful Mimka, like any cautious Russian peasant, sewed all the jewels of her mistress in the lining of her petticoat, the safest place of all. The unexpected loss of the ring was felt keenly by Olga, who regarded it as yet another sign of the curse that seemed to hang over the Romanov jewels.

In the autumn of 1951 her husband's health took a turn for the worse. His old spinal trouble deepened and made it more and more difficult for him to drive a car and even to move about. "I had so hoped never to have another move again, but there was nothing to be done," the Grand Duchess said.

So in the spring of 1952, the farm in Halton County was put on the market again. Their faithful friend, Mr. A. H. Creighton, arranged the auction, had the farm sold very well, and also found a four-room cottage on the outskirts of Cooksville. It stood in a small wilderness of its own. It had two bedrooms, a kitchen, and a living room. Neither of the Koulikovskys wished for more space.

The move was made just in time. By the summer of 1952, the Colonel's condition worsened, though he struggled on for as long as he could to help his wife with the ordinary household tasks. About the same time, the faithful old Mimka, aged eighty-seven, had a stroke which left her completely paralyzed. Well-meaning friends urged the Grand Duchess to have Mimka

The four-room Koulikovsky home in Cooksville, just outside of Toronto.

sent to a home for the aged infirm. Olga was indignant. Mimka, she said, was her oldest and closest friend in the world, and friends were not treated as though they were outworn gloves. So Olga turned into a nurse. She would not let any of the neighbors help her, and she bathed, dressed, and fed the old woman herself. Mimka lingered until 1954, her mind wholly back at Gatchina, the Anitchkov Palace, and Olgino, and she died in the arms of the mistress whom she had served so lovingly and loyally all her life. When the coffin was lowered into the Canadian soil, the Grand Duchess knew that yet another dear link with the past had gone forever.

In Halton County she had had Mimka and occasional outside help to share the housework with her. In Cooksville, Olga had to manage on her own. Most of her ready cash had been spent and rigid economy had to be practiced in the cottage. In spite of it all, her financial affairs were always in a tangle. Never had Olga learned how to manage money. It either was or was not there. The mere idea of a budget was Greek to her. She would do without outside help because having it would have meant sparing herself. Whatever funds there were must go on necessary comforts for her husband, her sons, and her friends, whose requirements, in Olga's opinion, were always more pressing than her own.

So in Cooksville she had not even a weekly char. Hard work, as such, never frightened the Grand Duchess, but she had not the faintest notion about the details of domestic organization on however humble a scale. The kitchen became chaotic, with crockery piled up here, there, and everywhere. Someone once described Olga's culinary efforts as being "charmingly primitive." Her own ideas went little further than tinkering with the can opener, and heating the contents of the can in the most handy saucepan. She did not mind flies getting into the milk or occasional cockroaches running across the kitchen floor.

It was a humble enough pattern for a Grand Duchess still remembered

Grand Duchess O[...]
living room in Co[...]
Behind her are hu[...]
icons presented to [...]
Russians all over [...]

by the entire world. In the eyes of the scattered émigrés, the fragile old lady remained the living symbol of a great and ancient tradition. Nor was Olga forgotten by her royal kin. In the summer of 1954, the Duchess of Kent had found time during her very crowded visit to Canada to drive out to Cooksville to see her Cousin Olga. The Grand Duchess described that occasion in a letter to a friend dated September first, 1954:

> Yes, wasn't it sweet of Marina to come and see her old aunt[2] whom she could not even remember, as she was but two years old in St. Petersburg when her two elder sisters and herself used to come with their nurse to play and have tea with me.... [She] rang up and said she could just come for a short visit in between her engagements on Saturday morning at ten-thirty. I kept this news secret not to have an inquisitive crowd gaping—you know what a crowd is!... Lots of police (nice people) arrived beforehand here and there 'round about our little house and garden. Marina is really a lovely person indeed and so friendly and sweet. She looked at our little house and ate some sandwiches in the

*rand Duchess Olga in her
ving room in Cooksville
underneath a portrait of her
father, Tsar Alexander III.*

kitchen. She had a lady-in-waiting and her secretary with her. We sat and talked but one can't really have a good intimate talk with so many in the room and the rooms are too small to get away. . . . We got photographed together . . . a photographer drove up from somewhere in the blue . . . and before Marina left a little daughter of one of our neighbors came up with a basket of peaches and was snapped at the door of her car. The nearest neighbors came rushing to speak to us after Marina's departure and some of them had coffee and the remains of the sandwiches in the garden with us to talk over events. . . .

She kept in touch with the émigrés to the very end. Members of her old Akhtyrsky Hussar Regiment, scattered all over the world, were not forgotten by her. Olga had a phenomenal memory and remembered most officers and even some of the men by their name and surname. Once Colonel Odintzov came to Cooksville to accompany the Grand Duchess to a regimental memorial service at the Russian Cathedral in Toronto. He brought with him a list of all the men fallen in the First World War. Olga read it through carefully. Then she said:

"Oh, you have forgotten to put in Vassily. . . . Oh, what was the man's surname? Never mind, it is certain to come back to me, and of course I shall pray for him just the same."

Colonel Odintzov replied that he did not think there had been a single Vassily among the officers.

"He was not an officer," the Grand Duchess said quickly, "but a sergeant, and I was very fond of him. Now, I have remembered his surname—Bazdyrev, Vassily Grigorievich."

Colonel Odintzov later checked the regimental records. There had been a sergeant—Vassily Bazdyrev. He joined the Akhtyrsky Hussars in 1898 and was killed in action in 1915.

She abhorred all purely social activities. She never ceased being interested in charities that stood closest to her heart. To the very end Olga continued giving her active patronage to all the émigré social endeavors in Canada. The Russo-American Aid Association in New York gives a big charity ball every year. They repeatedly invited their imperial chairman to

come over, and the Grand Duchess kept sending her regrets. One year, however, she decided that it was her duty to attend the ball and she began making all the preparations, but the United States immigration authorities barred her entry on the grounds of her not being a Canadian citizen.

The Grand Duchess was deeply offended and also bewildered. For the first time in her life, she came face to face with the maddeningly narrow outlook where identity is not recognized except by virtue of passports and visas. The incident certainly sharpened her consciousness of being an exile, with no hope of finding other roots in the world, but she spoke of it without bitterness.

"Really, those Americans should learn something about European history. How could a Grand Duchess be anyone's subject—except, of course, her own sovereign's—or citizen? It just doesn't make sense."

Intensely proud of her race as she was, the Grand Duchess had a curious streak of humility. She disliked being addressed by her title. Once, at the beginning of our friendship, I addressed her as "Your Imperial Highness" when she and I were having a meal at a restaurant in Toronto. She said quickly:

"Please never do it again. I am either Olga Alexandrovna or simply Olga to my friends."

Yet on another occasion when a neighbor's child ran up to ask her, "Are you really and truly a Princess?" Olga replied, "I am most certainly not a Princess. I am a Russian Grand Duchess."

Olga's correspondence was voluminous and she dealt with all of it. Letters reached her from many old servants of the households at Gatchina, Tsarskoe Selo, the Anitchkov Palace, and her own home in Sergievskaya Street in St. Petersburg. More than that, the Grand Duchess continued receiving letters from Russia itself. Two particularly moving ones were written by a valet of Prince Peter of Oldenburg and a nurse who had been in her own service at Olgino. Both of these were written on their deathbeds and finished in mid-sentence, an artless and unsigned post-script mentioning the identity of the writer. Another among Olga's correspondents was an old Cossack officer who had been imprisoned by the Communists for ten years, and knew well that he was putting his liberty into jeopardy every

Grand Duchess Olga, her grandson Leonid, and the author in Olga's living room in Cooksville. They are sifting through the heap of letters and cards she received each year from her royal relatives at Christmastime.

time he wrote to the Grand Duchess, but he could not help it, because, as he said, "this is all I have left in life—to write to you."

Four times a year, at Christmas and Easter, on the Grand Duchess's birthday, and her feast-day on the eleventh of July (old style), the living room in the cottage was swamped with letters and parcels from almost every country in the world—from Finland to Japan, from Norway to Australia, from South Africa to China—and those remembrances heartened her greatly. Her correspondents' social status meant nothing. Their affection stood for everything.

One Christmas Day I saw the table in the living room littered with cards and packages. There were messages from Buckingham Palace, from her royal relations in Sweden, Germany, Denmark, and Greece, and from famous people of many countries, but the little Grand Duchess looked concerned as she went on rummaging in one pile after another.

A letter to the author from William Shaw, Grand Duchess Olga's butcher from 1936 to 1960.

William Shaw

Area code 416
274-3907

apt 6,
328 Lakeshore E.,
PORT CREDIT, Ont.,
10th June 1965.

Dear Mr. Vorres.

We had a pleasant surprise reading TIME magazine of June 11 - the article covering your book on the grand duchess Olga, in which the duchess's butcher is mentioned. The writer is that butcher, & he would like you to know what pleasant memories he has of doing business with that lady, while acting as manager of the meat counter at McKee's in Port Credit (from 1936 to 1960).

She had one of the kindest dispositions, always reserved & polite, & at all times it was no trouble to do one's best for her & her husband when they came shopping together.

As time went on, I sent her Xmas cards, which as your article proves, she evidently appreciated, & now my wife & I are so happy that she thought so much of them. The last one we sent was in December 1959, as she died before the Xmas of 1960. The same year, 1959, we sent her a post card from Los Angeles, as we really wanted to let her know that she was in our thoughts.

One of my most treasured possessions is a Xmas card of flowers, originally painted by the grand duchess, & the greeting inside the card, in her own handwriting, is
     "Happy Xmas & New Year to you and yours".
          (Olga Koulikovsky).

It is like reading a golden tribute from the past, her mentioning "my dear butcher" : she needed all the kindness one could bestow, as after her terrible experience in that revolution, it must have been a great effort to appear normal, in the every day life of Canada.

One meets all sorts of people over a meat counter, & it has been one of the high-lights of my life, meeting the grand duchess Olga, whose graciousness will be in my memory to the end of time.

Her husband, the colonel, was a magnificient specimen of manhood - he was always so attentive to her - I am sure they were really happy in Canada, which became home for their two sons also.

When she smiled, & in the company of her sons, one felt that she had not lived in vain.

I am now 76 & in semi-retirement.

          Kind regards,
            from yours sincerely,

               William Shaw.

"I just can't understand it. I only hope the man isn't ill. It is the first time I've not had a card from him."

"From whom?" I asked.

"Oh, Mr. Shaw, my dear butcher in Campbellville. I do so hope he is all right."

Following the Romanov tradition, Olga stood close to the Orthodox Church all her life. The monks of a Russian monastery in the United States often sent her honey. One Christmas Eve they rang her up to sing a Christmas anthem over the telephone. Olga kept in touch with many other Russian religious communities and, well aware of their straitened circumstances, deeply touched by the absence of complaints in their letters, she would makeshift somehow and manage to send them little gifts from time to time. The Russian monks on Mount Athos prayed for her daily. On my visiting their monastery, they wept when I told them I knew Olga, and they asked me to take an icon for her back to Canada. The walls of the cottage bedroom were covered with icons bequeathed to the Grand Duchess by many men and women whose loyalty, when they died, was as fervent as it had been at the beginning of the Revolution.

"The Sunset Is Over"

In the winter of 1957–58 Colonel Koulikovsky's health got sharply worse. His spinal trouble developed some unforeseen complications. The doctor suggested that he should go to the Toronto General Hospital, and Olga, eyes flashing, retorted that it was nobody's place except hers to look after her husband.

The burdens grew that winter. Comforts were certainly needed for the Colonel, and Olga had occasional help for the household tasks. And money was scarcer than ever. A note to any among her royal kin would have brought an immediate reply, but the Grand Duchess, accepting unsolicited gifts with all the graciousness at her command, never begged from anyone. She decided to part with the very few jewels she still possessed.

They were few—two or three brooches, a pendant, a couple of bracelets, and some other oddments. They were mostly diamonds, rubies, and sapphires, their settings enchantingly old-fashioned. The Grand Duchess took them to be valued by a jeweler. The sum suggested was absurdly low, the man arguing that the setting greatly decreased the value of the stones. Olga decided to have the things sold privately. In the end, the Grand Duchess received a sum which, though significant, she felt was not enough.

"I'd much rather forget all about it," she said so curtly that I felt as though a curse had been hanging over all the Romanov jewelry, every separate disposal of them ending in disappointment.

In late spring of 1958, Colonel Koulikovsky became increasingly paralyzed. He lay on the sofa in the living room, and Olga nursed him to the end. In early summer, he died in his sleep. He was seventy-six. They had

Grand Duchess Olga enjoying the sun on her front porch in Cooksville, one year after her husband's death and a year before her own demise.

Grand Duchess Olga, in Cooksville. She always loved to paint. It kept her spirits up during the many cataclysmic events surrounding her life.

given each other forty-two years of married happiness which had withstood all the shocks and griefs they had borne together.

Olga certainly had her faith. Nonetheless, her husband's death left her with a sense of irreparable loss. He had been all things to her, the only man ever to have given the spiritual and mental support she needed. Colonel Koulikovsky had little head for business but his mind was practical enough to remedy his wife's total lack of business sense. They had stood so close to each other that all their reactions and their outlook on life and people had ended by being interwoven. In him the Grand Duchess lost not only the only man she had loved but also the very last remaining link with her dearest memories of imperial Russia. Her sons, born during the Revolution, belonged to a generation which knew of that Russia by hearsay only. They could hardly imagine its landscape, and its beauty was a closed book to them.

It was sadly obvious that with her husband's death Olga lost her own reason for existence. She retired into complete privacy in her cottage, and that cluttered living room became her world. There she would spend her entire days, exchanging its walls for her garden when the weather was fine. She still painted a little, and occasionally sold her delicate flower studies. She still received some old friends and her correspondence did not shrink in volume. But all zest had gone out of her life. She enjoyed lunching with the Queen on board the *Britannia*, and she was pleased by the visit of Lord and Lady Mountbatten of Burma, who, on an official tour of Canada, flew from Ottawa to see their cousin. That day in August, 1959, marked Olga's last personal contact with her royal kin. But those two great occasions, for all the sincere pleasure she took in them, did not touch her as closely as they would have done earlier. She now had no companion to share the day's chronicle in the familiar, warm, intimate way.

In the autumn of 1959, Olga's own health gave way, but she would not yield to what she called mere weakness of the flesh. She refused to see a doctor, preferring to find comfort in prayer. The idea of going to a hospital terrified her. She was determined to end her days in the cottage at Cooksville. Queen Louise of Sweden offered to send one of her maids to help her and the neighbors rallied when the unceasing challenge of brooms, dusters, and saucepans got beyond her. Every man and woman in Cooksville was willing and ready to do their share in easing her daily burden. Even the milkman, instead of leaving the bottles at the door, would enter the cottage and put them into the refrigerator.

Grand Duchess Olga and the author, preparing for a summer drive.

Grand Duchess Olga with her young granddaughter, Xenia Koulivosky, enjoying the afternoon sun on the author's car.

She kept receiving numerous invitations from friends all over the world. They all urged her to move to a milder climate somewhere in Central or South America or even in Europe. Olga refused them all.

"I am not moving anywhere," she told me firmly. "I have decided to end my days here, but the end is not very far and we must hurry, hurry. There is so much left for me to tell you."

One morning I found Olga reading a letter from an East German organization.

"I have had so many of them," she said and threw the sheet into the wastepaper basket. "They keep on offering to resettle me in Russia. It sounds almost a joke. If I were mad enough to accept, you would never see

Grand Duchess Olga in the author's car, smiling. She loved fast cars.

me again. They would probably announce that I had fallen suddenly sick. An illness out there, attended by some charming doctor of theirs.... That would be an end indeed!" and she laughed.

"I've seen you laughing so often," I remarked. "I have yet to see you cry."

"If I ever start crying," the Grand Duchess replied, her face suddenly grave, "I might never be able to stop. So I laugh instead."

Olga was adamant in her refusal to see a doctor, but she was perfectly willing to accept advice from friends and neighbors. Queen Louise of Sweden wrote suggesting that Olga should drink fresh lemonade every morning, a prescription religiously followed until its novelty wore off. Another friend, an enthusiastic vegetarian, persuaded the Grand Duchess that she should give up eating meat and fish. That counsel was rather difficult to accept: so much food was brought to her by neighbors, and Cooksville had no vegetarians.

She had obviously inherited her father's dislike and distrust of the medical profession.

"It's amazing what people suffer because of medical blunders. And doctors so often prescribe what they like taking themselves. I once had a doctor who kept telling me that vodka would do me much good. I never put it to the test. The man had a very red nose."

Soon enough I learned that the Grand Duchess enjoyed diagnosing her own ailments. It was not uncommon for her to determine—all within one week or so—that she was suffering from phlebitis, an unspecified heart disease, and arthritis. So she would write to a friend: "I had a heart attack yesterday.... Today I am all right again...but feel tired and sleepy so can't write a long letter," and another friend would suddenly hear of the Grand Duchess having been "laid up for weeks...but I enjoy life again...am out in the garden and...the sun shines and I feel in Paradise."

However fantastic her own diagnoses were, her ailments certainly increased. She had never been a glutton. Now, she merely pecked at her food. There were days when she felt all stiff and aching. "I suppose the pain will never leave me now, so I am trying to get accustomed to feeling like this. The sun shines and I look out of the window and feel happy—it would be so much worse to be blind...."

Day by day I sat in that room, which, for all its shabbiness and untidiness, seemed to have borrowed an
imprint of the Romanov grandeur. Day by day, following the Grand Duchess's journey from palaces to
peasant huts, from one continent to another, I grew
more and more amazed at her memory. She hardly ever
fumbled for a name. And there was also the refreshing,
effortless courtesy of a bygone age. With infinite
patience, Olga would spell out some names which, as
she knew, were unfamiliar to me, explain the neighbor-
hood of such and such town or village, pinpoint a landmark here and there
with a few words so telling that a corner of the landscape would at once be
flooded with light.

*Grand Duchess Olga also
loved to paint strawberries.
Here she is in Cooksville
retrieving her subjects from
her garden.*

But always there remained the sense of urgency. "So much left to say....
We must hurry..." she kept saying and yet, oddly enough, that urgency did
not quarrel with her deep-rooted tranquility of spirit. Olga looked upon
the end of her life as but another adventure, another new beginning. I very
much doubt if she ever had a single doubt in her life. Her faith was as clear
and true in color as her own exquisite flower studies.

"You know," she said, "tragedy and suffering seem part of the very
essence of life. There is nobody in the world who can escape either one or
the other. But, as I firmly believe, there is the hereafter to be happy in and
perhaps the greater one's sufferings here, the greater one's chance of happiness later on. But no matter what happens, one's faith in people and their
kindness should never be undermined."

Another day she said, "At Gatchina in the park there was a little bridge
over a cataract. It roared with a deafening noise. The bridge seemed so fragile that most people were afraid of crossing it. If they did, they would just
run, never linger for an instant. Well, my brother Michael and I would often
go there and stand on the bridge. It would probably be no more than a few
minutes. It always seemed hours to me. We were terribly scared and we
shook as we stood looking at the thundering, foaming water below. But it
was well worth it every time. We left the bridge, conscious that we had
achieved something. However unimportant, it was an achievement. I

wanted you to know about that little bridge because I am going to die with the same sense of achievement. However little I had to give, I don't think I withheld anything to serve my dear country as a Romanov."

She said it all so simply, not a breath of any boasting in her voice, and I knew that she had indeed remained a true Romanov with all their idiosyncracies. Olga never quite lost her fear of assassination. She always looked behind a door and under her bed when retiring at night, so she told me. When a water-pipe burst with a deafening bang, her first reaction was to telephone the police, not thinking of any water-pipes but of bombs. Like all genuinely courageous people, Olga neither disguised her fears nor was ashamed of them. Toward the end, however, many ancient terrors came to the surface again. One morning she told me that she had seen a red star move from wall to wall in her bedroom at night.

"It was just frightful.... Must they be after me even here?"

She had told me the story of her life without once laying an exaggerated emphasis on any incidents she had either witnessed or heard about, but her very austere objectiveness told me that the severe agonies of those years continued to haunt her.

Early in April, 1960, her doctor decided to pay a call at the cottage. He was so shocked at the weak state of the Grand Duchess that he rushed her to the Toronto General Hospital. She was far too exhausted to make much of a protest. She had given up the struggle to keep alive. All she prayed for was the mercy of a quick release. That mercy was not granted.

"What's the use of their trying to do all these things?" she said when I called at the hospital. "I know I am dying. Why can't they let me go in peace? Oh yes, they are most kind, but what is the good of trying to x-ray me? I am so tired. And they expect me to eat, too. I don't want to think about food." The Grand Duchess sniffed at her bowl of soup and attempted a smile. "Do you know, half the fun in life is smelling the food, not eating it."

She found the hospital too impersonal. All the regulations irked her, but even here, her frail body one big pain, the Grand Duchess came out with an occasional quip.

"Do you know there are some very good-looking doctors here? One came to see me this morning, tall, dark, incredibly handsome, and I said to him, 'What a pity we didn't meet fifty years ago!'"

A few weeks went by, and Olga began having spells when her mind failed her. She slipped back into the past, she again walked with her father in the park at Gatchina and climbed a palace roof with young Michael at her heels, mimicking a guest's disappointment at the plain food offered at Gatchina. Side by side with those tranquil excursions, the Grand Duchess's mind went on far more perilous journeys. One day she ordered a nurse out of the palace gates for having spied on her and threatened the girl with imprisonment at the fortress. So imperious was Olga's order that the nurse was afraid to go into her room again.

"What a tyrant she is!" said the nurse and looked amazed when I shook my head.

"Of course she is," repeated the girl. "All her family were, weren't they?"

I might have told the girl that her helpless old patient was one of the gentlest and most compassionate women it had ever been my privilege to know, who had fought for her own liberty and never failed in her respect for her neighbor's right to freedom. But I felt that it would have fallen on uncomprehending ears and I said nothing.

The Grand Duchess's friends wisely kept from her the news of the death of her elder sister, Xenia, who died in London on April twentieth, 1960, aged eighty-five. The telegram of condolence sent by the Queen and Prince Philip was not given to Olga.

Yet even toward the end, the misty spells were not continuous. Some mornings when I called, the Grand Duchess would astonish me by her keen interest in all that was happening in the outside world.

"Hasn't there been a photograph of Prince Andrew published anywhere?" she asked once and was very pleased with the newspaper clipping I brought the next day.

One afternoon in May, when she heard about the destruction a tidal wave had wrought in Japan, she said she felt very sorry, adding: "Why, I think I am developing a soft spot for the Japanese." Hearing it, I could not help smiling. For Olga, Japan had been a *bête noire* since the days of the 1904–05 war.

Someone told her about the Soviet sending a dog into space, and I found her very angry and agitated that day: "It is cruel and also cowardly to use animals for such a purpose. A dog couldn't know what was being done to it or why."

As the summer went on, it became obvious to all the doctors that nothing more could be done for the Grand Duchess. All the physical ailments apart, and in spite of the interest she showed in outward events, she had lost her will to live. There was much in the hospital routine to irk and disturb her, and it was decided to let her end her days away from all the official and impersonal pattern. The cottage in Cooksville was naturally out of all question; it could no longer be a matter of an occasional meal or an hour's housework done by a kindly neighbor. In the end, Olga's old friends, an elderly guards officer, Captain K. N. Martemianov, and his wife, offered to look after her. They lived in humble enough lodgings over a beauty parlor in one of the poorest quarters of Toronto, a far cry indeed from the spacious splendor of Gatchina and the Anitchkov Palace, but the dying Grand Duchess was greatly refreshed by her very last move on earth. The Martemianovs' flat evoked so much in her memory. She could see candles burning in front of the icons in her bedroom. She could hear the soothing accents of her dear mother tongue. Captain and Madame Martemianov did not spare themselves in giving every possible help and comfort to their last Emperor's last surviving sister.

A dispossessed exile for more than forty years, the last Grand Duchess of Russia was dying in poverty, but the mere magic of a great name was still strong enough to evoke homage all over the world. Messages of sympathy, anxiety, and hopes for her recovery poured into the flat day by day. At the liturgy, all the Russian churches and monasteries throughout the free world had a petition added to the litany, "For thy infirm servant, our sovereign lady and Grand Duchess Olga Alexandrovna" (*Za bolyashchuyu rabu tvoyu velikuyu knyaginyu Olgu Aleksandrovnu*) and special little services were held, the so-called *molebni o zdravii*. The Russian convent in New York lent their miraculous icon of Our Lady and it was brought to the Grand Duchess's bedside. Her friend, former Prince John Chekovsky, Orthodox Bishop in San Francisco, came all the way from California to administer the last sacraments.

The last home of Grand Duchess Olga in a working-class district in east Toronto.

One of the last people to come and be recognized by Olga was Sir Edward Peacock. He came on September twenty-seventh. She made an effort, opened her arms wide, and kissed his hands, whispering: "One of my oldest friends...."

After that, nothing but a flicker remained—though it went on burning steadily for nearly two months longer. On November twenty-first the Grand Duchess passed into a coma. She never regained consciousness. She died three days later, on November 24, 1960, at 11.35 p.m., in the seventy-ninth year of her life.

That evening I had to go to Brantford in the neighborhood of Toronto to give a lecture. It was late when I started driving back to Toronto. The night air was crisp with frost and the skies were studded with stars. Nearing the city, I had a feeling that death's wings had brushed against the darkness. I looked up. The stars shone brighter than ever, and I knew Olga had been released from all her burdens and gone into the eternal light. I knew that she was dead.

Early in the morning a telephone message confirmed my intuition. Later that day, a few from among Olga's intimates—her son Tikhon, the Martemianovs, and myself—were gathered together in that bedroom for the

Grand Duchess Olga's deathbed in the apartment in east Toronto.

very first *panikhida* sung by Father Diatchina, rector of the Russian Cathedral in Toronto. All of us, lighted tapers in our hands, knelt facing the bed. The Grand Duchess looked wholly at peace. More than that: her face reflected a serenity I had never seen before. I heard the words of the Kontakion with their fervent hope that she might be granted rest with the saints of God. But, as I looked at her face and at the plain wooden cross between her emaciated fingers, I felt that the prayer had already been answered. The last Grand Duchess of Russia was truly at rest, all her tears wiped away and her great griefs assuaged by the love of the God who had been her friend and defender through so many bitter years.

What followed in the days before the funeral seemed rather a pathetic pretense to revive splendors which had ceased to exist. For five days the Grand Duchess lay in state in the cathedral, her open coffin guarded day and night by the surviving officers and men of her faithful Akhtyrsky Hussars.

They buried her on November thirtieth, the Requiem Mass lasting nearly three hours. A short memorial sermon was preached by Bishop Athenagoras, head of the Greek Church in Canada, and representatives of Orthodox communities throughout the New World took part in the service.

The open coffin,[1] the imperial standard draping it, stood on a catafalque surrounded by sheer walls of flowers. An exquisite piece of silver and gold embroidery with the imperial crown and the cipher O.A., for Olga Alexandrovna, lay at the foot of the coffin. All through the lengthy service, officers and men of the Akhtyrsky Hussar Regiment stood on guard. At the end of the service, the last homage having been paid, the coffin was closed and covered with the imperial standard and the regimental colors rescued by a Hussar and brought over to Canada soon after the Revolution.

The cathedral was packed from end to end. Many of the mourners had to stand outside in the street. Members of the old nobility, Canadian and American friends, and hundreds upon hundreds of Russian exiles of hum-

The funeral service for Grand Duchess Olga at the Russian Cathedral of Christ the Saviour in Toronto on November 20, 1960.

ble origin all stood together. It was obvious that they had not come in obedience to a mere hollow convention, still less for the purpose of paying lip service to a blurred symbol of a dead past. They were there to take a last farewell of a greatly loved friend.

Many royal names appeared on the wreaths. Olga's kin from all over Europe had remembered her, and a Romanov cousin of hers, Princess Vera of Russia,[2] came over from New York.

All through her life Grand Duchess Olga had, to use her own words, despised politics. Certainly she had kept aloof from them. Yet she was not spared a touch of political expediency at her funeral. With the exception of the Danes, the large consular body in Toronto sent no official representatives to the cathedral. The Greek consul explained the predicament by saying that he would have come as a private individual but that he could not attend as an official representative since his country had recognized the Communist régime. The Estonian had a far more violent reason for keeping away: "We used to oppose Tsarism as much as we have opposed Communism," he said. At the American Consulate, nobody knew anything about the funeral the day before. An official asked about the time and the place but refused to say if any member of the Consulate would be present.

A little after noon at York Cemetery, the tiny coffin, still draped with the imperial standard, and the old Russian flag of white, blue and red, was lowered into a humble grave next to that of Colonel Koulikovsky. Hardly an eye remained dry when Father Diatchina stepped forward and scattered a handful of Russian soil over the coffin.

It was a cold, gray day, and the cemetery was swept by icy winds. The golden domes and spires of old St. Petersburg, the pageantry of imperial weddings and burials, the roar of the cannon announcing imperial births and deaths, all of it seemed to belong to another world. And then, standing under those wintry skies of Canada, I remembered the last words Olga spoke to me.

On the day before she finally lost consciousness, I was standing very still by her bed. Some sixth sense told me that this was to be our last meeting on earth. She recognized me. Her eyes, for all the infinite weariness in them, lit up for one brief moment and one bony hand reached out from under the bedclothes. I stooped and kissed it, and heard a barely audible whisper:

"The sunset is over. . . ."

So often, when she and I sat either in the living room or in the garden in Cooksville, Olga would tell me that she thought her entire life had been something of a gradual sunset. "I can see every event in my life bathed in the light of the setting sun, and all of it seems to assume a new clarity. It is a good thing I have waited so long to tell my story. I can see and judge much better now than I would have done years ago."

So now her story has been told—the facts about her greatly beloved niece, the truth, as Olga saw it, about Rasputin; the splendor and the terror together; the luxury and the privation; and, always, weaving a clear golden thread across its darkest reaches, Olga's simple childlike faith in the God of her fathers and her nation.

Epilogue

rand Duchess Olga never had a governess. She had a number of masters who tutored her somewhat indifferently in humanities and other disciplines. Never in her whole life had she either time or occasion for a course of extensive reading. She was not an intellectual. She could never reason about a problem. She either grasped it or left it alone. Had she been born a commoner, she would undoubtedly have made a name for herself as a landscape painter.

Considering the lack of all academic opportunities, it is a matter for marvel how informed the Grand Duchess was in certain subjects, such as botany and history. The latter, in particular, remained an inexhaustible source of study to her. She studied it in her own fashion. She often leapt at wrong conclusions, gave free rein to inherited prejudices, and formed opinions wildly at variance to most recognized authorities. But Olga's studies never fell to the level of a dusty habit. History remained a living subject to her, more immediately the history of her own country and of her house.

The Romanovs ruled Russia for three hundred and four years. Elected by the will of the nation in 1613, they were overthrown not so much by the will of a powerful minority as by the violent impetus of abnormal conditions for which, be it admitted, they were responsible, however partially. The never-ebbing anxiety of Grand Duchess Olga was concerned with their future place in history. She said:

"It might indeed appear trivial to be so troubled about the judgment of history, but to me it is important not because I happen to be a Romanov but because a just appraisal should not be denied to future generations. Justice should mean everything."

Olga knew that the tendency of Western historians and writers was to portray her race as oppressors of their people, greedy for absolute power, grandeur, self-indulgence, and as enemies of all liberty in action and in thought. Olga readily admitted that some of the Romanovs of her own generation had not remained true to the family tradition, but it was the wholesale condemnation of the dynasty that troubled her, the endless mis-representations of their motives, the invidious coloring given to their actions, and the occasionally grotesque caricatures of their personalities. Books in two or three languages appeared in Olga's lifetime in which the portrayal of her father, Emperor Alexander III, was grossly untrue, and one need not be an overzealous monarchist to admit that the European reports of Bloody Sunday in January, 1905, were painfully distorted.

"All the mistakes my people made would always receive such promi-nence. So much has been written about our barbaric penal system—but what about England when even under Victoria people were hanged or transported for life for stealing a leg of mutton or a loaf of bread? So much has been said about our prisons—but what of the conditions in Spain and Austria, to say nothing of Germany? Yet the mere sound of 'Siberia' was like a red rag to a bull in the West. Actually, in spite of the police and censorship and the rest, there used to be more freedom in Russia than in Austria and Spain, and certainly far more than there is today under the hammer and sickle. And nobody troubles to remember the vastness and complexity of the task which faced three great reformers—Peter the Great, Catherine the Great, and my grandfather, Alexander II."

Olga went on to tell me about a fact virtually forgotten today—that it was a Romanov who instituted the principle that the sovereign, for all he was an autocrat, was the servant of his people. The idea was embodied in the Order of the Day given by Peter the Great to his troops on the eve of the Battle of Poltava when the power of Sweden was crushed by the Russians. The principle lay at the root of the Tsar's dedication at his anointing.

She told me much about her ancestors, pointing out that most European historians saw them out of focus, as it were, occasionally ignoring the cause of a particular effect, and just as often basing their conclusions on unreliable evidence. The Grand Duchess had once read a book which said that the murder of Alexander II had produced hardly any effect on the people—they heard of it with absolute indifference.

"Heavens!" Olga's eyes flashed with anger at the memory. "In my youth I would meet hundreds and hundreds of eyewitnesses of the national sorrow. Yet I suppose it is so much easier to remember the cruelties of Peter the Great, the lovers of Catherine, the pseudo mysticism of Alexander I, and all the rest of it. And naturally the Rasputin legend proved a gold mine for Hollywood producers. Will anyone ever write honestly about Nicky and Alicky? The stories invented about them are incredible, and I suppose all the genuine material will never be released by the Kremlin—if it has not been destroyed already."

Olga always maintained that it was the abysmal ignorance of the West about Russia that lay at the root of it all. She gave as an example the fact that when the novels of Tolstoy, Turgenev, and Dostoevsky became known in the West, some of the critics said that the novel was the only literary form known to the Russians, there having been no poets in the country.

"That was said in the '80s and the '90s—nearly half a century after the death of Pushkin and Lermontov, to quote but two of our great names. And again, the world went mad over our music and our ballet. Yet how many people know that it was the Romanovs' love for the arts that established the cradle of the Russian ballet and laid the foundations of the great Hermitage collection? That it was their money—not just the Treasury grants—that maintained theaters, concert halls, and art galleries?"

During her years of exile the Grand Duchess heard frequent references to "the German rulers of Russia."

"Did the British call King George VI a German? He had not a drop of English blood in him. Had he in his turn married a foreigner, the present Queen would also have been a German by blood. Yet there is hardly a book about my family which does not regard their foreign blood as some kind of a contamination. Moreover, blood is not everything. It is the soil you spring from, the faith you are brought up in, the language you speak and you think in. My father's mother was a Princess of Hesse—but to look at him, he might have descended from an old Kiev warrior, and his personal habits were as simple as those of a Russian peasant."

Olga once said to me: "The growth and the incredible strength of Communism are the direct result of the blunders and the selfish policy of the West. I feel no pity for the countries which bear the brunt of the cold war today. They have asked for it."

She had clung to that belief all through the years of her exile. She insisted that when, during the First World War, Russia was engaged in a deadly struggle against Germany, the Allies purposely hampered and delayed the dispatch of supplies and munitions Russia needed so badly to bring the struggle to an end.

That did not make sense to me and I said so.

"It does make sense," she retorted. "The Allies wanted to kill two birds with one stone—to crush Germany and to exhaust Russia. I loathe the very name of Stalin, but he and his henchmen, well remembering Russia's past experiences at the hands of the Allies, were perfectly justified in suspecting the same intrigues during the Second World War. They were not wrong when they accused the Allied High Command of purposely delaying the invasion of France."

The Grand Duchess was convinced that, at the end of the First World War, the Allies treated Russia as though she were an enemy. On the thin excuse that the Communist government had signed the Brest-Litovsk Treaty, the Allies barred all Russians, whether White or Red, from the peace conference at Versailles. They forgot that the Communist régime had not been chosen by the whole nation and that the White Armies were fighting the Reds on several fronts. It never occurred either to Great Britain or to France that all true Russians regarded the Brest-Litovsk Treaty as a shameful blot on their history and that all its clauses would have been immediately annulled if the White Army had proved triumphant in the end.

"The Allies chose to remain blind to that truth because at long last they had an opportunity of falling upon Russia and of throwing pieces of her flesh to the waiting vultures. All the countries bordering on my brother's Empire extended their frontiers at our expense. Poland, Hungary, and

Roumania were not slow to help themselves. Finland, Lithuania, Estonia, and Latvia were created out of territories Russia held by virtue of lawful treaties in the past. Japan had a bite of the Far East. Even Georgia and Azerbaijan appeared as independent states at the peace conference, and no protests were made against the treachery.

"Do you know," Olga went in fierily, "my mother and I were still in the Crimea when my brother-in-law, Grand Duke Alexander, sailed for France? We all felt that one of our men should go to Paris and put the Russian case, as it really stood at the time, before the Allies. And what happened? They treated Sandro as though he were a traitor. He was refused the courtesy of an interview with Clemenceau, whose secretary had the effrontery to answer Sandro's warnings about the grave danger by a remark that Communism was a disease to attack none but defeated nations. Of course, nobody at Versailles troubled to remember the tremendous sacrifices made by the Empire for the Allies. It was my brother's army which was used as some kind of a human shock absorber against the German attack. By the heroism of my countrymen the French were given enough time to strengthen their own positions. The hundred and fifty thousand Russians, trapped to their death at Tannenberg, helped to ease the German pressure against Paris. And all of it came to be forgotten.

"When things went from bad to worse with us, it would have been so easy for my brother to sign a separate peace. The Kaiser would have been only too willing to bring the matters to such a conclusion on the Eastern front. But Nicky's loyalty to Britain and France never wavered for an instant. When the Germans, hoping to start negotiations, offered him surprisingly generous terms, Nicky would not even discuss them with his commanders. His honor forbade him to do anything except send an immediate refusal. Had he accepted the Kaiser's terms, he might well have saved his throne and his life, and the horrors of the Revolution might not have fallen upon the Empire.

"And, oh, the ineptitude of Western statesmen at that time!" she went on. "They just played into the hands of the Reds. Even if the Western Powers had no great love for imperial Russia, it would surely have been in their own interest to stem the tide of Communism. Clemenceau was of the firm opinion that the pressure of a blockade would bring that about! Could blindness and stupidity have traveled any further? It was precisely the Allied blockade which, added to appalling transport conditions in Russia and a succession of poor harvests, helped to create an ideal background for absolute chaos, and thus the Great Famine started. Naturally, the Communists turned the blockade to their own advantage. The foreigners were strangling the country, they told the people, and millions of peasants believed it. Did anyone in the West even begin to try and understand what was happening in Russia at the time? President Wilson and Orlando, the Italian Prime Minister, frankly confessed their inability to grasp the Russian problem. It was not simple, but the world's future welfare depended on the West grappling with its complications in time."

In the opinion of the Grand Duchess, the spring of 1919 was one of the most crucial moments in the history of the twentieth century. Lenin and Trotsky were aware of their precarious hold upon the country. To the northwest, General Yudenich, the former commander of the Caucasian army, had reached the outskirts of Petrograd. In the southeast, General Denikin had assembled a sizable force in the Caucasus. In Siberia, Admiral Kolchak's large army strengthened its position from day to day. But all of them were in need of support, and they relied on their Allies in the West to send them munitions and other supplies.

"It was a golden opportunity. The Soviets were pressed on every side. The activities of the Tcheka in towns and in the countryside had not endeared that government to the population. Their own forces were under-fed. They lacked boots and ammunition. They had no commanders to compare either with Yudenich or with Kolchak. Even Trotsky gravely doubted the fighting potential of the Red Army at the time. But the opportunity was wasted. A blockade was imposed—and it hit not so much at the Kremlin as at the millions of men, women, and children who had never bothered about any political matters. And what was the actual help given to the White Armies? Certainly, some was offered by the West, but on such conditions that the White Russians could never accept them. Then the British landed at Baku. They went to Batum and declared it a free city, and gave independence to Azerbaijan. What was the motive behind it all? Help for the White Armies? Restoration of order in Russia? Not at all! Oil for the West....

"Next, the Italians, anxiously keeping an eye on those rich manganese mines of Georgia, marched into Tiflis to the sound of drums and the waving of banners, and Georgia was created an independent state by the will of Italy. The French, not to be outdone, occupied Odessa, Russia's most important port, and started intriguing for the independence of the Ukraine. Ammunition, artillery, and planes which should have gone to Denikin and Yudenich were given to the Poles, who, led by Pilsudsky, invaded Russia and occupied Kiev and Smolensk. As the crowning gesture of blind stupidity, the Americans landed a contingent at Vladivostok and were soon joined by the Japanese."

And the outcome of all those policies, the Grand Duchess argued, was a terrific moral victory for the Kremlin. To the Russians, the Bolsheviks suddenly became guardians of Russia's sovereignty threatened on every side. Almost overnight, as it were, the Allied action transformed the Communists from red devils into guardian angels of the country. The White Army commanders saw that there was no further purpose in continuing the struggle. One by one, their units began to disintegrate. Many thousands just returned to their homes. Thousands more joined the Bolshevik forces to fight their ancient enemy, the Poles.

"It was General Brussilov, the great hero of the imperial army, who summed up the whole situation," said the Grand Duchess. "When the Polish guns began hammering at the walls of Kiev and Smolensk, Brussilov made a momentous public declaration. Its psychological effect was worth more than a dozen army corps to the Soviet government. He said: 'The Poles are besieging Russian fortresses with the help of the nations whom we rescued from a certain defeat at the beginning of the war. With every drop of my blood I wish success to the Red army, so help me God.'"

By 1920, the exhausted and disorganized White Armies had virtually ceased to exist. The sporadic skirmishes they made here and there had no other effect than that of infuriating the population. Any army, its discipline, purpose, and unity in tatters, would be prone to commit fearful excesses.

"And look at what happened after the Second World War," the Grand

Duchess went on. "The Allies were just like innocent children led by the nose by Stalin and his thugs. President Roosevelt imagined himself capable of handling the Kremlin government! Nothing will ever absolve him from the consequence of those disgraceful Yalta agreements. The U.S.A. helped to create the Iron Curtain. All the warnings given by Churchill fell on deaf ears. I have no sympathy for the Americans who now suffer from all the pressures and the nervous tension of the cold war. They were strong enough in 1945 and later not only to prevent whole countries in Europe from falling victims to the Communist yoke but to insist on free elections in Russia. They missed their chance and the whole world is paying dearly for it today."

Olga spoke of the creation of independent states out of the Empire's Baltic Provinces. That happened forty years ago. "People who did not know much history went mad with joy that the victims of the imperial oppression should at last have been given their place in the sun. Those provinces were ceded to my country more than two hundred years ago after a victorious war against Sweden. But nobody that I know of went mad with grief when, after the Second World War, those countries in the Baltic fell victim to a terror few people in the West know much about. And nobody today seems to complain about the continued entombment of Estonia and Latvia."

I did not feel I could ask Olga any questions about the part played by thousands of Russian émigrés during Hitler's war, but she herself broached the subject. There was great sadness in her voice.

"General Vlassov and his men were no more traitors than you or I. They remained committed to their loyalty to Russia all through their exile. They did not profess the Nazi creed, but they were compelled by their conscience to join the Germans because, as they believed, it was a chance to free Russia from Communism. As I know but too well, many thousands of those émigrés, settled in Allied countries, were faced with a terrible dilemma, but what possible choice could they have when the Allies were on Stalin's side? Of course, those unfortunate émigrés were let down by the Germans in the first place; they blundered so badly when they broke into Russia. Hitler kept saying that he meant to free my country from the Reds.

The Germans should have formed units of local government composed wholly of Russian members and set up a national administration. Instead, they rushed in to pillage and to murder, sparing neither women nor children, and they lost on all counts."

One by one, our sessions at the cottage were drawing to a close. It had not greatly surprised me to find how well the Grand Duchess remembered the past, but her grasp of current events certainly took me aback. It was with something of a shock that I heard her say, "I have always followed Soviet foreign policy with great interest. Hardly anything in it is different from the course adopted by my father and by Nicky."

When we came to consider the details, she was proved right. The strictly nationalistic policy of Alexander III has indeed been faithfully reflected in the course followed by the Kremlin. The fear and mistrust of Germany, the apprehension of the growing population in China, the insistence on a demilitarized zone in Central Europe, the Pan-Slavic ambitions, the hunger for more and more ports, the administrative measures taken along all the borders even in times of peace, indeed all the salient features of Tsarist policy are as evident today as they were under the Romanovs.

Olga was convinced that many ideological shifts have been forced upon the régime by rapidly changing conditions in the world outside Russia. "Peaceful coexistence is a glaring departure from Marxism which taught that war was a sine qua non of capitalism. Now the Russians are told that they are expected to coexist with capitalist countries. It can't make any sense to them. I tell you that the least educated Russian can and does think for himself—whatever his rulers may do. It is precisely these changes in ideology which will lead to the downfall of Communism someday. Each one of them makes the average Russian a little more confused. Each one of them makes him lose a little more confidence in a régime which moves further and further away from the tenets it preaches."

In Olga's opinion, the religious persecution of the earlier years, with all the terror it brought in its wake, was in keeping with the Soviet system. The present tolerance, however conditional, is a glaring contradiction of Communism. It helps to create a world within a world. To the Kremlin, such tolerance is an expediency. They saw years and years ago that the hunger for religion could never be eradicated among the masses. "From the Communist point of view," argued the Grand Duchess, "all religious practice must introduce a subversive element. Of course, they try to counteract it by teaching atheism in their schools but, sooner or later, the influence and the example of believers, whoever they be—Orthodox, Catholic, Protestant, or Muslim—will present a problem. And it will by no means be the only one."

Olga thought that the ever-increasing numbers of the intellectual stratum, a fact which she admitted to be a Soviet achievement, would ultimately prove to be a double-edged sword.

"Their educational standards grow higher and higher every year. I don't believe in the boast that there is no illiteracy today, but it is idle to deny that they have made vast strides—particularly since the end of the Second World War. But intensive education and government apron-strings are unlikely to coexist, as it were, for an indefinite period. Sooner or later, the desire for freedom and for individual rights as distinct from those of the state will assert itself. The Kremlin will not find it easy to satisfy an enlightened nation with nothing but a series of hollow slogans, spectacular nuclear successes, and grandiose demonstrations in Red Square.

"Poverty-stricken China looks much more like a champion of Communism than Russia. Since the radical teaching of Communism condemns the maldistribution of wealth, Russia, now among 'the haves' in the world, can no longer be considered fit to carry the Red banner. Why, it is just as though Rockefeller began representing himself as the leader of the world's paupers. Little wonder that China disputes the Russian claim to leadership. There is something else to weaken that claim: In China, Communism was established by the will of the people thirty-seven years after the fall of the imperial government. The Bolsheviks seized power in my country eight months after my brother's abdication, and the nation was never given a chance to make its will heard. The so-called Soviet elections are a hideous perversion of the word."

Long before recent events, the Grand Duchess predicted the widening of the rift between Moscow and Peking. "It may well be that Russia will come to be regarded as the only brake on China and the only effective barrier between Europe and Asia. I only hope that when it happens, the West will be supporting a freely elected democratic government in my country," she said.

One day, after a long discussion of the possible future of Russia, I asked the Grand Duchess if she thought it likely that the Romanovs would return.

"I am sure that there will never be any restoration," she replied. "If the Communists were ousted, Russia would most likely become a republic. Even if there are people who still dream of a restoration, whom could they restore? There is no heir to the throne."

"But there are two claimants," I reminded Olga, and she shrugged.

"I know. Prince Vladimir who lives in Madrid and Prince Roman who is in Rome.[1] All my personal prejudices apart, Prince Vladimir's marriage has put him out of the line of succession. However, these are such details. I am convinced that to dream about a Romanov restoration is a pure waste of time today."

There was no sadness in the reply. Olga had long since seen the fact and accepted it. Those few words of the last Tsar's sister seemed a very brief requiem to three hundred years of Russian history.

She envisaged the future fall of Communism as a slow disintegrating process. "And I would greatly prefer to have it happen in some such way because a sudden and inevitably violent collapse could only come about as a result of a military defeat from the West. And I am wholly Russian and far too proud to hope for any alien intervention at that time."

More than anything of what the Grand Duchess had told me, those words of hers stressed the tragic predicament fate had chosen for her personal lot. Most of her life having been spent in the twilit world of exile, Olga was burdened with the consciousness that those same people who so warmly befriended her belonged to a nation which had refused justice to her country.

"It is indeed appalling," she once admitted to me. "My best friends and so many of my relations are British, and I am devoted to them and to much in the English way of life. I am not quite like my father in my attitude to England. I disliked Victoria as much as he did, but I could never see why, respecting Uncle Bertie as my father certainly did, he had such a dislike for him. I loved Uncle Bertie and Georgie and so many others, and they have done so much for me. But, of course, it has never been possible to discuss with them the utterly vile politics of successive British Parliaments. They were nearly all anti-Russian—and so often without the least cause. So much of British policy is wholly contrary to their own tradition of fair play."

"Does that ever enter into politics?" I asked, and Olga sighed.

"I suppose not—but I am ignorant enough to think that it should. Now had a braver and more imaginative man than Buchanan been at the British Embassy in Petrograd in 1917, I feel sure that Nicky's life would have been saved. I felt so sorry for Buchanan's daughter, Meriel. She met Duke Alexander of Leuchtenberg, and they fell in love with each other, but Sandro never dared to marry her, so bad was her father's reputation in Petrograd, except among the Leftists. Yet these are all such trivial matters. It is the big things that count in the long run."

"Which among them would you put first?" I asked her.

"The free future of my dear country," the Grand Duchess answered.

It was during those final discussions of ours that I came to appreciate her kindness, her insight into human nature, her love for her homeland standing above all personal interest, her staunch refusal to be defeated by all the storms of her generation. All this considered, Olga's vehemences and prejudices might well be forgiven her. She bore a great name and she bore it in the grand manner. But she was also the daughter of an Emperor who preferred a peasant shirt to any other garment and looked upon his exalted rank in terms of responsibility and hard work.

It is good to realize that the very last Grand Duchess of Russia should have been a woman capable of carrying the imprint of her race through sorrows, hardihoods, privations, and humiliations rarely encountered together in a single life. She, having hated all false glitter, lent a true radiance to the sunset of the great house.

Appendix

The Massacre of the Romanovs

he Grand Duchess rarely spoke of the massacre of her brother's family, but the tragedy haunted her all her life. "It must have been terrible," she once exclaimed, recalling the agony suffered by her brother's family during the long imprisonment that began in Tsarskoe Selo in August, 1917, and ended in their massacre in Ekaterinburg in July, 1918. She spoke the words with a shudder that transformed the simple sentence into a searing memory which had nagged her heart for forty years.

"All the girls and even the poor boy were by temperament gay and vivacious," she said, "but they all had inherited that certain sense of tragedy from their mother. They all knew they were going to die. I am sure of that.

"The only consolation of that last night was that all was done with quickly. The speed of execution was not the result of humane consideration, of course, but because of necessity. . . ." The armies of White Russian Admiral Kolchak were rapidly advancing on Ekaterinburg and the Bolsheviks were forced to deliver their coup de grâce in haste.

The Grand Duchess knew Admiral Kolchak personally and greatly admired him. She described him as a brilliant, methodical man. And it is because of his methodical nature that historians have been able to reconstruct in detail the last moments in the lives of the Tsar and his family.

When his army entered Ekaterinburg on July 25, seven days after the murder, Kolchak ordered an immediate investigation. Besides carefully collecting personal belongings of the imperial family which had been left in their last residence, the Epatiev house in Ekaterinburg, his special investigation tribunal examined dozens of witnesses. Among them were several of the Bolshevik guards who had been in charge of the impe-rial family to the very end and who had been captured by the White Russian soldiers.

It was just after midnight when the imperial family was aroused by Abraham Yurovski and brusquely ordered to get dressed. The prisoners dressed themselves well, believing that the sudden awakening meant they were to be taken from Ekaterinburg quickly. Some of them carried cush-ions and small private belongings. Yurovski led the way from the first floor down to the cellar. Bewildered, some of the children still half asleep, they followed Yurovski. Behind the Tsar, who was carrying Alexis in his arms, came the Empress and the four Grand Duchesses. Following them were Dr. Botkin, the Tsar's private physician; Demidova, the maid; Troup, a footman; and the cook—all that remained of the several hundred servants and atten-dants once at the service of the Emperor. The only prisoner not included was Leonid, the kitchen boy. In a sudden show of pity, the murderers decided at the last moment to spare him. The Empress, half fainting, had to be helped down the last few steps. Behind them marched the fierce Latvian guards, hand picked by Yurovski to assist him in the execution.

Then the Bolsheviks, with a peculiar sense of protocol that could only be described as monstrous, proceeded to position members of the group at one end of the cellar in much the same manner as would a court photogra-pher. The Tsar was ordered to sit on a chair, his son was placed on his right while the rest of the family and attendants were grouped around them. The torches flickered eerily as Yurovski, according to one version of the death scene, stepped forward and quickly pronounced the sentence: "Nikolai Alexandrovitch, your agents tried to save you but they failed. We are now forced to put you to death."

"What!" cried the bewildered Tsar as Yurovski shot him in the head. At the same moment, the guards opened point-blank fire on the screaming victims who futilely attempted to shield themselves with their arms.

(According to another version, as the death sentence was read the Tsar leaped up and managed to utter a few unintelligible words as Yurovski shot him and the horrified Tsarina automatically crossed herself. It has also been said that the Tsarina, realizing what was about to happen, pleaded with the executioners not to shoot the children—if they must shoot someone that it be her alone.)

All reports generally agree that death was instantaneous for the Tsar, the Tsarina, three of the Grand Duchesses, Dr. Botkin and the cook. Alexis, the Tsarevitch, slumped to the floor but remained alive and groaning with pain. Yurovski struck him with a pistol, then emptied its bullets into the boy's body until he stopped moaning. The maid Demidova lived the longest, having protected herself behind two cushions. She died under the savage bayonets of the guards. Grand Duchess Anastasia rolled about screaming, even struggling with her executioners, before she was subdued by blows. Eighteen bayonet marks embedded in the flooring of the cellar marked the spot where the young, horrified girl writhed her last.★

After the massacre, the cellar was filled with the eye-stinging smoke of powder, but Yurovski and his henchmen had not yet finished their work. While some of the guards held torches, the others calmly stepped through the blood and began the ghoulish task of robbing the victims. Personal belongings—bracelets, necklaces, rings, watches—were torn from the bodies and given to Yurovski.

"The Jew most certainly got his money," the Grand Duchess said bitterly.

But not all the priceless jewelry fell into the hands of the assassins. Undiscovered were some gems sewn into the clothes of the family.

Then, according to one report, the still-bleeding bodies were thrown into sacks and carried on stretchers to the yard, where they were dumped on the back of a truck. The rickety vehicle broke down repeatedly on the trip to the old mine in a nearby forest and its driver, Liuchanov, had difficulty finding his way. At the thirty-foot gaping pit of the Mine of the Four Brothers, named for the four lofty pine trees standing guard at the site, the bodies were unloaded and soaked with petrol and sulphuric acid.

If any of the millions of Russian peasants who adored their Little Father, the Tsar, as passionately as the Russian earth itself could have ventured into the well-guarded forest, they would have seen a roaring fire burning

★ This exact spot was shown by one of the Communist guards, captured by the White Russian armies, to British General Sir Alfred Knox, head of the British expeditionary forces in Russia. Sir Alfred was asked to investigate the murder of the imperial family by the Marchioness of Milford-Haven, eldest sister of the last Tsarina.

stubbornly through the night. But they could never have known that this brilliant pyre was offering to heaven the earthly remains of the Romanov family and that with these bodies was consumed the glory of Old Russia.

Back at the empty Epatiev House, the Bolsheviks continued to stand guard as though the imperial family was still imprisoned there. Their actions misled the public, probably preventing a popular uprising.

A few days later, White Russian troops entered Ekaterinburg and went to the Mine of the Four Brothers. There they found mute proof of the bloody deed: a heap of ashes, a few scraps of bones, clothes and jewels trampled in the mud.

Notes

Preface

1 Queen Olga was one of the two daughters of Grand Duke Constantine, second son of the Emperor Nicholas I and uncle to Alexander III, the Grand Duchess's father. After the Russian usage, the relation was that of a "cousin aunt" (*Dvourodnaya tetka*). The Queen was also the Grand Duchess's godmother.

2 Grand Duchess Xenia died in London on 20 April 1960.

3 "Born in the purple" (in Russian, *porfirodny*) was applied solely to sons and daughters of a sovereign who were born after his accession. The Romanov dynasty reigned for three centuries (1613–1917), but there were comparatively few *porfirodny* members: Paul's youngest son, Michael, born in 1798, Nicholas I's three younger sons, and Alexander II's two younger sons. Grand Duchess Olga was the only child of Alexander III to be born in the purple. On the other hand, all the five children of the last Tsar, Nicholas II, were born after his accession in 1894.

Chapter One

1 A parallel case occurred in England twenty-seven years later when Princess May, the fiancée of the Duke of Clarence, became engaged to his younger brother Prince George (later King George V) when the Duke died suddenly of pneumonia in 1892.

2 See pages 11–14.

3 The manor of Gatchina belonged to the Orlov family. It was originally a small farm, a mysa. Catherine gave it, together with some few thousands of acres, to her lover, Gregory Orlov, who built a villa there. On his death she bought it back from his executors and gave it to her son, Paul, who enlarged the villa to its present size and turned the place into a miniature Potsdam. Alexander III was the first to live there after Paul's murder in St. Petersburg in 1801.

4 During Nicholas II's reign, the great Anitchkov Palace in St. Petersburg was occupied by his mother.

5 One such example is the Popov family: Popov, a peasant from the Novgorod province, was a confidential footman under Catherine II, the only domestic allowed to dust her study. His son, grandson and great-grandson were in service under Alexander I, Nicholas I, and Alexander II. It may well be that a

still later descendant was in the imperial household during Grand Duchess Olga's childhood and youth.

6 The Mopsopolis album was the joint effort of Alexander III and his elder brother Nicholas. *Mops* in Russian means "pug," and the inhabitants of the city had pug-faces. Both Grand Dukes seemed to possess enough subtlety not to make their satire too obvious by choosing bull-dogs instead of pugs. The sketches were made in 1856 when Alexander III was eleven and the result of the Crimean War embittered everyone in Russia against Great Britain and France.

7 When Alexander II was assassinated in broad daylight in a street of St. Petersburg in March, 1881, the first bomb injured a few of the Cossacks in the escort and some passers-by. The Emperor's carriage was badly damaged, but he was unhurt. Regardless of his own safety, Alexander II insisted on leaving the carriage to see what he could do for the wounded, and it was on his turning toward his equerry's sledge that another bomb was thrown. (That second explosion also killed ten people and injured fourteen.)

8 The river and the many lakes at Gatchina were under the care of the Admiralty.

Chapter Two

1 Two only among the nineteen Romanov sovereigns were properly prepared for their station in life: Alexander I, pupil of Frederick La Harpe, and Alexander II, whose tutor was Zhukovsky, the poet. For the younger sons, languages and military science were the most important parts of the curriculum.

2 The Grand Duchess's talent developed and matured. Her nature studies were exquisite, and she painted to the very end of her life.

3 A shop in St. Petersburg which might be compared with Asprey's in London. All the others mentioned were of the same kind.

4 See Preface footnote 1.

5 It was Prince George of Greece who saved the life of Nicholas in 1890 during a visit to Japan. The two young princes were riding in an open carriage through the narrow streets of Otsu. Suddenly a Japanese fanatic, brandishing a sword, attacked the Tsarevich and would have killed him if Prince George had not leaped up and with his own walking stick struck the attacker about the head and then held him until the Japanese police arrived.

6 The Princess of Wales, later Queen Alexandra of England.

7 The only member of the imperial family who liked Queen Victoria

was the Grand Duchess's eldest brother, Nicholas, and the fact that his bride, Princess Alix of Hesse, was the Queen's favorite granddaughter had a great deal to do with it.

Chapter Three

1   Princess Helene Kotchoubey, Mistress of the Robes, was one of the most extraordinary women of her time, perhaps the last grande dame of the past century. Enormously wealthy, authoritative on imperial matters and fully aware of her position, she gave magnificent receptions at her St. Petersburg palace which rivaled in brilliance those of the imperial court itself. She was on intimate terms with every crowned head of Europe and was even reputed to know by memory the Almanac de Gotha from beginning to end.

2   All three sons of Alexander III were on board the train. Had they been killed together with their father, the crown would have passed to Grand Duke Vladimir. Until 1797, succession in Russia was governed by an act of Peter the Great which empowered the sovereign to name his or her successor and gave them freedom to disinherit their own children. In 1797 the Emperor Paul I had that

law repealed, and the new act (which held until the end of the dynasty in 1917) established male primogeniture as the only right to succession.

3   In January of 1889, the Empress Marie planned to open the season with a particularly brilliant ball. All the invitations had been sent and preparations completed when St. Petersburg heard that an archduke had died in Vienna. Society was in despair, but the Empress reissued her invitations. The ball would be un Bal Noir, all the ladies having to wear black. The Empress, having remembered an earlier occasion when the Austrian court had taken no notice of a mourning in Russia, thought that her idea of a Bal Noir was something of a polite retaliation.

4   Bieloviecz was a forest of nearly 30,000 acres, the only place in Europe, except for the Caucasus, where wild bison could still be found.

5   Nicholas and his bride-to-be first met in St. Petersburg in 1884 at the wedding of her elder sister, Elizabeth, to Grand Duke Serge, Alexander III's brother. Between 1884 and 1891 Alicky visited Russia twice, and it was obvious that they were deeply in love, but she kept refusing him. She knew she would have to become

Orthodox if she married him, and she felt she could not forsake the Lutheran creed. Not until 1894 did Nicholas succeed in winning her. His parents had begun by opposing the match. The Emperor was afraid of the possible growth of British influence in Russia, since Princess Alicky was known to be Queen Victoria's favorite granddaughter. The Empress disliked the girl's reserve and interpreted her shyness as pride. In the end, however, the Emperor gave his consent to the betrothal.

6   The dates here are given in the old style. The date was November thirteenth in Europe.

Chapter Four

1   As a matter of fact, the Grand Duchess had no lady-in-waiting until 1901 when the Empress Marie forced her to have one. The appointment, made by the Empress, was an unfortunate one. Mme. Alexandra Kossikovsky, well bred, intelligent, and very pretty, soon enough won the confidence of her young mistress, who called her "Dina." But the relationship could not last: Dina promptly fell in love with Grand Duke Michael, and was eventually dismissed.

2   Young Olga was given violin lessons by Vlatislav Kournakovitch, a talented musician who was the first violinist of the imperial orchestra. Emperor Nicholas presented his sister and her famous tutor each with a priceless violin—one of them belonged to the poet Lvoff who wrote the Russian national anthem. This violin was subsequently stolen under mysterious circumstances and Kournakovitch, turning detective, spent three months looking all over the world for it. Eventually he found it displayed in a London antique shop.

3   The young Empress's four daughters, Olga, Tatiana, Marie, and Anastasia, were born between 1895 and 1901.

4   From the days of Peter the Great, some among the lesser German reigning houses, such as, for example, the Princes of Hesse-Homburg and others, would enter Russian service. As the century advanced, their number increased, most of them preferring to be dictated to by Elizabeth and Catherine rather than by Frederick the Great. They did not necessarily forfeit their lands in Germany. By the end of the century, Princes of Holstein-Gothorp, Oldenburg, and Mecklenburg-Strelitz were firmly established in Russia. A daughter of Paul I was the wife of Prince George of Oldenburg and another Grand Duchess had a Duke of

Leuchtenberg for her husband. The three families, i.e., Oldenburg, Mecklenburg-Strelitz, and Leuchtenberg, were thus incorporated into the dynasty. They were all "Highnesses," but not "Imperial."

5   The Grand Duchess said to me: "I retained all the jewels to the Oldenburgs when my marriage was annulled in 1916. I was particularly glad at having done so when I heard that Prince Peter and his mother lived very comfortably in exile on the proceeds of the jewelry they were able to take out of the country after the Revolution."

Chapter Five

1   The expenses of a sovereign's household.

2   Later the Grand Duchess told me the story of Countess Kleinmichel's escape when the Revolution broke out. She had every window shuttered and every door locked. A great notice was hung in the porch: "Trespassing prohibited. This house is the property of the Petrograd Soviet. Countess Kleinmichel has been taken to the Fortress of Peter and Paul." The trick worked because of the general confusion and tumult. The Countess had enough time to pack some of her treasures and make arrangements for her escape from Russia. Only

after her flight did the local Soviet discover the trick.

Chapter Six

1   At the beginning of this chapter, I quoted the Grand Duchess as including herself among the transgressors. In fairness, it should be pointed out that the dissolution of her own marriage to Prince Peter of Oldenburg cannot be regarded in the light of a divorce. The marriage was never consummated, and the official documents, issued by the Holy Synod, refer to its dissolution as "an annulment." Nor did the Grand Duchess marry a divorcé. Colonel Koulikovsky was a bachelor.

2   His wife was Princess Alexandra, daughter of King George I and Queen Olga of the Hellenes. There were two children of the marriage: Grand Duke Dimitri, implicated in the murder of Rasputin, and Grand Duchess Marie, whose own marriage with Prince William of Sweden ended in a shipwreck.

3   Grand Duke Serge's wife, Princess Elizabeth of Hesse, retired from the world and founded the Abbey of Martha and Mary in Moscow.

4   Grand Duke Nicholas Mikhailovich, brother of Sandro, Olga's brother-in-law and a historian, was reputed to be the greatest landowner in the Empire.

5   King George V of England.

Chapter Seven

1   In this chapter I have had to depart
slightly from the chronological
order of the rest of the biography
in order to deal comprehensively
with one of the most controversial
characters in history. If much of
what follows seems novel, if not
incredible, to many readers, I ask
them to remember that this is
Grand Duchess Olga's own story. I
have neither colored the facts she
gave me, nor interpreted them in
my own fashion.—I.V.
2   Grand Duchess Marie Pavlovna,
wife of Grand Duke Vladimir.
3   Lady-in-waiting to the Tsarina.
4   The Grand Duke was Dimitri, only
son of Grand Duke Paul, youngest
son of the Emperor Alexander II.
The scion of a great house was
Prince Felix Yusupoff, whose wife
was Princess Irene, only daughter
of Grand Duke Alexander and
Grand Duchess Xenia. The
Emperor sent Dimitri into exile on
the southeast border of Russia, not
far from the Persian frontier. The
penalty proved Grand Duke
Dimitri's salvation in the end.

Chapter Eight

1   Apart from the Crimean party, the
Grand Duke Dimitri, exiled to the
borders of Persia after the Rasputin
murder, and the three sons of
Grand Duke Vladimir, few of the
Romanovs survived the Terror.
2   See Appendix.
3   The French evacuated Odessa in
April, 1919; that move enabled the
Red Army to occupy Perikop
Isthmus, within a stone's throw of
the Crimea. At Harax, the Dowager
Empress gave way. On receiving an
urgent letter from Queen
Alexandra, she went on board
H.M.S. Marlborough, but not
before she had got the British to
agree to the evacuation of all her
friends in the neighborhood of
Yalta. That, though not in strict
accord with Admiralty instructions,
was done. The Empress Marie left,
together with Grand Duchess Xenia
and her children, Grand Dukes
Nicholas and Peter, and all the other
Romanovs in the Crimea. The
Marlborough left Yalta on 11 April
1919. Just as she was weighing
anchor, a troopship carrying soldiers
passed her very close. Evidently the
imperial standard was hoisted on
H.M.S. Marlborough because the
men on board the troopship stood
in salute and sang the national
anthem. The Empress Marie kept on
deck, waving her hand, until she
could see them no longer. To all
who witnessed the scene it seemed
the swan-song of an era.

4   Many years after this incident Vice-Admiral Sir Thomas N. James, C.B., M.V.O., told me about the Grand Duchess's visit to H.M.S. *Cardiff*. "In my cabin she saw a photograph she had given me at Olgino. It was a group which included Grand Duke Michael. She looked, and said, "I feel sure he is still alive." I asked her where she thought he might be. She replied, "I think he is at Hong Kong." I then remembered the report published in the *Times* about the Grand Duke having been murdered in Siberia. I did not dare break such tragic news to her."

5   Grand Duchess Vladimir, on leaving Russia in February, 1920, went to Switzerland, but died a few months later.

Chapter Nine

1   In a letter to the author in 1961, the Duke stated his disbelief in Mrs. Tchaikovsky-Anderson's claim. Among his reasons were: (1) Mrs. Tchaikovsky did not speak or understand Russian, English (except what she learned in lessons taken at Lugano and Oberstdorf before coming to Seeon) or French. She spoke only German with a north German accent. Anastasia, on the contrary, spoke Russian, English and French but no German; (2) Mrs. Tchaikovsky did not know the Russian Orthodox rite, whereas Anastasia was brought up in this rite; (3) the Duke was present during the surprise meeting between Mrs. Tchaikovsky and Felix Schanzkovsky when the latter recognized her as his sister Franciska Schanzkovsky; (4) Dr. Kostrizky, the dentist of the imperial family, testified that the jaws of Mrs. Tchaikovsky-Anderson had nothing in common with the jaws—of which there was a plaster impression—of Grand Duchess Anastasia.

2   Queen Marie of Roumania, daughter of the Duke and Duchess of Edinburgh and first cousin of Emperor Nicholas II.

3   For the part played by Grand Duke Cyril during the 1917 Revolution, see the Epilogue. Grand Duchess Olga and many other members of the Romanov family never forgave him for his premature recognition of the provisional government.

4   Russian Minister of Finance, 1914–1917. He settled in England after the Revolution, was befriended by the King, and subsequently knighted.

Chapter Ten

1   Literally, "little one," a term of endearment used by the imperial family when they spoke to or

about Grand Duchess Anastasia.

2   Princess Marina is the daughter of the late Grand Duchess Helen, Princess Nicholas of Greece, who was Olga's first cousin. According to the Russian usage, Grand Duchess Olga was *dvourodnaya tetka*—roughly, "cousin aunt," to the Duchess of Kent.

Chapter Eleven

1   According to the Orthodox usage, the coffin remains open all through the funeral service to enable the relatives and all the others present to pay their last homage to the dead.

2   One of the two daughters of Grand Duke Constantine, the poet, who died in 1915 and, incidentally, was the very last Romanov to be buried in the family mausoleum in the Cathedral of SS. Peter and Paul in Petrograd. The Grand Duke's other daughter, Princess Tatiana, is now abbess of the Russian Convent in Jerusalem. Their family, known in old Russia as the "Constantinovichi," suffered most during the Terror. Three of Grand Duke Constantine's five sons, Princes John, Igor, and Constantine, were thrown alive down a disused mine shaft near Alapaevsk in Siberia in July 1918. Grand Duke Constantine's brother, Grand Duke Dimitri, was shot in

Petrograd in January, 1919, an eyewitness later deposing that his last words were a prayer for the men about to murder him.

Epilogue

1   Prince Vladimir of Russia is the only son of the late Grand Duke Cyril by his marriage with Victoria, the divorced Grand Duchess of Hesse, daughter of the Duchess of Edinburgh. From the point of view of seniority, Prince Vladimir's claim to the throne of Russia is certainly more valid that that of his cousin, Prince Roman, son of the late Grand Duke Peter. Prince Vladimir is sometimes erroneously described as Grand Duke. There are no Russian Grand Dukes living today. The Emperor Alexanfer III established the so-called Romanov Family Statue whereby only sons and grandsons of sovereigns in the male descent bore the grand-ducal title. The father of Prince Vladimir was a grandson of the Emperor Alexander II and his children were therefore debarred from the grand-ducal title. It is true that on receiving definite proofs of the Ekaterinburg and Perm massacres, some émigrés recognized Grand Duke Cyril as Emperor, but this recognition carried no dynastic validity. Grand Duchess Olga's preference of Prince Roman's claim

was due to the fact that Prince Vladimir's father, Grand Duke Cyril, yielded to the provisional government almost before the Emperor's abdication became known. Cyril commanded the Marine Guards, and marched at the head of the entire regiment to the headquarters of the provisional government (at Taurida Palace in Petrograd) to take his oath of allegiance. As a member of the Romanov family, the Grand Duke had sworn an oath of allegiance to his sovereign and cousin, who alone could release him from it.

Photo Credits

All photographs appear by permission of the author, with the following exceptions:

The photograph on page 60 appears by permission of the Royal Danish Library;

The photographs on pages 82, 168 and 172 appear by permission of Madison Press Limited;

The photographs on pages 132, 179, 190, 191, 192 and 193 appear by permission of Paul Kulikovsky.

Every effort has been made to contact all copyright holders. The publisher welcomes any queries or additional information on this matter.

Index